1

6

2

4

3

5

9

J-2

16

19

20

BULLDOG
The Bristol Bulldog
Fighter

BULLDOG
The Bristol Bulldog Fighter

DAVID LUFF, C Eng, MI Prod E.

with Foreword by
Air Vice-Marshal Charles George Lott,
CB, CBE, DSO, DFC, RAF (Ret'd)

Airlife
England.

This book is dedicated to those young former Bulldog squadron pilots of pre-war days, who became the backbone of Britain's air defence during the Second World War.

Copyright © David Luff 1987.

ISBN 0 906393 94 9

First published 1987,
by Airlife Publishing Ltd.

Printed in England by Livesey Ltd., Shrewsbury.

Airlife Publishing Ltd.

7 St. John's Hill, Shrewsbury, England.

Contents

Acknowledgements

Any serious work of non-fiction must, inevitably, only be possible by the combined contributions from many sources. This book is certainly no exception and my sincere thanks must go to the people and organisations listed below.

Martin Longbottom, Dick Wood, George Lambe, Duncan Greenman, Arthur Gregory and Ray Westaway of British Aerospace plc, Filton; John Heaven, Jack Barnard and Janet Rugman of Rolls-Royce Engines plc, Patchway; Ken Hunter, Matt George, Gordon Leith and Reg Mack of the Royal Air Force Museum, Hendon; Richard Searle, Chief Librarian and his staff at the Royal Aircraft Establishment, Farnborough; Arnold Nayler, Librarian and his staff at the Royal Aeronautical Society, London; Mr R. W. Elliott, Librarian of the Shuttleworth Collection, Old Warden; Jim Halley and Ray Sturtivant of Air Britain (Historians) Ltd; Mr I. D. Blackwood of RAF Records, MOD Gloucester; Mr G. Clout of the Imperial War Museum, London and John Janaway of Surrey Local Studies Library.

Overseas countries have been particularly helpful in supplying me with material, especially Mr R. E. Cowley, Curator at the Australian War Memorial, Canberra; Flight Sergeant D. W. Gardner of the RAAF Museum, Point Cook; L. A. T. Ege of the Royal Danish Air Force Historical Section; Paul E. Branke for help with the Baltic States; Timo Heinonen, Curator of Keski-Suomen Ilmailumuseo, Finland; Patrick Laureau for help with Bulldog's involvement in the Spanish Civil War; Axel Carlsonn, Director of Flygvapen-museum, Malmen, Sweden; F. Robert van der Linden, Assistant Curator of the National Air and Space Museum, Washington, D.C., and H. W. Raines, Jr. of the Department of the Navy, Virginia.

I wish to acknowledge my grateful thanks to Christopher H. Barnes and The Bodley Head for permission to reproduce line drawings from "Bristol Aircraft since 1910". I also thank Macdonald & Co (Publishers) Ltd, for permission to include the extract from *Fighter over Finland* by Eino Luukkanen.

It is now almost sixty years since Bulldog first took to the skies and not so many of the pilots of that era are still with us. The written contributions by those who flew this colourful fighter are therefore all the more valuable today and, for me, the highlight of the book. I am deeply indebted to Sir Harry Broadhurst, GCB, KBE, DSO and bar, DFC and bar, AFC; Sir John Grandy, GCB, KBE, DSO; Sir Edouard Grundy, KBE, OBE, CB; Air Vice-Marshals George Lott, CB, CBE, DSO, DFC; John Rotherham, CB, CBE; Air Commodore Paddy Heffernan, RAAF; Group Captain Edgar Glennie-Carr; Wing Commanders W. G. Easton; Leslie Holman, AFC; Ray Love, DSO, DFC; John Rye, AFC, and Carl-Erik Bruun, FAF.

It is with similar gratitude that I wish to record my appreciation to Ted Robins and Arthur Strudwick, the only members of the RAF ground staff at the time of Bulldog that I was able to contact, for the information they supplied on life at Upavon, circa 1932. Their role was a less glamorous one than that of the pilot, but an equally important one and well worthy of inclusion in the aeroplane's history.

Background to the design aspects of Bulldog were vital and for this I am indebted to those few remaining members of the original design teams, Sir Archibald Russell, CBE, FRAeS; Fred Pollicutt and Frank Owner, CBE, who were so generous with their help. My appreciation also extends to Mrs Sidonie Frise for personal recollections of her late husband.

Maybe one day we shall see *K2227* back in the air again but until then we must rely on our memories and the written impressions kindly supplied by Godfrey Auty and Sir John Rogers, KCB, CBE, in the penultimate chapter.

I feel privileged to include Richard Ward's superb coloured illustrations of Bulldog in this volume and trust that they will give the reader as much pleasure as they have given to me.

Finally, much nearer home, I wish to express my thanks to Peter Sharman, Gayle Peacock and Elizabeth Hardman of Lytham Library, and to Debbi King for her extreme patience and single-mindedness in typing the manuscript.

David Luff.

Foreword

On 3 June 1931, while I was serving in 19 Squadron at RAF Duxford, I was sent to Filton to collect one of the first two Bulldogs to be allotted to the squadron. It was always a thrill to fly a new type of aircraft, but this occasion gave me special pleasure. I had been flying Siskins for three years, and the improved handling and flying characteristics of the Bulldog were impressive. It was a milestone in the development of the single-seat fighter, and it is proper that its story should be researched and recorded.

In this book the record is complete. It has been most carefully and comprehensively researched, and it has obviously been a labour of love for its author, David Luff. The full story has been told in a graphic and most readable manner, profusely illustrated with pictures of the aircraft, in many of the liveries it wore, and of many of the pilots who flew it.

It is an absorbing account of a fine aircraft, worthy of a place on the bookshelf of anyone with an interest in aviation.

George Lott
Freshwater
Isle of Wight.

Preface

In the 1930s the Bristol Bulldog fighter biplane aroused excitement; from that of the schoolboy with capped hand over eyes squinting into the sky at the air display, to the pupil-pilot easing himself into its instrument-crowded cockpit for the first time, whilst glancing along its silver-doped fabric-covered wings. Palmer wheels with their coloured disc covers nudging at the chocks, dirty big nine-cylinder Jupiter thumping away up front, oil-spotted windscreen and the smell of burnt oil and fresh cut airfield grass — all contributed to the magic. Who with any soul could fail to be moved by the sight of a squadron of Bulldogs in flight? Brightly coloured squadron markings on wings and fuselage, drogue pennants from wingtips and tail of the squadron leader's aircraft — reminiscent of the heraldry of bygone knights — truly 'la belle epoque' of the biplane fighter.

Bulldog was not a perfect aeroplane and it had its share of detractors but by far the large majority of those who flew it came to love it. One very eminent pilot has recorded that 'it was a rugged, friendly to fly fighter providing one recognised its limitations and did not take liberties with it. But then taking liberties with any aeroplane is a questionable pastime!'

Aeroplanes just don't happen, their stories are about people as well as themselves; people who dreamed them, built them, flew them and maintained them. This book is about them, as well as Bulldog.

Frank Sowter Barnwell and Leslie George Frise were a formidable design partnership for 22 years at Filton, Bristol. Their innovation and flair in design was a credit to their company and resulted in military aircraft such as the Brisfit, Blenheim and Beaufighter which contributed a major part in the successful defence of this country in two world wars. In addition, their vision extended to the realisation of the air freighter long before it became a reality. At the time of Barnwell's tragic death in 1938 he had, if one includes design studies which did not materialise as prototypes, laid out over 150 types at Bristol during a 26-year period —- such was this man's energy and vigour! I stood by Barnwell's unkempt grave in Alveston's Parish churchyard earlier in the year and reflected upon this 'gentleman pioneer of aviation' with some considerable emotion. Our people are not the best for honouring their great men and their deeds, at least not for long, and they are soon forgotten. Inscribed on the headstone was an added tribute to his three young sons who were to perish whilst on active service with the RAF, within three years of their father's death. John and Tony were killed in Blenheims in 1940, and the youngest, nineteen-year-old David, was last heard over the R/T of his Hurricane with the words 'Baling out — engine cut — am baling out' as it descended into the sea off Malta on 13 October 1941. What a courageous and incredible family were the Barnwells!

Many of those who flew with the ten Bulldog squadrons during those somnolent pre-war years were destined, within a short time, to be fighting air battles in more modern aircraft over these and other shores. By 1939 they had five or six years' experience under their belts, and were therefore to become the leaders of the squadrons which bore the brunt of Göring's *Luftwaffe* offensive on Britain in 1940. Perhaps the best known of them was to be Douglas Bader, who lost his legs whilst carrying out low-level (too low) aerobatics in a Bulldog over Woodley in 1931. Bader and Bulldog complemented each other; he exhibited those qualities that one associates with the breed — a tenacity and aggression when under attack that is typically British. Maybe it is fashionable nowadays, in the age of the anti-hero, to deride such qualities but none should forget that we owe our freedom to such men.

Bulldog has long departed, apart from a static display *BU-59* in a Finnish air museum, but it still has two strong links with today's aviation. Frise's first design work began in 1916 on Brisfit, and yet today his Jet Provost still fills a vital role as the basic trainer for the RAF. His assistant in the Filton design office *circa* 1926 at the time of Bulldog's conception was a young stressman named Russell who was knighted in 1971, as Sir Archibald Russell, for his design contribution to Concorde. I like to think that there is a little bit of Bulldog in both of these aircraft!

If my praise of Sir A. H. Roy Fedden and L. F. G. 'Bunny' Butler, together with their brilliant design team at Patchway, is somewhat muted, it is because more capable pens than mine have told their story in fuller detail. Suffice it to say that without their contribution on the engine side Bulldog would never have achieved the success that it did.

Many have asked me for my *raison d'écrire* about this particular aircraft. For me it has always held a fascination and enchantment, born many years ago as a young schoolboy living not so very far away from Hornchurch at the time when it equipped No 54(F) Squadron. What started as a hobby became a way of life.

Strictly speaking a history should preclude comment so perhaps this book cannot be placed in that category. I have attempted, within the scope accorded me, to give as full an account as possible — no doubt there are many omissions and perhaps a few errors for which I readily apologise.

Without the help and encouragement of so many people, to whom thanks and acknowledgment have been given elsewhere, this book would never have been written. I don't know if all researchers are as untidy as I am but my special thanks and gratitude go to my wife who has acted as typist, coffee-maker, part-time researcher, etc, and who has so patiently tolerated her dining-room in disarray for so long.

Lytham St Annes, October 1986

Chapter 1
The *Old Man* and his team

On Tuesday 2 August 1938 George Matthews — a Bristol tramdriver — had been enjoying a leisurely day off work as compensation for the previous Sunday's duty. It was late during the warm afternoon when he decided to walk, together with his wife and six-year-old daughter Jean, to the nearby airport at Whitchurch. Upon arrival they entered a fenced area where they sat down and spread out the picnic that they had packed before leaving home. Jean was quite excited as she watched the aeroplanes soaring, almost it seemed, above their heads. Suddenly they could hear the sound of an engine and then a small single-seat low wing monoplane appeared from behind a nearby hangar and climbed into the brilliant cloudless sky. Jean waved and the pilot, who could be clearly seen, waved back. The small aeroplane made a partial circuit of the aerodrome whereupon it seemed to lose flying speed, nose-dived from a height of 100 feet and crashed onto a nearby road. So ended the life of the Bristol Aeroplane Co's Chief Engineer, and one time Chief Aircraft Designer, for he was killed instantaneously.

Frank Sowter Barnwell was born in Lewisham, Kent, in 1880, the second of three sons, two of whom were to make their mark upon the history of aviation in Britain. A year later the family moved to Scotland where his father became the Managing Director of the Fairfield Shipbuilding Co at Govan, near Glasgow. All three brothers, Harold, Frank and Archibald were educated at Fettes College, Edinburgh, the 'Eton of Scotland', where none of them particularly distinguished themselves. It is patronisingly on record that 'Frank came no higher than eighth on the Modern side in his last year and, as the vast majority of anyone with brains were on the Classical side, that was no great achievement'.

Upon leaving Fettes at the age of eighteen Frank served a six-year apprenticeship at his father's firm, backed up by attendance at evening school and full-time study at Glasgow University where he obtained a BSc in naval architecture in 1905. To widen his experience he went to America where he spent a year as a draughtsman with a firm of shipbuilders. It was during this period that he became interested in aviation when he met, and was enthused by, the Wright brothers before he returned to Scotland in 1907. Upon his return he joined up with Harold and Archie to form the Grampian Engineering and Motor Co, Causewayhead, Stirling (a firm still in existence) which began to design and construct aircraft. After unsuccessful attempts with an underpowered monoplane in 1908 and a large biplane, pushed by two chain-driven propellers, in 1909, Frank succeeded in piloting a new monoplane in January 1911 which rose to a height of fity feet and flew a third of a mile before nosing over in a ploughed field. Two weeks later the repaired aircraft, this time with Harold at the controls, won the Law

Captain Frank Sowter Barnwell in RFC uniform circa 1914 *(British Aerospace, Filton).*

Frank Sowter Barnwell, OBE, AFC, BSc at the time of his death circa 1938 *(British Aerospace, Filton).*

prize of £50 donated by the Scottish Aeronautical Society for the first half-mile flight by an all-Scottish aeroplane.

Frank's interests were not entirely devoted to aeroplanes, for in 1910 he married Marjorie, the eldest daughter of Lieutenant Colonel Charles Lansford Sandes of Stirling. However, the two elder brothers were soon to move south to take up careers in the emerging and fast-growing aviation industry. By March 1911 Frank Barnwell had joined the newly founded British and Colonial Aeroplane Co at Filton, Bristol, as a draughtsman whilst Harold had decided to take up a post with Vickers at Brooklands as their Chief Flying Instructor and test-pilot. Archie remained to manage the business until 1914, when, being an Army reservist, he was called to the colours, initially as a Captain, and finally, after service in France, rose to the rank of Major.

The British and Colonial Aeroplane Co had been formed in February 1910 by Sir George White, Bart., and his brother Samuel, with the modest capital of £25,000; they were men of vision and imagination who had realised the potential of the aeroplane. Sir George had already pioneered the use of electric tramways in Bristol and other major cities in the country and was now determined to establish an aircraft industry in the south-west of England. The company's first venture was to manufacture, under licence, the Zodiac biplane of French design which was not a success. This failure was to be a mixed blessing for it gave Sir George the impetus to engage his own design staff and it was soon after this time that Barnwell took up his appointment.

Barnwell's first task, working under the direction of Lieutenant C. D. Burney, was to develop one of Gordon England's biplanes as a seaplane for use by the Royal Navy. He was given the assistance of Clifford Tinson who had joined the company in January 1912, but the project was not to succeed. It resulted in an abortive attempt to fly the aircraft off the water which it failed to do, even when towed at speed by a destroyer. This failure in no way reflected upon Barnwell, for he had been given an impracticable specification which severely limited his freedom of design.

It was not long, however, before he revealed his true design talent when with Harry Busteed's assistance as test-pilot, he produced the highly successful Bristol Scout in March 1914. Barnwell, at that time, made all his own design and stressing calculations in a penny exercise book, whilst Tinson recalls that 'we had no printing machine or equipment of that sort for copying drawings, so we made all our drawings in manifold-books, giving the carbon copies to the Shops'. This small (24ft 7in wingspan) biplane, originally designed for reconnaissance purposes, was not only the first single-seat military aircraft to be put into quantity production but the first Allied aircraft to be equipped with a synchronised gun firing through the propeller. It was very popular with RFC pilots in France because of its strength and ease of handling, and by 1916 almost 400 had been built. The Bristol Scout was the aircraft used by Major Lanoe G. Hawker when, on 25 July 1915, he was awarded the Victoria Cross, the first to be awarded for an aerial combat, for shooting down three German aircraft in one day.

Soon after the beginning of the 1914-18 war government policy dictated that all aircraft manufacturers should standardise their production and build Royal Aircraft Factory-designed aircraft only. Barnwell was disgusted by this restriction on his talent and left the company in November 1914 to join the RFC. After receiving his wings at the Central Flying School in March 1915, he was posted to No 12 Squadron where he was soon to fly, amongst other aircraft, one of his own Bristol Scouts — now nicknamed Bullet. (Tinson was to follow Barnwell in the exodus of staff from B & C A Co's design office and after a short spell with the Air Department of the Admiralty he became Chief Designer to Frederick Sage & Co at Peterborough in January 1916.)

Two factors combined to bring about the release of Barnwell, on indefinite leave without pay, from the RFC in August 1915 — by which time he had attained the rank of Captain. Firstly, the heavy losses suffered by the RFC in 1915 had led to a lobbying of the government by the Press for the War Office to reverse its earlier decision to allow only official designs. Secondly, it was soon realised that Barnwell was more valuable as an aircraft designer than as a probably below-average pilot.

He rejoined the company as Chief Designer, since the post had fallen vacant when Henri Coanda returned to Romania upon the outbreak of hostilities, and resumed his work with a new-found zest and enthusiasm. He was soon to justify his new appointment by following up the successful Scout with two further brilliant designs — the M1 monoplane and the renowned Bristol F2B Fighter. Unfortunately, the former was to suffer from an ill-founded prejudice by officialdom against monoplanes in general, and its adoption was restricted, ostensibly, on an excessively high landing speed (49 mph) and insufficient downward view. The M1C did, however, serve as a fighting Scout in the Middle East where 125 were used during the 1916-17 period. It was fast, extremely manoeuvrable and regarded by some as the finest fighting machine of the war — a fitting tribute to Barnwell's advanced thinking.

By the time Barnwell had commenced work on the Bristol Fighter in 1916 as a replacement for the much-maligned BE2c, he had been joined by Leslie George Frise as his assistant. It was to be a harmonious and long-lasting partnership during which time the history of the company's design office was practically the history of the aeroplane.

Barnwell's canard biplane which flew 80 yards at an altitude of 12 feet in 1909
(Grampian Engineering Co Ltd, Causewayhead, Stirling; Stirling Field and Archaeological Society and Stirling Smith Art Gallery and Museum).

Barnwell's brother Harold in the cockpit
of a Vickers monoplane, 19 December 1913
*(Grampian Engineering Co Ltd, Causewayhead, Stirling; Stirling Field and
Archaeological Society and Stirling Smith Art Gallery and Museum).*

Frise had recently been released from his commission as a Sub-Lieutenant with the RNAS, having graduated with honours in Mechanical Engineering from the University of Bristol a year earlier. It is on record that when they first met Frise recalled:

'I was interviewed by Captain Barnwell; he seemed to think I could help, and so I was sent over to the big house where the financiers dwelt. When I came back he asked "How much are they going to give you?" I replied "Thirty-five bob a week". He pulled the lobe of his ear and said "Good God! You have first class Honours, haven't you?" I said "Yes". He said "A ruddy tram driver gets more than that". I replied "Yes, but I took mechanical, not electrical".'

Barnwell, the older and more experienced man, took Frise under his wing and no doubt taught him much about aircraft design in those early days. Although dissimilar in outlook they complemented each other in what was to be a happy partnership. Barnwell displayed the public school image; quiet polished Edinburgh accent with a slight Scottish burr, neat and well-dressed, and giving the impression that he took a cold bath every morning. He was a man without enemies, kindly affectioned and quite slow to anger, although on one occasion he exploded in an uncharacteristic outburst when frustrated by a

blind bureaucratic decision with the words, 'We struggle against a sea of bloody fools'. As an engineer he was meticulously careful and neat in all his calculations and notes, writing with a large upright boyish hand. During his later years at Filton his unwillingness readily to seek the opinions of his colleagues on design problems, often resulted in submissions that were, whilst soundly based, rather too orthodox and conventional.

Frise was described by friend and colleague, Fred Pollicutt, as 'a brilliant thinker' with great inventiveness and flair. His ideas and thoughts were often far ahead of his time which meant that he was not always readily understood. On such occasions, especially when confronted by the technically illiterate, he could, if provoked, become quietly belligerent and resort to sarcasm. His family were descendants from the Huguenots — a town in France bears the family name — and his father as well as his headmaster wanted him to take a career in the Civil Service. However, even at an early age he displayed what was to become a lifelong trait of farsightedness and characteristically chose to become an aeronautical engineer. Unlike Barnwell, who was never happier than when in the air, particularly if he was at the controls, Frise had no great love for flying and much preferred to be at the drawing-board engaged in the solution of some new problem. Barnwell and Frise were in the years to come to gather around them a brilliant design team which was to make an impact upon the history of aviation.

The prototype Bristol F2A Fighter first flew in September 1916, after Frise had completed the whole of the stress calculations and made drawings for a large proportion of the parts. However, by the time quantity production finally commenced in April 1917 the design had been refined as the F2B, and in its final form was fitted with the Rolls-Royce 'Falcon' III 275 hp engine. The 'Brisfit', as the F2B came to be affectionately known, was considered to be one of the most successful military machines to participate in World War 1. In spite of being a two-seater carrying its observer/gunner in the rear seat, it had the manoeuvrability and aerobatic qualities of a single-seat fighter. In the hands of an experienced pilot who flew it as a single-seat fighter, confident in the knowledge that he had ample protection from the rear gunner, it was lethal. Apart from the rear gunner's Scarff-mounted Lewis gun, the F2B employed a single Vickers gun synchronised to fire forward through the propeller. This gun was set on the longitudinal axis of the fuselage and below its surface where it passed through the upper fuel tank. This meant it was conveniently positioned to receive warmth from the engine which prevented it from freezing up. Barnwell had sent his young assistant off in March 1917, to the School of Musketry at Hythe, where he attended a course of instruction on the Vickers gun. Within a fortnight he was back at the design office with a gun, making the necessary drawings for its installation in the F2B.

This was Frise's first experience with aircraft armaments but it was not to be his last by any means for, in 1930, galvanised by his contributions to F2B and Bulldog, he was to design and take out patents on the first Bristol power-operated gun-turret. During the Second World War he was not only to design gun-turret and hydraulic systems of wartime aircraft, such as the Blenheim and Beaufighter, but was to produce the first all-electric cannon turret in the UK — such was his versatility. Eventually, after leaving Bristol in 1948 he was to establish the Armaments Division of Hunting Percival Aircraft Ltd.

In the end some 4,747 'Brisfits' were to be built by B & C A Co and other licensed firms, and the type was to see service with the RAF up until 1932.

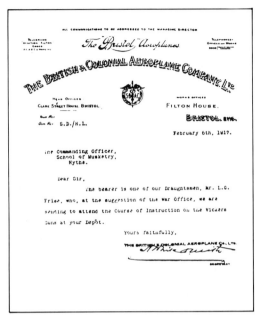

Frise's letter of introduction to the School of Musketry, 1917 *(Mrs Sidonie Frise)*.

Bristol Bullet, Type 32, *G-EATS* the first Bristol aircraft to be designed around a Bristol engine *(British Aerospace, Filton)*.

So successful was the design that Tourer and Coupé versions were built in 1919. Barnwell was now firmly established as a leading aircraft designer and in recognition of his services he was awarded an OBE in 1917, to which was added the AFC. It was in the same year that his elder brother Harold was to be killed near Dartford, Kent, whilst flying a Vickers FB26. Meanwhile his younger brother Archibald, who had been a reservist, had entered the Army as a Captain with the Royal Artillery and gone to France, where he was awarded the DSO and the Belgian *Croix de Guerre*. Certainly the Barnwells had made their contribution to their country's need in time of war.

Two further types were to emerge from the Barnwell stable in 1918 — the all-metal MR1 biplane and the single-seat Scout F — neither of which were to see wartime service. However, both were significant steps in the development of Bulldog, as yet unconceived.

The MR1 — Bristol's first all-metal aeroplane — was a two-seater reconnaissance biplane constructed from high tensile steel, aluminium alloy and small amounts of mild steel. Bristol had shown a strong interest in an aircraft using this type of construction since 1914, and in November 1916 a contract was placed for two prototypes to be used in evaluation and testing. At this time Barnwell was heavily involved, along with Frise, in the Bristol F2B Fighter, which meant that the detail design work on MR1 was assigned to W. T. Reid. The aircraft bore a strong resemblance to the F2 designs and employed a duralumin monocoque fuselage, one of the first examples of double-skin construction, built up from four sections bolted together. By mid-1917 the first of the two aircraft, *A5177*, was complete except for its wings; it had been found that their construction in duralumin was unsatisfactory, owing to excessive flexing, and it was eventually finished using wings of wooden construction. The second prototype *A5178*, now fitted with steel wings and 180 hp Wolseley Viper engine, was first flown late in 1918; it was, however, never destined to fulfil its role of evaluation by the Royal Aircraft Establishment. Barnwell, unlike Frise, was never happier than when flying an aeroplane and it was whilst he was making the delivery flight to Farnborough that he collided with the top of a tree on his landing approach and crashed near the north gate of the RAE. Fortunately Barnwell was unhurt but the aircraft was considered beyond repair and reliance had to be made upon the information received from the structural tests carried out on *A5177*.

By the end of 1916 the limitations of the rotary engine were becoming apparent and Barnwell set out to design a single-seat fighter biplane known as the Scout E capable of accepting more powerful in-line and radial engines. The result was that by May 1917 he had drawn up a revised version of the Scout E known as the Scout F, designed to accept the 200 hp Hispano-Suiza 8Ab engine. However, because of reliability and supply problems with this engine, the specification was changed a month later for installation of the 200 hp Sunbeam Arab, and it was with this engine that the first Scout F flew in March 1918. Its performance was remarkable for its time, achieving a maximum speed of 138 mph at sea level and 128 mph at 10,000 ft. The second Scout F was well received by experienced pilots of the CFS who, whilst enthusiastic about its flying qualities, were less impressed by its vibration-prone Arab engine. Quite fortuitously at this time A. H. Roy Fedden had received a contract for 200 Cosmos Mercury radial engines and was looking for a suitable aircraft as a test-bed. Fedden approached Barnwell and a 315 hp Cosmos Mercury was installed in Scout F *B3991*. It was test flown on 6 September 1918 by F. P. Raynham, and was subsequently delivered to Farnborough where in April 1919 it put up unofficial records by climbing to 10,000 ft in 5.4 minutes, and to 20,000 ft in 16.25 minutes, with a maximum speed of 143 mph at sea level. The Cosmos Mercury contract was cancelled due to the Armistice though, and no further development took place on the Scout F, only four having been built.

The success of the Mercury in the Scout F encouraged Fedden to work with Barnwell on similar exercises for his new 400 hp nine-cylinder Cosmos Jupiter radial engine. Barnwell had been working on a new design of two-seater reconnaissance fighter biplane designated the F2C, officially named Badger, when a contract was placed in September 1918 for three prototypes. With the cessation of hostilities, production contracts were cancelled and the second Badger was not to fly until 24 May 1919, but it was to be instrumental in launching the Jupiter engine on its long and illustrious career. In addition, Badger was to be the impetus which caused Bristol to install their own wind tunnel, rather than sending 1/10th scale models to the National Physical Laboratory to confirm aerodynamic design. The Badger had shown in full-scale flight tests, control inadequacies which had not been revealed in the 1/10th scale tests; eventually this led to the installation at Filton, in June 1919, of their own NPL-type equipment. This 4 ft square, closed-jet type of tunnel, with a parallel length of 24.5 ft, was to remain in service until destroyed by the

Bristol MR1 metal biplane (originally *A5177*) at Filton, 1918 *(British Aerospace, Filton).*

Luftwaffe in 1942. The Jupiter I's excellent performance in the Badger was instrumental in an order being placed for a fourth aircraft, this time to full military standard. In the meantime, Frise had re-designed the ailerons to give better control, but was met with a claim from A. V. Roe & Co that they already held a patent on the design. This sent Frise back to the drawing-board and led to the introduction of the Frise-aileron, on which he took out a patent in 1921. By setting the aileron hinges back from the rear spar fixings, the design gave light and progressive control loads at speed, without snatch. Although Frise only received the princely sum of £1 for his idea, his company was to receive royalties from various manufacturers, including A. V. Roe & Co, for many years. It was eventually adopted as practically standard practice throughout the world, and such was its efficacy that it enabled the Spitfire to have superiority of manoeuvre over enemy aircraft such as the Messerschmitt Bf 109E, not so fitted. It was not until 1932 that Frise was given recognition for this

work when he was awarded the Wakefield Gold Medal by the Royal Aeronautical Society.

The B & C A Co had by the end of the First World War firmly established itself as an aircraft manufacturer of world-wide repute and quickly realised the need to maintain this reputation. Barnwell had again been encouraged by Fedden, this time to design an aircraft specifically around the new Jupiter engine, now that it had shown such promise in the Badger. The outcome was to be the Bullet (not to be confused with the wartime Scout D), a single-seat biplane specifically designed to keep Bristol's name to the fore in international air-races, and at the same time to act as a test-bed for the more powerful 450 hp Cosmos Jupiter II engine. On 31 December 1919 the B & C A Co was to become the Bristol Aeroplane Co, and by July 1920 the Cosmos Engineering Co had become its Aero Engine Department. This meant that when the Bullet finally appeared on 24 July 1920 at the Aerial Derby, it was to be the first aircraft to combine a Bristol airframe with a Bristol engine. It

Alveston House Hotel — formerly Alveston House,
residence of Frank and Marjorie Barnwell
(Alveston House Hotel).

was to become one of the fastest aeroplanes of its
day, distinguishing itself in the Aerial Derby and
King's Cup Air Races of 1920, 1921 and 1922,
whilst in its final modified form it achieved a
maximum speed of 170 mph. Although only of
wooden construction — the standard practice for
that time — it had of necessity great structural
strength, and was to be the progenitor of similar
high-performance single-seat Bristol biplanes,
such as the Badminton and Bulldog, yet to come.

The early 1920s were years of slump and
depression for the aircraft industry, and the Bristol
Aeroplane Company was forced to rely upon the
production of aero-engines from their newly
acquired Cosmos concern in the post-war period.
Naturally with the rapid decline in orders for
military aircraft the company's interest was
directed mainly towards civil aircraft, which meant
that Barnwell's and Frise's fecundity produced
several innovative designs, amongst them being the
Babe and the Tramp. The Babe was a single-seat
sporting biplane, hardly more than a toy, but it
stoked up Barnwell's interest in the light aeroplane
to a fascination, which was to lead ultimately to his
untimely death. Their vision and foresight were
highlighted in the design of the Tramp, a four-
engined triplane freighter, a concept far ahead of
its time and one which was to culminate in the
Bristol Freighter/Wayfarer some 25 years later.

The financial stringency exercised towards
military aircraft contracts was truly reflected in the
economy of design shown by the Bullfinch fighter
— an aircraft capable of being built in two forms.
As a two-seater fighter it was a sesquiplane with a
rear cockpit for a gunner, whilst by detaching the
lower wing and the rear cockpit section of the

fuselage, it became a single-seat parasol fighter.
The failure of the Bullfinch to achieve a production
contract in 1921 led Barnwell to become as
frustrated and depressed as he had been in 1914
and he decided that his future lay elsewhere.

The company made every effort to dissuade
Barnwell from leaving them, but in October 1921
he resigned and took up a technical commission,
with the rank of Major, in the Royal Australian Air
Force whereupon W. T. Reid was appointed Chief
Designer. Barnwell was to work closely with
Squadron Leader L. J. Wackett (later to become
Sir Leonard — founder of the Australian aircraft
industry) who was to establish the first
Experimental Air Station for aircraft design and
development at Randwick, a suburb of Sydney
NSW. To the Australians, Barnwell was just
another 'Pommie' for whom they had little regard
and after a time he again found himself to be
under-used — the sum total of his endeavours
being, to use his own words, 'to design a tail-skid'.
He returned to Bristol in October 1923 at an
opportune time, for W. T. Reid had just resigned in
order to take up an appointment with the
Canadian Vickers Co. The 'Old Man', as he was
known, received a warm welcome back at the
Filton design office, where he resumed his old post
as Chief Designer. Several factors had over the
years combined to earn him this affectionate title.
Firstly, his prematurely balding appearance allied
to a quiet and thoughtful manner; secondly, the
fact that he walked with a limp — the legacy of an
RFC crash when he broke both of his ankles — and
lastly the position he held within the company. He
was delighted to be back and took up residence
with his wife and three children at Alveston House,
some ten miles north of Bristol. Hilda Shepherd,

Bristol Bullet, Type 32
(Drawings by kind permission of C. H. Barnes/The Bodley Head).

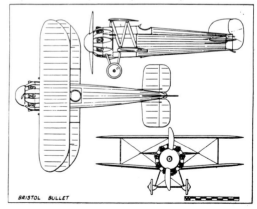

now an 82-year-old living in a retirement home in Alveston, remembers that time when she worked as a nineteen-year-old chambermaid at the Barnwells' residence — now a hotel. She recalls that:

'Captain Barnwell was a very quiet gentleman who mostly liked to sit reading in his study during the evenings. Sometimes at weekends he would go for walks, or use his Rudge-Whitworth bicycle on country rides.

'Mrs Marjorie Barnwell was a very dignified and kind lady who liked to relax by playing bridge, but the family would always worship at the parish church on Sundays.'

The period 1923-1925 was to see the coming together of a very strong and powerful design team at Filton, comprising Barnwell, Frise, Tinson, Pollard and Russell. Tinson had left the employ of Frederick Sage & Co in 1921 when they lost their contract for amphibian machines. He then found himself with no more challenging a task than re-designing the wooden laths used on sun-blinds (Sage's pre-war business was shop-fitting) in order to prevent sag, by forming sheet brass in the section of a wing-spar! Leaving Sage's for A. V. Roe & Co at Hamble, where he worked as an assistant to Roy Chadwick, had been hardly more challenging and on 1 January 1923 he returned to Filton as a leading draughtsman. When Barnwell returned from Australia he appointed Tinson as his Chief Draughtsman, a post he was to hold for ten years.

Harold J. Pollard joined the team in 1922,

having previously worked with Boulton & Paul Ltd, where J. D. North had led the firm in the development of constructing aircraft in steel. Consequently Pollard, a tough but likeable north countryman, had acquired a specialist knowledge of high tensile steel strip fabrication. He worked closely with Tinson in developing methods of rolling the flat steel strips into tubular sections. This knowledge was soon to be exploited by the company, when Air Ministry specifications started to preclude the use of wood in the construction of RAF fighter aircraft. The use of fabricated steel was to last for a period of ten years, whereupon it was superseded by the use of stressed-skin constructions, as aluminium alloys were perfected. Pollard was, in 1951, awarded the Royal Aeronautical Society's bronze medal for his contribution to the development of aircraft construction.

Archibald E. Russell (to become Sir Archibald in 1972 when he was knighted for his contribution to the design of Concorde) joined the company in 1925 as a young 22-year-old stressman. He had graduated from Bristol University with an honours degree in Mechanical Engineering a year earlier, and had then spent some time at the Bristol Bus Co at Eastfield, working under Professor Morgan. He recalls that his employment with Bristol came about quite by accident because his friend Adams, a co-graduate at university, had gone to Filton and hated it. After twelve months they were both offered jobs in the Midlands, but Russell did not

Bristol Badminton I, Type 99, *G-EBMK*, April 1926 *(British Aerospace, Filton)*.

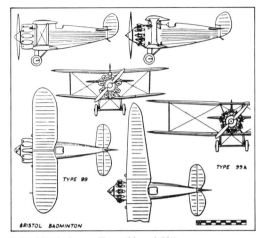

Bristol Badminton, Types 99 and 99A
(Drawings by kind permission of C. H. Barnes/The Bodley Head).

want to take his because he had a girl-friend in Bristol. They decided that if Adams could get the job in the Midlands, then he would recommend Russell to his old employer as an immediate replacement. His first task as a complete novice in the design office, where he was the only one with a slide rule, was to calculate the size of orifice needed on the shock absorbing oleo-leg for the Berkley. This was a two-seater day bomber biplane which eventually lost out in competition to the Hawker Horsley. He was later to work very closely with Frise whom he considered to be 'the best aircraft designer in the country by a long way'.

The mid-1920s were lean years for Bristol as well as for other aircraft manufacturers, and Russell

remembers that 'things were pretty quiet in the Filton design office when I started there in 1925'. Two years earlier the Air Council had decided, in spite of the prevailing financial restraint, that the Royal Air Force should be increased over a period of time to 81 squadrons. At the same time design, performance and strategic requirements were changing. Increased power from aero-engines was imposing higher stresses on aircraft structures which meant, among other things, that wooden construction was no longer adequate. Apart from the strength factor, wooden aircraft were proving difficult to maintain during service use in the Middle East and on the North-West Frontier of India, where the heat and humidity played havoc with their correct rigging. The complexity of fighter and bomber aircraft was also increasing as higher service ceilings meant the carrying of oxygen, whilst the need for improved communications called for installation of radio telephony equipment. Parachutes were to become compulsory equipment for the RAF in 1926 — a measure long overdue — and this was reflected in a design requirement for parachute-type seats.

The first all-metal Bristol aircraft, MR1, had been followed up in 1923 by the Bloodhound — a two-seat fighter biplane designed by Reid during Barnwell's absence — which first flew in June 1925. It was intended to be a replacement for the successful F2B, and used tubular steel in its construction, a method which unfortunately proved unsuitable for production purposes. Hawker were to develop their own successful method of using tubing in a bolted-construction which obviated the need for welding. Pollard's method was to form a tube by rolling flat high

Bristol Badminton I, Type 99, in skeletal form *(British Aerospace, Filton).*

tensile strip steel into cusped and flanged sections which were then joined by riveting. In this way he produced tubes for use as longerons, or struts, which were then joined together by using pre-formed gusset-plates, rather than the more expensive and conventional machined end-fittings. Not only was the ensuing structure stronger and lighter, but it was cheaper to produce and more easily repaired when damaged than were other methods of fabrication. The efficacy of the latter aspect was to be amply demonstrated in his contribution to the construction of the Boarhound, a two-seat fighter biplane, which first flew in 1925. Cyril Uwins had crashed *G-EBLG* at Odiham on 11 August 1925, severely damaging it, but within a week it was quickly repaired at Filton and delivered back for its service trials.

Air Ministry performance specifications were to be drastically revised when the Fairey Fox, a two-seat light bomber biplane, embarrassingly appeared on the scene in March 1925. It had been designed around the Curtiss D12 vee-twelve liquid-cooled engine, a product which had already distinguished itself in the Schneider Trophy races. Its small frontal area enabled the Fox bomber to have a clean low-drag form which, when combined with a Fairey-Reed metal propeller, gave it a top speed of almost 160 mph — a 50 mph advantage over its predecessor, the Fawn. In October of that year it was demonstrated to Air Chief Marshal Sir Hugh Trenchard, where it proved its superiority in rate of climb as well as speed, even over contemporary RAF fighters. Ironically No 12 Squadron, Barnwell's old RFC squadron, was the first to be equipped with the new aircraft. It now became apparent that new and faster fighters would be required if an adequate air defence was to be maintained. Barnwell and Fedden became more determined than ever that a Bristol product should meet that need.

The unwarranted stigma that had unfortunately been attached to the monoplane during World War 1 by those who held the purse strings, meant that aircraft designers were still encouraged to keep with the biplane configuration. There is no doubt that had the main thrust of aircraft design effort in 1914 been placed in the monoplane rather than the biplane, then the air battles of World War 1 might well have been fought at much higher speeds than they were. There was, however, some compensation in the biplane layout for its good manoeuvrability and rate of climb were factors not to be ignored. It was to be shown during the air battles over Malta during 1940 that the agility of the Italian Fiat CR42 biplane often made it a match for the Hurricane monoplane, and more

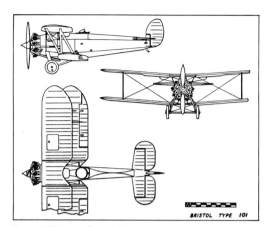

Bristol Fighter, Type 101
(Drawings by kind permission of C. H. Barnes/The Bodley Head).

than one British pilot found it a very difficult aeroplane to shake off once engaged in combat. Nor should it be forgotten that the Hawker Fury's rate of climb up to 20,000 ft was fractionally faster than that of the more modern Hurricane when it first appeared. Fortunately for Britain, the fighter biplane was to reach the peak of its development by the mid-1930s, marginally in time to allow the RAF to meet the *Luftwaffe* on equal terms in quality, if not in quantity.

Apart from Beaver — a derivative of Boarhound — two more new Barnwell biplanes were to fly before Bulldog was to be conceived. These were the single-seat Badminton racer, and the Type 101 two-seat fighter, with which he hoped to repeat the

Bristol, Type 102A.
(Drawings by kind permission of C. H. Barnes/The Bodley Head).

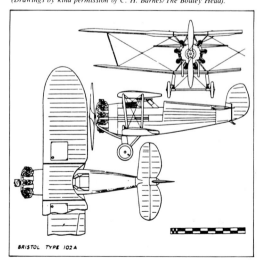

Bristol Badminton II, Type 99A, in which Captain F. L. Barnard was killed on 28 July 1927
(British Aerospace, Filton).

success of the F2B. Barnwell's design method when a new prototype was in the offing was to disappear for three or four weeks. He would then return to the design office with a GA drawing meticulously finished, with weights and performance estimates as well as most of the preliminary stressing completed. Frise did not work like that at all but would use a more imaginative and consultative aproach. He would gather others around him listening and discussing, thereby pooling ideas to produce a design. The purpose of Badminton was to produce an aircraft that could win the King's Cup Air Race and at the same time promote Fedden's developing range of Jupiter engines. Barnwell had already produced sketches by March 1924 but it was not until September that he was given authority to commence design. A one-fifth scale model was built and put through a series of wind tunnel drag tests before a full-scale model was built. It was virtually an all-wooden construction with a fairly restricted forward view, owing to the shrouding of the top wing attachments to the centre-line of the fuselage.

As first flown by Cyril F. Uwins on 5 May 1926 using a 510 hp Jupiter VI engine, it gave an encouraging performance. Captain Frank L. Barnard, chief pilot of Imperial Airways, who had been the winner of the 1922 and 1925 King's Cup Races, was hired by the company to fly Badminton I in the 1926 event. Success was to elude him in this race when on the third lap he made a forced-landing owing to a faulty fuel feed supply. Barnard was undeterred by the set-back and expressed a willingness to try again in the 1927 event. Under

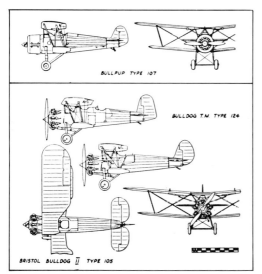

Bristol Bulldog II, Type 105; Bullpup, Type 107 and
Bulldog TM, Type 124

(Drawings by kind permission of C. H. Barnes/The Bodley Head).

Barnard's guidance modifications were carried out, resulting in an increased wingspan (26 ft 7 in) and removal of the upper wing centre-line attachment and shroud, thereby improving forward vision. In this form and using an Orion (Jupiter VI) engine it was known as the Badminton II. For the 1927 King's Cup Race further modifications to take advantage of handicap rules were implemented. This again meant an increase in wingspan (33 ft) but with a high degree of taper from root to tip, whilst the outer wing struts were replaced by single I struts. Using a 525 hp Jupiter VI of reduced diameter, it handled well and was known as the Badminton Type 99A. Barnard took the aircraft up from Filton on a test-flight on 28 July 1927 but, having reached a height of only 200 ft, the engine seized. In an attempt to turn and land in a nearby field the aircraft stalled and nose-dived from a height of 80 ft and Barnard was killed instantly. His death was a great blow to the company as well as to aviation in general, for he was a pilot held in high esteem; but much useful knowledge had been gained which was soon to be utilised in Bulldog.

The company was beginning to recognise the advantages of designing aircraft as private ventures rather than to official orders; it meant that they were free from official restrictions and could sell abroad as they pleased. It was on this basis that Barnwell was directed to design a two-seat fighter designated Type 101, and in January

1926 he produced a GA plus the usual calculations. This high-performance aircraft was an attempt to challenge the Fairey Fox and it was therefore designed originally for the 480 hp Mercury II, but owing to delays in this engine's development the 450 hp Jupiter VI was fitted instead. The 101 was an equal-span (33 ft 7 in) biplane with a plywood monocoque fuselage, and steel wings constructed by Pollard's method with flat steel-strip. It carried seventy gallons of fuel in two upper wing-mounted tanks, whilst the lower wing was mounted at a mid-way gap by pylons and faired into the fuselage. The aircraft's armament consisted of two Vickers guns mounted in troughs in the fuselage and synchronised to fire through the propeller, whilst the rear cockpit carried a single Lewis gun mounted on a Scarff ring. In spite of being turned down by the Air Ministry in March 1926 because of its wooden fuselage, the prototype (registered *G-EBOW*) was completed, but did not fly until 5 August 1927. With the rear cockpit partially faired in, armament removed, ailerons now operating on the upper instead of the lower wings, and a Jupiter VIA engine installed, it took second place in the King's Cup Race on 21 July 1928 with Cyril Uwins at the controls. It was subsequently relegated to the role of test-bed for the Mercury engine, but on 29 November 1929 it was destroyed when it broke up in the air during an overspeed test dive; the test pilot, C. L. Shaw, abandoned the aircraft and made a parachute descent landing unhurt.

In March 1924 the Air Ministry had issued specification F17/24, which called for a fast interceptor fighter using the Rolls-Royce Falcon XI engine, and Barnwell had sought to respond with a design incorporating the in-line engine. Fedden, however, challenged the specification, objecting to the power requirement which excluded the use of his Jupiter and Mercury radials, and consequently a design was not submitted. The arrival of the Fox in early 1925 convinced the Air Staff that a replacement was needed for the obsolescent Woodcock and Gamecock, as well as for the ageing Siskin, and by April 1926 specification F9/26, for a day-and-night fighter, had been issued. This revived Barnwell's interest in the single-seat fighter, and by September of that year he had submitted a design based on the Badminton racer and designated Type 102. It was detailed and drawn up by a young draughtsman, H. W. 'Micky' Dunn, who had recently arrived from F. Sage & Co. Type 102A was for a landplane, whilst Type 102B was for a floatplane that would also meet specification N21/26 — a naval version of F9/26. Barnwell's design was rejected, which was very bad news for the company as well as the design office during that time of economic depression. Bristol had over the past ten years produced some eighty designs, only two of which, apart from the F2B and M1C monoplane, had achieved production. These two were the Type 83 two-seat light trainer biplane, and the Type 89 Jupiter School trainer which was based on the F2B; only a meagre 24 of each had been produced.

Frise, who was particularly disappointed by the failure of Barnwell's 102, decided to approach the directors of the company with two further designs of his own. It was a move which needed delicate handling, for he was virtually going behind the back of Barnwell to whom he had no wish to be disloyal. In retrospect it can be seen that Frise had a determination not unlike that of Roy Fedden in the Engine Department; neither man was easily baulked by seeming failure and both equally saved

the company as an aircraft manufacturer during those very difficult times. (Frise's willingness, almost ruthlessness, in adopting unorthodox methods to achieve a justifiable end was to be highlighted later in 1941. The Beaufort, which was designed to carry a torpedo inside its fuselage, was being used to attack German shipping in the North Sea but on many occasions aircraft were arriving at their targets at the limit of their range. In this situation the Beaufort was an easy victim for *Luftwaffe* fighters scrambled from their Norwegian coastal bases. Frise, after discussion with Beaufort operational crews, saw the Beaufighter with its greater speed, manoeuvrability and heavier armament as the answer, if it could be modified to carry a torpedo on the underside of its belly. Attempts to obtain a torpedo with which to experiment were met with a negative bureaucratic response. 'As the specification for a Beaufighter

Bristol Fighter, Type 101, with rear cockpit partially faired and armament removed and as flown in the King's Cup Air Race in July 1928 *(British Aerospace, Filton).*

Bristol Scout F, Type 21, (*B3991*) with close fitting cowling around its 315hp Cosmos Mercury engine, Filton, October 1918 *(British Aerospace, Filton).*

did not call for a torpedo carrying requirement, one could not be supplied.' Frise, who knew exactly what he wanted, and having the correct Ministry code and reference for such a torpedo, decided to take the law into his own hands. He set out from Filton with a company vehicle and driver, and headed for the RN Stores at Gosport where he asked for 'the' torpedo, adding that the paperwork would follow in due course. His persuasiveness was effective, for the torpedo was loaded on to the vehicle without question and he quickly headed back to Bristol, no doubt already turning over in his mind exactly how he would fit it. Within a few months Frise was inviting Air Ministry officials to Filton in order to witness trials of Bristol's new torpedo-carrying Beaufighter, and such was their enthusiasm that they asked how quickly they could have 25 modified aircraft!)

Frise was given permission to proceed with an F9/26 design which was Type 105, and an F17/24 design which was Type 107. These designs had

been drawn up by Frise during the late summer of 1926, with Russell, his protégé, assisting in the stressing calculations. Design criteria in those days were largely derived empirically, knowing from past history what could and could not be done. Russell had developed a great admiration for Frise whom he considered to be one of the finest aircraft designers of his day. He recalls:

'I can see Frise now in my mind's eye at his board, drawing the first lines on Bulldog — he liked me to watch him. He'd have the tenth-scale plastic man put in the seat and he would draw the field of vision from his eyes, and that was where the leading edge of the lower-wing was going to be. Then he would fix the relative areas of the wing, and position of the upper wing stagger, wholly by the pilot's visual requirements. There were no aerodynamics in that whatsoever — it was solely to give the pilot the best view.'

Wind tunnel tests had given encouraging results,

Sir Archibald Russell, CBE, FRAeS
(British Aerospace, Filton).

J9051 — to be known as Bullpup — was ordered. At the same time the company decided to proceed with Type 105, now known as Bulldog, and a prototype was built as a private venture. Owing to difficulties being experienced in the supply of the Mercury engine, a Jupiter VII was fitted, and on 10 May 1927 with Cyril Uwins — Bristol's Chief Test Pilot — at the controls, it took to the air for the first time.

Leslie George Frise, BSc, FRAeS
(Mrs. Sidonie Frise).

and so mock-ups were built in February 1927 and given Air Ministry approval. In all, there were to be three layouts of Type 105; the first, drawn up on 13 August 1926, had wings of equal span; by November, in the second layout, the wings had been reduced in span as well as in chord; finally, in March 1927 the third and final design, although slightly larger than Type 107, closely harmonised with it. By this time specification F20/27, an up-date of F17/24, had been issued for an interceptor, and Type 107 was detailed to meet it using a geared Mercury III engine which was then being developed. The design was accepted by the Air Ministry for development, and one prototype,

Chapter 2
The four stars from Patchway

Alfred Hubert Roy Fedden was born in Bristol on 6 June 1885, the youngest son of a wealthy Victorian businessman and County Magistrate who had a propensity for philanthropic work amongst orphan children. He was educated at public school, where his headmaster encouraged him to make a career in the Army and recommended to his father that he should enter Sandhurst. Roy, however, had other ideas, born out of his passion and interest in motor cars, and wanted to become an engineer. Such a profession was at that time socially unacceptable to the middle-class into which he had been born, where it was associated with an 'oily rag and cloth-cap' image — an attitude which, unfortunately, still persists to a certain degree in our present day society. Roy's father reluctantly agreed to his desire to become an engineer, and in 1904 he began a three-year apprenticeship with the Bristol Motor Co where he received a thorough practical training. Realising the need to consolidate this training with a theoretical knowledge of automobile engineering, he attended the Merchant Venturers' Technical College during the evening where he studied under the direction of Professor William Morgan. (A. E. Russell was himself to come under the influence of Morgan, some twenty years later, when he worked for the Bristol Bus Co prior to joining the Filton design office.)

Upon completion of his apprenticeship Fedden took up employment as a junior draughtsman with Brazil Straker & Co, Fishponds, a local firm of motor manufacturers. It was not long before his single-mindedness, allied to his natural ability as a design engineer, encouraged his employer to appoint him as their Chief Engineer. Fedden's reputation was soon to be enhanced by the design team that he had inherited, which included men of great talent such as L. G. 'Bunny' Butler, the chief designer, and Fred Whitehead, a production engineer of outstanding ability. By 1909 the firm was producing its successful 15 hp Straker Squire, a car which was to compete at Brooklands and other events, sometimes with Fedden himself at the wheel. Although he was elected a member of the Institution of Mechanical Engineers in 1910, he by

no means confined his interests to automobile engineering, for amongst the racing fraternity with whom he now mixed, particularly at Brooklands, were those who flew and maintained aircraft. By the time war was declared in 1914, Fedden had firmly established himself as an engineer of some repute and was appointed Technical Director of Brazil Straker, with a seat on the board of directors. At the same time the company was to be involved with aero-engines, for it had been given an Admiralty contract to overhaul Curtiss OX-5 engines, which at that time powered the Curtiss JN-4s being used by the RNAS. Careful examination of these engines by Fedden and Butler not only revealed lack of quality control in their manufacture, but also basic design faults. Within a few months they had redesigned more than a half of the major components, which they then produced and built into a more reliable engine.

So impressed were the Admiralty by Brazil Straker's contribution to the redesigned Curtiss engine that by January 1915 the Fishponds factory was given over totally to war production. The company's reputation was soon to be firmly established when it was entrusted with the manufacture of two of Rolls-Royce's recently designed aero-engines; the six-cylinder 125 hp Hawk and the vee-twelve 280 hp Falcon which was to power the Bristol F2B Fighter. Fedden's and Butler's appetite for original design, rather than solely manufacturing, had been partially whetted by their revised Curtiss design, but was to be fully satisfied early in 1917 when the Admiralty drafted and issued a new specification. This called for a static air-cooled radial engine weighing no more than 600 lb and to give a maximum power of 300 hp. The specification of a radial, rather than an in-line engine, pleased Fedden, partially because he had been forbidden by a clause in his Rolls-Royce licence to manufacture or even to produce a rival in-line engine. The result of his submission to the specification was to be the prototype Mercury, a 14-cylinder 300 hp two-row radial, which soon received an order for 200. The engine was, however, never to reach the production stage for it was subsequently cancelled with the cessation of

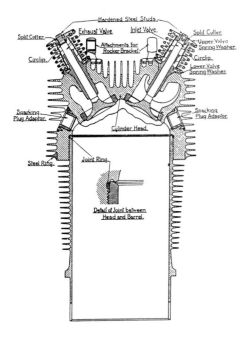

Fig. 1 — Section of Cylinder Jupiter VIIF

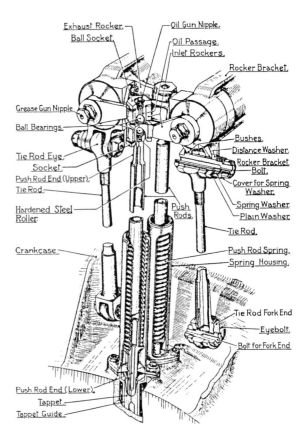

Fig. 2 — Details of Jupiter Push Rods and Tie Rods.

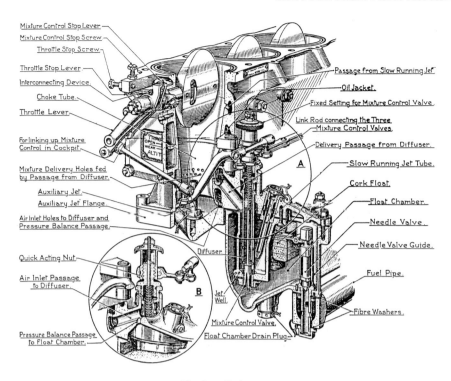

Fig. 3 — Carburettor

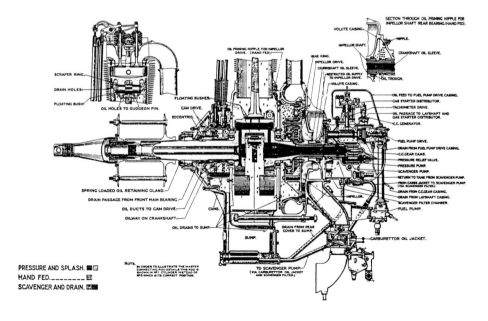

Fig. 4 — Jupiter VII Lubrication Diagram

Sir A. H. "Roy" Fedden *(Rolls Royce plc, Aero Division Bristol).*

hostilities in November 1918. The second prototype — the first of Fedden's design to fly — was fitted into Barnwell's Scout F, and took to the air on 6 September 1918. Its performance was such that in April 1919 it set up a record for the rate of climb of an aircraft to 20,000 ft; a record which was to stand for three years. Brazil Straker & Co had in the meantime been taken over by a financial group and renamed Cosmos Engineering Co.

In an attempt to obtain greater power and more simplicity in design, Fedden and Butler drew up a nine-cylinder air-cooled radial of 400 hp, which was to become known as the Jupiter. It had a bore and stroke of 5.75 in (146 mm) by 7.5in (190 mm) giving it a capacity of 1,753 cu in (28.7 L), and used a one-piece single throw crankshaft which carried the split master-rod and its eight articulated connecting rods. The steel cylinders incorporated their own four valve integral cylinder heads, to which were added separate finned aluminium heads for efficient heat dissipation. Its crankcase comprised two machined aluminium castings, split vertically, and secured together on assembly by nine close-fitting bolts which correctly aligned the two halves. Carburation was by three adjacent carburettors, connected to the nine cylinders via

the main induction annulus, inside of which was housed a spiral deflector plate to give an even distribution of gas charge. Like all good designs it was simple and therefore relatively cheap to produce, whilst at the same time it was robust and easy to maintain.

The Air Ministry accepted the design and the first prototype was bench-tested on 29 October 1918, but again as in the case of the Mercury the Armistice thwarted its production. In spite of the cancellation of orders, Fedden was officially encouraged to continue with the development of the Jupiter, and in the early part of 1919 a second prototype was built, this time incorporating reduction gearing. This engine, now known as Jupiter I, was fitted to the Badger II and first flown by Cyril Uwins on 24 May 1919.

Cyril Frank Uwins was to play an important role, not only in the development of Jupiter and Mercury, but also in the Bristol Bulldog itself. He was, in a sense, the vital link between the two design teams; Barnwell and Frise on the aircraft, and Fedden and Butler on the engine side. He had joined the British and Colonial Aeroplane Co on 25 October 1918 — just at the time Fedden and Butler were producing their prototype radials. As a Captain and pilot in the RFC he had, in January 1917, experienced an engine failure and crashed whilst taking off from St Omer airfield. He sustained injuries which included a broken neck, and subsequently earned him the tag of 'the man who couldn't be killed'. Within six months he was back again on flying duties, but now on a secondment which relegated him to ferrying aircraft from B & C A Co's Aircraft Acceptance Park, at Filton, to their various destinations. These duties included giving each aircraft a short test-flight before delivery and this naturally gave him an intimate knowledge of the company's products. He became a familiar figure at Filton and was eventually offered a post by the company which included test-flying, and oversight of their Flying Schools at Filton, Amesbury and Brooklands.

In December 1919 the Cosmos Engineering Co went into liquidation, leaving Fedden, and his staff in a precarious and uncertain position, for the firm was soon to be placed in the hands of the Official Receiver. Various established aircraft manufacturers, such as the Bristol Aeroplane Co, Vickers and Armstrong Siddeley were interested, but empty order books in the industry, and a surplus of aircraft resulting from the aftermath of war, made them indecisive. Bristol was the natural choice as purchaser by virtue of their close proximity and existing ties as a customer. After some pressure from the Air Ministry, they made a

Cosmos Jupiter engine
(Rolls Royce plc, Aero Division, Bristol).

decision to purchase, and on 29 July 1920, Cosmos Engineering became the Aero-Engine Department of the Bristol Aeroplane Co Ltd. The result of this decision, probably unforeseen at the time, was without doubt to be the salvation of the company in those lean post-war years. It must be remembered that from the end of the war until the production of Bulldog, early in 1929, the company was only to sell some fifty aircraft, apart from the F2B and its derivatives. In contrast, the Engine Department was to be building and selling engines at home and abroad in substantial numbers, and was eventually to occupy larger premises than its parent firm.

Fedden moved his equipment and staff from Fishponds to the village of Patchway which was on the north side of the Filton aerodrome, and conveniently near to its flight sheds. He now had a staff of some thirty engineers whom he worked, as he did himself, extremely hard, putting in long hours to survive in those difficult post-war years. He employed what was for that time modern techniques to maintain quality, such as materials testing, fatigue testing, failure analysis and quality control, all of which were to pay rich dividends in establishing a reputation for reliability in his engines. Meanwhile, on 24 July 1920 the Bullet Type 32 racer — the first Bristol aircraft designed specifically for a Jupiter engine — was flown by Uwins in the Aerial Derby, where it achieved the third fastest time.

The Jupiter II 385 hp engine appeared in 1921, incorporating an automatic compensating device which corrected valve and rocker clearance as it

varied when the heated cylinder expanded. Not only did this maintain correct valve timing but it also produced a quieter engine with reduced wear, and therefore less need for maintenance. Its effectiveness was soon to be proven for in September 1921 it became the first engine ever to pass an Air Ministry Type Test. This accolade virtually became a seal of approval, and it was not long before the Gnôme Rhône Co of Paris requested, and was granted, permission to build Jupiter engines under licence. Within seven years of the licence being granted, so successful were Fedden's engines that the French aircraft industry became alarmed when one of their newspapers reported that almost eighty per cent of the aircraft on display at the 1929 Paris *Salon de l'Aéronautique,* were powered by the Jupiter. Little did Fedden imagine, at that time, that the Jupiter would eventually be built by a further sixteen foreign licensees, or that a grand total of 7,100 engines would power more than 262 different types of aircraft!

In 1923 the Jupiter IV 436 hp engine was put through a revised Type Test, which included a 100-hour test at almost maximum power, during which time no replacement parts were allowed to be fitted. It successfully passed these arduous tests and was subsequently stripped down for examination and measurement, whereupon wear

Jupiter IVF *(Rolls Royce plc, Aero Division, Bristol).*

L. G. "Bunny" Butler *(British Aerospace, Filton).*

was found to be negligible. The Air Ministry were so impressed that in September 1923 they placed an order for 81 of the engines, which they had earmarked for fitment to the Hawker Woodcock II. This aircraft had previously, in its Mark I form, been fitted with the Armstrong Siddeley 358 hp Jaguar II fourteen-cylinder, two-row radial engine. Fedden and his team were delighted and were more determined than ever to improve the design and to increase its power output. For some time Fedden and Butler had not been completely happy with the design of the crankshaft assembly on the Jupiter, for the split master rod, which was a highly stressed member, relied upon bolts to hold it around the crank pin. They decided therefore, on Jupiter V, to use a one-piece master rod and make the crankshaft in two halves. This meant that the master rod, complete with its fully floating bearing, was assembled on to the completely parallel crank pin, which itself was integral with one half of the crankshaft. The remaining parallel portion of the crank pin then entered the other half of the crankshaft, where it was secured by a pinch-bolt, which was fully tightened after precise alignment of the crankshaft halves. The integrity of these design modifications were soon to be assured, for in 1924 the engine was subjected to another of the Air Ministry's ever increasingly

stringent Type Tests, which it successfully completed.

Now that the Jupiter was being fitted into several different types of aircraft, Fedden realised the importance of it being correctly installed if it was to give its best performance. He had learned from his experience with Barnwell, on the installations in Scout F, Badger and Bullet, that close liaison was needed between the aircraft manufacturer and his department if his engines were to sell. So in 1923 he appointed Freddie Mayer as his Chief Installation Engineer, and made him not only responsible for supervising engine installation at home and abroad, but also for the supervision of engine-servicing in the Bristol Flying Schools. He became a focal point for customer liaison, which meant that he travelled extensively and to many parts of the world. Mayer had begun his career with the Royal Aircraft Factory (later to become the Royal Aircraft Establishment) at Farnborough, where he was employed as an inspector. In 1915 he was seconded to the B & C A Co, Filton, as a Chief Engine Examiner, before being transferred to their Aircraft Acceptance Park, where he was involved not only with engines, but also in flight-testing and armaments of Bristol aircraft. After the Armistice he was invited to join the company itself, and did so in 1919 before transferring to Fedden's Engine Department in 1921. As the Jupiter and other engines were developed and sold, Fedden came to respect Mayer and the important role he played in the success of the department.

Two new members were to join Fedden's design team in 1922; both were to become experts in their particular discipline and to make major contributions in engine design. Fred Whitehead was a machine tool specialist and production engineer 'par excellence', and had worked with Fedden and Butler during their early days at Brazil Straker & Co. He had left the Fishponds firm to join Vickers where, during the war, he had been engaged on the production of munitions. His intimate knowledge of machining methods, allied to an appreciation of design requirements, enabled him to influence the design of vital components. One such contribution was to be made in 1928 when he suggested ways for machining the fins on the forged cylinder head, making it a design fifteen years in advance of world competition. His introduction of improved machining methods and tooling were to enable the holding of closer tolerances, thereby giving interchangeability of parts, something taken for granted today but then quite rare. This aspect of his contribution was to be amply demonstrated when in 1923 six Jupiter

Freddie Mayer *(British Aerospace, Filton).*

Owner mentioned the name of a colleague who had left the design team after an altercation, Fedden remarked, 'Never ever mention his name, my heart is as stone towards him'. No doubt all men of genius are flawed and Fedden was no exception. His single-mindedness and strivings for perfection did not endear him to many people and, unlike Barnwell who was the perfect gentleman, he did make enemies. Unfortunately, these included the Bristol board of directors, who found Fedden a difficult man to control. Being managers who were largely technically ignorant, they were unable to challenge his continual demands for money to be spent on development, and regarded him with suspicion as an empire-builder. These misunderstandings were to sow the seeds of a rupture in relationships that would eventually,

Frank Owner, CBE *(F.M. Owner).*

engines were taken at random off the production line, bench tested in the presence of the AID inspectorate, and completely stripped down into individual components. The parts were then mixed up, and then rebuilt, whereupon they produced six engines that ran satisfactorily.

Frank Owner — the first graduate to join the Engine Department — was 21 years of age when he started with the company as a stressman, on a wage of two guineas a week. He had a fine brain (he eventually became Chief Engineer in 1947) and was able to analyse and solve complicated vibrational problems that were to occur in the later Schneider Trophy Mercury engine. Working closely with Butler, he was also to be responsible for the introduction of automatic boost control on the company's superchargers. Owner's impression of Fedden in those days was that he was much more of an organiser than an engineer, Butler having the greater strength in that direction. Although he had great respect for the man, he found him to be a hard taskmaster, perfectionist and completely devoid of any sense of humour. He could be petty and grudging too, and on one occasion when some twenty years later, lead to his dismissal from the company.

The Bristol Bloodhound Type 84, a two-seat fighter biplane that had been designed by W. T. Reid during Barnwell's absence in Australia, was to play a vital role in the development of Jupiter. The prototype, no 6222, which first flew in May 1923 registered as *G-EBGG*, was to act as a test-bed for Jupiter V, as well as the recently introduced 450 hp Jupiter VI. The VI now incorporated drop-forged duralumin machined crankcase halves and a reduced frontal area which, when combined with improved machining methods for the valve cam-ring, resulted in a power increase of 12 hp as well as an 80 lb weight reduction. In October 1925 Bloodhound *G-EBGG* was fitted with long-range fuel tanks and the improved Jupiter VI engine which had been sealed by the AID. From 4 January until 8 March 1926 the aircraft was flown, under adverse weather conditions, regularly between Filton and Croydon by Colonel F. F. Minchin and Captain F. L. Barnard, both pilots being on loan from Imperial Airways. At the end of this period, the aircraft had logged 25,074 miles in a total flight time of 225 hours and 54 minutes, during which time the engine had given trouble-free service without any part being replaced. Subsequent stripping and examination of the engine showed it to be in perfect condition, apart from the need to replace one exhaust valve. Imperial Airways were so delighted with the performance of the engine, which they now intended to use in their own aircraft, that *G-EBGG* was flown from Croydon to Cairo return in 56

Jupiter VI
(Rolls Royce plc, Aero Division, Bristol).

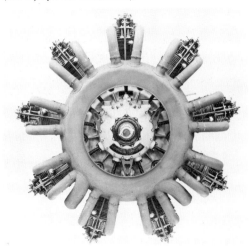

hours using the same engine, and again without trouble. These successful flight-tests not only created a widespread interest in the aircraft industry, at home and abroad, but also within the RAF who were soon to use it in, what was to become their front-line fighter, the Bulldog. Its supreme reliability and ease of maintenance now placed it irretrievably in front of its main rival and competitor, the Armstrong Siddeley Jaguar.

In the early 1920s engineers were well aware of the limitations of the normally aspirated aero-engine. As an aircraft climbed into the rarified atmosphere of, say, 20,000 ft, its power output was only approximately a half of that obtained at sea level. Fedden's engineers were to try five different methods of overcoming the problem, as follows:

(a) Use of a higher compression ratio combined with a gated-throttle.

(b) Use of a higher compression ratio combined with a means for varying the inlet valve timing.

(c) Use of a higher compression ratio combined with a bi-fuel system.

(d) Use of a turbo-supercharger.

(e) Use of a mechanically-driven supercharger.

Method (a), by restricted throttle opening, limited the power available at the lower altitudes of high density, but allowed the increased compression ratio to give maximum power at higher altitudes.

In method (b), the pilot could, by a mechanical linkage from cockpit to engine, rotate the fixed outer annulus of the epicylic gear which meshed with the cam sleeve, and retard the inlet valve timing. This reduced the engine's volumetric efficiency and power at take-off, but allowed, by advance of the control, maximum power at altitude. Both methods (a) and (b) were widely used before the introduction of superchargers.

Method (c) was used successfully in a Bloodhound Jupiter IV by the addition of a tank carrying alcohol fuel for use during take-off and climb, whereupon a switch to normal fuel enabled the engine to take advantage of the increased compression ratio at higher altitudes. The idea was never seriously pursued in production because of the possible dangers from incorrect fuel replenishment.

Superchargers, whether turbo-driven as in (d), or mechanically gear-driven as in (e), are used to force more air/fuel mixture into the engine cylinders as the density of air decreases with altitude. The RAE had already designed a turbocharger whereby the exhaust gases from the engine were used to drive a turbo-blower, and this had been jury-rigged to a 435 hp Jupiter III in the Bristol Seeley Tourer Type 85 in 1923. The Air

Jupiter VIIF *(Rolls Royce plc, Aero Division, Bristol).*

Ministry were encouraged by the results obtained with the Seeley, and invited Fedden to submit a design incorporating the RAE's device. The result was to be the Orion which was basically a Jupiter VI, and when developed was, in 1928, to power a Gloster Gamecock to 20,000 ft in less than thirteen minutes, whilst maintaining its sea-level power of 495 hp. This was a reduction of seven minutes over its performance when fitted with its standard unsupercharged Jupiter VI. However, cooling problems resulting from increased exhaust back pressure, meant that the design was dropped in favour of method (e). By 1926 Fedden had made the optimum choice with a supercharged Jupiter VI incorporating an impeller, which was gear-driven from the crankshaft, through an automatic clutch in order to overcome shock loads.

Fedden was an engineer who believed in the triumph of development over design and in order to prove a proposed design modification he would have a single cylinder test-rig engine built and run. In this way he could predict the effect of design changes in components such as pistons, valve-gear or connecting-rods quickly and cheaply. Since the original Jupiter design, Fedden and Butler had used a cylinder, integrally incorporating its own combustion chamber at one end, on to which was bolted an aluminium cast head, in order to dissipate heat. The reason for this design was to eliminate the sealing problems encountered when

jointing a separate cylinder head to its cylinder. Apart from machining difficulties, the limitations imposed by this design become more apparent as the power output of the engine increased, the main one being that of cooling. By 1926 they had gone over to using a separate cast aluminium cylinder head, which did achieve a suitable cylinder head/cylinder joint. Excessive build-up of heat in the cylinder head continued because of the lack of suitable finning that could be achieved with a casting. They solved the problem in 1928, with the introduction of a drop-forged duralumin cylinder head which was subsequently machined to create finning that gave adequate cooling. The new cylinder head, which now meant the suffix 'F' being added to the engine mark, was screwed on to its cylinder barrel and permanently shrunk into position using a joint seal. Not only did the forged head provide a good seal and adequate cooling, but it enabled a higher induction chamber pressure to be employed from the supercharger.

When the Jupiter VIIF engine finally came off the production line at Patchway in March 1929, it produced 480 hp at the rated altitude of 8,000 ft and had a slightly reduced overall diameter over its predecessor series VII. This reduction was achieved by raising the base flange of the cylinder barrel, thereby allowing the cylinder spigot to enter deeper into the crankcase. The VIIF's carburettors now employed a pump-fed jet which was linked to the throttle, thereby improving acceleration, whilst the supercharger used an automatic boost control (ABC) which ensured that rated boost was not exceeded, irrespective of throttle opening. The ABC was largely Butler's idea and used a barometric capsule linked to an hydraulic servo. Frank Owner recalls being asked by Butler to calculate the size of the capsule needed, which he did, at four inches diameter by fourteen feet in length! Butler was not pleased, so Owner suggested using an hydraulic servo, which controlled the boost so well that pilots complained of being made redundant. In addition, automatic centrifugally controlled ignition was fitted to the VIIF which made the engine more responsive. The series VIIF was to be the engine that powered the bulk of the Jupiter-engined Bulldogs when fitted to the Mark IIa, (the earlier Mark I and II used the VII) whilst the dual-seat trainer TM used the VIF.

Fedden had, with the Jupiter, firmly established the company as the leading manufacturer of reliable air-cooled radial aero-engines. However, the performance of the recently introduced Fairey Fox had made him more than ever aware of the growing popularity of the vee-type liquid-cooled in-line engine for military use. Although the radial

Mercury (short stroke)
(Rolls Royce plc, Aero Division, Bristol).

had the advantage of compactness, lightness, simplicity and ability to operate in extremes of climate without the complications of the radiator and coolant, it did lack the reduced frontal area, and hence low-drag characteristics, of the in-line engine. He sought a solution to this problem in two directions. Firstly, by the initial use of helmet fairings and then Townend cowling rings on the Jupiter Bulldogs; and secondly, by a radial engine of reduced overall diameter, which was to be the Mercury.

The Gnôme-Rhône Jupiters were the first to try separate helmet fairings over each of the nine cylinders, whilst the RAE Farnborough were to experiment with them later on a service Bulldog. The increase in performance (which was marginal) was at the expense of increased cylinder head temperatures and impaired access for maintenance, which meant that they were never implemented on service aircraft.

Two types of Townend engine cowling rings were tried on Jupiter-engined Bulldogs by the RAE. The thin polygonal plate type which were subsequently fitted only to *K1657* of 32 Squadron and *K2206* and *K2227* of 56 Squadron, increasing their top speed by 7 mph; and the thick exhaust type ring which decreased both top speed and rate of climb. The plate ring increased cylinder temperatures by as much as 45°C, even producing a noticeable belt of warm air over the cockpit when the engine was run up with the wheels against the chocks, and its use was never extended. Experiments were subsequently made by the RAE in January 1932, with an NACA type cowl on a

Jupiter VII Bulldog, and whilst top speed was increased by 6 mph the maximum rate of climb decreased from 1,280 to 1,240 ft/min. Again unacceptably high temperature increases were recorded, with the lower two cylinders rising by as much as 80°C, and success with this type of cowling was not to be achieved until it was allied to the Mercury engine.

Fedden and Butler set about the design of the new Mercury engine in 1925; unlike its 1917 Cosmos predecessor of that name, it only used nine cylinders with a bore and stroke of 5.75 in (146 mm) by 6.5 in (165 mm), giving it an overall diameter of 47.5 in against that of 53 in for the Jupiter. It used separate cast-aluminium cylinder heads, which carried their inlet and exhaust valve pairs inclined to each other in a penthouse form, giving improved breathing and reduced overall height. Drop-forged instead of cast-aluminium pistons were used, as well as an extended propeller drive shaft to give a lower profile at the front. With its mechanically-driven supercharger it was to become a worthy successor to the Jupiter which, by the early 1930s, was to have reached its peak. Fedden was anxious to obtain as much publicity as possible for his new engine, having obtained a contract for three prototypes. It was decided to fit the first engine into the Short Crusader racing seaplane, which was a contestant in the 1927 Schneider Trophy event. The engine went through a development stage where Owner had some reservations about the lengthened crankshaft, because his preliminary calculations had shown that it would be running on its firing-order torsional critical speed. The outcome was an agreement to run the engine quickly through its critical speed and operate well above it. The engine was bench-tested, using 100 octane fuel, where it developed 960 hp over short periods, and it was eventually installed in the aircraft. Unfortunately, in spite of preliminary trials in which a speed in excess of 270 mph had been achieved, the aircraft was damaged during a practice, owing to a fault in the rigging of its controls, and had to be withdrawn from the race.

Fedden and Butler were well pleased by the results obtained with the new engine in the Crusader, but were to run into many development problems over the next two years, which seriously delayed the Mercury programme. One aircraft to suffer from this delay was the Bullpup Type 107, a scaled-down version of Bulldog, which had been designed to meet the F20/27 interceptor specification using a Mercury engine. Although it first flew in April 1928, having to use a Jupiter VI, it was not until March 1929 that it was to be fitted with its Mercury IIa. The Bullpup was, however, to eventually demonstrate the superiority of the Mercury installation in 1931, when it was fitted with a short-stroke (5 in) version, enclosed by a close-fitting long chord cowl, and achieved a better performance than when fitted with the more powerful Jupiter VIIF.

By 1930 both of the prototypes of the geared Mercury III and IV engines had been tested in flight. The result was to be the series IVA, which after type testing was installed in Bulldog Mark IIIA, No 7560, carrying Class B registration markings, as *R5*, and flown to the Aeroplane and Armament Experimental Establishment at Martlesham Heath for evaluation on 7 December 1931. The series IVA eventually went into production in 1932 as the IVS2, where it developed 560 hp at 16,500 ft at 2600 rpm. By April 1934 the Mercury had been developed to the 640 hp series VIS2 — the final one for Bulldog — with which it powered the Mark IVA fighter to 224 mph, an increase of 46 mph over Bulldog IIA. In its series VIS2 form the Mercury incorporated some important design changes, which included a far greater area of cooling-fins to its cylinders and heads than in the case of Jupiter, for if it was to take advantage of close-fitting cowls then it needed to dissipate heat more effectively. Increased engine revolutions, resulting from the squarer

Mercury IVS2 *(Rolls Royce plc, Aero Division, Bristol).*

bore/stroke of the Mercury, also meant the need for a stiffer and heavier crankshaft. Owner recalls that he was concerned with possible flexural vibration from the Mercury crankshaft and it occurred to him, whilst calculating its flexural resonance speed (which turned out to be uncomfortably close to its running speed range), that the crankshaft would make an ideal tuning fork. Being blessed with a good ear for musical pitch, he visited the Experimental Fitting Shop in order to make a preliminary test for frequency by striking a suspended crankshaft. Unbeknown to him, the shop foreman was anxiously watching from a distance and soon reported that Owner had gone round the bend, and was knocking hell out of a Mercury crankshaft whilst moaning to himself! He later devised a capacity type of strain gauge, using the crankweb as one element of a condenser, and this showed that his previous estimates were not far out. This was not only one of the first researches on crankshaft flexural vibration, but also one of the few occasions when trouble had been predicted before it occurred.

Cyril Uwins was to play a large part in the development of the Mercury IVA, IVS2 and VIS2, when it was used with and without controllable gills, and various lengths of cowlings, including those of the Townend and NACA type. In one of his reports dated 4 March 1932, whilst flying *R5*, he recorded that the Townend ring remained steady when diving to an indicated 270 mph, adding that recovery was made from the dive at 12,000 ft owing to the presence of clouds at 8,000 ft.

The power from an engine must be converted into useful thrust if it is to give of its best, and therefore the importance of propeller design held great interest for Fedden and Barnwell in particular. It was said on one occasion by Uwins that it seemed as if Barnwell was designing a new propeller every day. In January 1927 he had given a paper, illustrated by 'lantern' slides, entitled *Some notes on the design of Airscrews*, for which he was later awarded the Taylor Gold Medal. Even today his notebooks, which are kept in the library of the Royal Aeronautical Society in London, can be perused, where they show his neat pencilled calculations on tip-speeds, bending-moments due to centrifugal pull, and all that goes to make up propeller design. By the early 1930s the limitations of wooden propellers of fixed pitch were beginning to be realised. Four-bladed wooden propellers had been tried on a Bloodhound with a geared Jupiter VIII engine, and on Bulldog *R1* with its geared Mercury III, but these were to give way to metal designs. Bulldog *J9580* had been used experimentally in 1932 with magnesium-alloy blades, which could be pre-set and locked to different angles before flight, and these had given a better rate of climb than the standard two-bladed wooden Watts propeller. It had long been recognised that variable angles of pitch were needed for optimum efficiency in flight; fine pitch for take-off, so that all available power could be used, and coarse pitch, for cruising economically once airborne. The problem was how this could be achieved. The solution for Barnwell and Fedden was to be the three-bladed Hamilton variable-pitch metal airscrew, which was first tested by the company in 1934, when fitted to Bulldog Mark IVA *R8*. The Mercury VIS2 was, in 1935, to become the first British aero-engine to be approved for use with a variable-pitch propeller. The Mercury was to shine long after the darkness had overtaken Bulldog, and in its later series it was installed in other well known military aircraft, including the Gauntlet, Gladiator, Lysander and Blenheim.

Fedden, like Sir George White (founder of the Bristol Aeroplane Co), was a visionary and one never content to sit back and be satisfied with present achievements. By 1926 he realised that if he was to keep the company's aero-engines to the forefront as a world competitor, then he must move away from the limitation of the poppet-valve mechanism, with its complexity of moving parts, and look for an alternative.

The earliest form of sleeve-valve engine was credited to the American Charles Y. Knight who used two reciprocating steel sleeves, one inside the other, and assembled between cylinder-wall and piston. The sleeves, which had shaped ports cut in them, moved up and down to align with inlet and exhaust ducts in the cylinder-wall, thereby enabling the four-stroke cycle to take place. The system operated reasonably well, and the result was a very quiet engine which came to be known as the 'Silent Knight' when fitted to Daimler and other cars. The real breakthrough was not to come, however, until 1909, when a Scottish engineer named Peter Burt, who worked for the Argyll Co, a firm of motor manufacturers, patented the single sleeve-valve mechanism. The sleeve had a rotary as well as a reciprocating movement, and did the work of Knight's two sleeves. The idea had simultaneously and quite independently been patented also by the Canadian engineer James McCullum. The result was to be an agreement between the two men, whereby the device was patented and known as the Burt-McCullum sleeve-valve mechanism. In 1913 the Argyll Co produced an engine using the patent, which caught Fedden's eye when it won the Naval and Military Aircraft

Engine Competition a year later. Great interest was shown in the new engine particularly by the RAE who experimented with it for a short period, but the war curtailed its development for use in aircraft. However, in 1922 the Scottish firm, Barr and Stroud Co, used the Burt-McCullum mechanism to produce a range of twin-cylinder sleeve valve engines for use in British motor cycles.

Fedden was not alone in considering the possible advantages of the sleeve-valve engine, for in 1925 the American aero-engine manufacturer, Continental Motors, had purchased a patent right on the Burt-McCullum mechanism and used it to produce a radial engine two years later. After much research in looking at all the possible options to the poppet valve, and with the financial help and encouragement of the Air Ministry, Fedden and his engineers decided that the Burt-McCullum single-sleeve valve system offered the best possibilities. As in the design of the poppet-valve Jupiter and Mercury, they turned to the use of single-cylinder test-rig engines for development purposes. They began to build the first such unit in November 1927, using a 5.75 in by 6 in bore and stroke cylinder which was taken from a proposed design of inverted vee-twelve air-cooled engine that Fedden and Butler were working on. It was to be the first of many in the development of their

Aquila I
(Rolls Royce plc, Aero Division, Bristol).

sleeve-valve engines, and little did they realise at that time, that by February 1939, more than 35,000 hours' research would have been put into such units. Many difficulties were to be encountered, particularly with the design of the sleeve, during the next four years before their first air-cooled radial sleeve-valve Perseus was to run. The sleeve, which achieved a rotating and reciprocating motion from a ball-coupling at its lower end, had four precisely profiled ports cut into its wall at the top end. These ports aligned alternately with ducts in the cylinder wall — two exhaust at the front and three inlet to the rear. The problem was to obtain a wear-resistant material capable of resisting distortion from the high temperatures under which it operated, whilst maintaining the correct clearances between piston and cylinder wall. A long and tedious process of material selection was made before the breakthrough came with the use of an austenitic stainless steel, which was given its ground finish before being hardened by nitriding.

A company demonstrator, Bulldog IVA registered *G-ACJN* with experimental marking *R8*, had the privilege of being the first aircraft to be powered by the first complete sleeve-valve radial engine in the world — the Perseus IA — when test-flown by Cyril Uwins in October 1933. It was a nine-cylinder radial engine, using Mercury size cylinders of 5.75 in by 6.5 in bore and stroke, with a 24 litre capacity, and first ran in July 1932. Later in that year it had completed its type test, having a nominal rating of 515 hp at 2,200 rpm with a maximum power of 638 hp. It was first seen by the public in the New Types enclosure at Hendon in June 1934, when *R8* appeared in its pristine pearl and black paint finish. A few days later it was demonstrated at the SBAC trade show, where Uwins put it through a spectacular display of almost vertical climbs and dives. The quietness and smoothness of the engine was quite unlike the stacatto bark of a Jupiter or Mercury, as it emitted a faint whistling noise which was caused by the rapid displacement of air between the cylinder heads and engine cowling.

Not only was the sleeve-valve engine considerably quieter than its poppet valve counterpart, for now the noise from valves, rockers, push-rods and tappets was eliminated, but it produced more power. It could use higher compression ratios, and its volumetric efficiency was greater because the sleeve ports improved cylinder filling and scavenging, all of which resulted in improved fuel economy. In addition maintenance costs were reduced because of the smaller number of moving parts. The top overhaul became a thing of the past, for the top cover, or

Perseus 100 *(Rolls Royce plc, Aero Division, Bristol).*

'junkhead' as it was called, only carried two spark plugs. The Perseus was soon to establish itself in its later series by powering RAF aircraft such as the Vickers Vildebeest, Westland Lysander II, Blackburn Botha, Roc and Skua whilst its use in civil aircraft included the D.H. Flamingo and Imperial Airways Empire flying boats.

So confident was Fedden in the sleeve-valve development that he did not confine his energies to Perseus but extended it to other designs. One such was the Aquila, a smaller version of Perseus, with a 5 in by 5.375 in bore and stroke of 15.6 litre capacity which was designed to meet the civil aircraft market. A single-cylinder test-rig engine gave promising results in October 1933, which resulted in Aquila I passing its type tests a year later whereupon it was fitted into the prototype Bullpup. This aircraft was displayed at the 1935 SBAC show, when it was flown by Chris A. Washer, a New Zealander, who worked as a member of Uwins' team of test pilots. Russell remembers Washer as 'the' supreme aerobatic pilot on Bulldog remarking that 'when he took off at Filton, work practically stopped — people would get outside to watch him'. Tragically, he was to be killed at Filton during the early part of the war whilst testing a Beaufort which suffered engine failure.

The 500 hp Aquila I's test programme during 1934/35 included endurance flying in both Bullpup and Bulldog *G-ABBB*, the former over a 200-hour, and latter over a 100-hour period. These two engines were eventually installed, in January 1936, into Barnwell's twin-engined monoplane Type 143, which was a variant of the Lord Rothmere sponsored 'Britain First' — the forerunner of Blenheim.

As in all good marriages the two constituents must harmonise into a working partnership if it is to be successful. Such was the case with the four Fedden/Butler engines and the Barnwell/Frise airframe. The result — a classic fighter biplane — the Bulldog!

Chapter 3
Design, Development and Production

By the end of the First World War, in 1918, a nucleus of knowledge in aircraft design, mostly derived empirically, had been acquired in the UK. It had come from various sources, one such being the Air Department of the Admiralty who had, in April 1915, issued the document *Some contributions to the theory of engineering structures, with special reference to the problem of the Aeroplane* by H. Booth & H. Bolas. In addition, a further milestone was to be the issue, in February 1918, of a publication known as HB806 and entitled *Handbook of Strength Calculations* by A. J. Sutton Pippard and Lieutenant J. L. Pritchard, RNVR. It was in essence a design manual explaining methods to be used in calculating the strength of aeroplane structures. Concurrently with these foundational works the Royal Aircraft Factory at Farnborough (it was later to become the Royal Aircraft Establishment in June 1918) was also gathering valuable design criteria, accrued as a result of direct involvement in their own wartime designs such as the BE2c. These combined sources of aircraft design knowledge were finally distilled, in 1918, into the Air Ministry's Air Publication 970, using the identical title to that of HB806. It became the bible on the bookshelf of every aircraft designer in the country, especially as it featured prominently in Air Ministry specifications for military aeroplanes, and needed to be complied with in order to gain a certificate of airworthiness. In its second edition, issued in October 1924, it covered a description of methods of calculation for a single-seat biplane of normal design, and was therefore pertinent to the design of Type 105 in the Filton design office in 1926. Among the subjects covered were methods of dealing with torsion on a fuselage, and wingtip corrections; the strength of undercarriages; formulae for calculating engine thrust and torque, as well as pin-jointed parallel struts; the stressing conditions to cover the case of inverted flight; the consideration of tail and spar loads arising in a limited nose dive; and the ratio of wing loading as a function of stagger. It was against this background of limited knowledge that Frise, Russell, Pollard and to a lesser extent Barnwell, made their contributions for a day-and-night fighter that was to eventually become known as Bulldog.

The Air Ministry's specification F9/26 which was issued in April 1926, was very much conditioned by the concept of aerial warfare in World War 1 terms, where the biplane was supreme. Official prejudice against the monoplane, combined with a lack of knowledge, and materials, for the construction of an unbraced cantilevered mainplane still held aircraft manufacturers to the biplane configuration. This failure to keep up with fighter development meant that priority was placed more upon manoeuvrability and low landing speeds rather than all-out performance. It was not until the advent of 'Alclad' in the early 1930s that the improved method of stressed skin construction was to permit the development of the monoplane. Admittedly there had been some progress inasmuch as there was now a requirement for an all-metal, rather than a wooden construction, fighter, but essentially the specification clung to outdated conceptions.

In the matter of armament, officialdom held to a requirement for the trouble-prone twin Vickers .303 in machine-gun, where a pilot needed access, in flight, to their breeches in order to clear jammed rounds of ammunition. Eventually an American weapon, the Browning .303 in, was to supersede the Vickers and become the main armament of RAF fighters, beginning with the four-gun Gladiator in 1934, and finally the eight-gun Hurricane and Spitfire in 1935/36. Finally, the specification did allow for the use of either the in-line water-cooled or the radial air-cooled engine, with the addition of a supercharger. The latter component had become an essential requirement as it was by then realised that future air battles would be fought at an ever-increasing height. As the power and calibre of anti-aircraft guns increased, so it was concluded that enemy aircraft would approach and cross the shores of Britain at altitudes of 30,000 ft or more.

The design team at Filton was virtually forced to

submit a design for F9/26 based upon a radial engine, for the company had become fully committed to the configuration ever since it had inherited the Cosmos Engineering Co in 1920. Fedden, who in his early days at Brazil Straker had been forbidden, by a clause in the Rolls-Royce licence to manufacture, ever to design or market a rival in-line engine, made the most of the radial and argued forcibly in its favour. In a paper entitled *Radial Aircooled Aero Engines*, read before the International Air Congress at Brussels in 1925, he had presented cogent arguments in its favour by virtue of its weight saving (a 33 per cent reduction over its 440 hp rival in-line engine), elimination of inertia torque, ease of reduction gearing, and simplicity by omission of radiator, piping and liquid coolant. What he could not deny, and what had been so powerfully demonstrated by the Fairey Fox, was the reduced frontal area, and hence low-drag characteristics of the in-line engine. It was to be a rivalry and argument that was to be waged for many years to come, even up until the demise of the piston engine itself. However, the fact cannot be ignored that history was largely on Fedden's side, for although the RAF and *Luftwaffe* entered the Second World War predominately equipped with in-line single-seat fighters such as Hurricane, Spitfire and Messerschmitt Bf109, by the closing stages of the war the radial-engined Tempest II and Focke-Wulf FW190A were being used to great effect. Post-war the Hawker Sea Fury, with its Bristol Centaurus radial, became the most powerful propeller-engined fighter in British service, achieving a speed of 460 mph at 18,000 ft. It can therefore be argued that the clause in Fedden's early contract actually worked to Bristol's advantage in the long run.

After Barnwell's unsuccessful submission for the F9/26 specification, with what was probably a too-conventional design based upon the ill-fated Badminton, Frise, with Russell as his assistant and stressman, produced a design. It was built as a private venture and went on to become the eventual winner of the F9/26 competition. Frise already had a great deal of experience in fighter aircraft design, much of it taught by his mentor Barnwell, and knew from his First World War dealings with 'Brisfit' that a pilot's visual requirements were vital. Its importance is stressed by the views of the highest scoring ace of World War 2 — Erich Hartman — who, with 352 victories to his credit, lived by the maxim that 'he who sees the enemy first, already has half the victory'. This meant for Bulldog, large cut-outs in upper and lower mainplanes, as well as unobstructed views fore and aft along the fuselage decking. Frise had

also given a lot of thought to control co-ordination, whereby changing from elevator to rudder, or to aileron, during flight, was smooth and did not feel like an abrupt change of gear. He had already, in 1921, made a major contribution to the design of control surfaces with the Frise-aileron which, through its patent, had earned his company a large revenue in licence to manufacture. All of this knowledge was to be built into Bulldog, earning it an accolade from Service pilots for its well harmonised controls. Some credit must also go to Cyril Uwins who was to play a significant part in this aspect of the design, for a designer was very much dependent upon an intelligent feedback from his test pilot.

The all-metal construction of Bulldog enabled Frise to use a clean tailplane design, free from any drag-inducing strut bracings which were quite common on Bulldog's competitors. Barnwell had gained some knowledge of metal construction for aircraft from the MR1 biplane in 1917, but it was Pollard's expertise in forming flat high tensile strip steel into cusped and flanged sections that was to make Bulldog's construction successful. It was to be a design that gained for itself a reputation of not only being easy to repair, but one that could take some severe knocks. More than one Bulldog pilot was to experience a mid-air collision in which the airframe held together and enabled him to land the aircraft successfully. Subsequent combat experience with the type in the Spanish Civil War of 1936, and Finnish Winter War in 1939/40, also bore testimony to its toughness and ability to stand up to constant heavy usage.

Bristol's nearest main rival at the time of Bulldog's conception was the Gloster Aircraft Co, some forty miles north-east of Filton, at Cheltenham. This company's brilliant chief designer, H. P. Folland, had scored some remarkable successes with Nighthawk, Mars, Grouse, Grebe and Gamecock biplane fighters in the early 1920s. Folland had pioneered the use of combined differing aerofoil sections in biplanes, enabling the Grouse, in 1923, to use a smaller wingspan for a given lift, thereby enhancing its manoeuvrability. Frise used a similar idea on Bulldog when he used the Bristol 1A section (this had been developed in conjunction with the RAE) on the upper wing, with the Clark YH section on the lower wing. This arrangement gave the aircraft the optimum combination of maximum lift with minimum drag at higher speeds, and enabled it to become the finest aerobatic fighter of its time. It has been suggested by some, that the combined aerofoil sections may have been a contributory factor in Bulldog's allegedly poor spin recovery.

However, subsequent investigations of the prototype at the A&AEE Martlesham Heath, and production types at the RAE Farnborough, were never able to confirm this.

Two prototypes were built during the spring of 1927, clearly showing their pedigree from Bristol progenitors. There was the external strut bracing from bottom wing centre section to fuselage, so familiar a trade-mark on the First World War 'Brisfit', but now with the addition of fairings to reduce drag. Again, there was the short stubby aggressive rounded fuselage blending into the familiar Jupiter radial, so redolent of Bullet and the Badminton racer — all unmistakably Bristol!

Successful test flights followed in May 1927, and a month later a prototype Bulldog Type 105 flew to Martlesham, very much a latecomer, to join the competition along with four other rivals. After the first stage of the F9/26 evaluation trial at Martlesham Heath in October 1927, the prototype, designated Bulldog Mark I, returned to Filton for incorporation of modifications recommended by the A&AEE. A Mark II prototype, now with lengthened fuselage in order to improve its spinning characteristics, returned to Martlesham in February 1928 for the final stage of the competition, whereupon it became the Air Ministry's choice for a contract in August of that year. The Bristol Aeroplane Co's fortunes had truly turned, firstly at Patchway with the production of Fedden's successful Jupiter engine, and now at Filton with what was to be a lengthy production run of Bulldog.

* * *

A total of 26 aircraft was laid down in the first production batch of Bulldog Mark IIs in May 1929 at Filton, with their completion being made by the October. The batch included 24 aircraft for RAF squadrons based at Upavon; eighteen for No 3(F) *J9567-J9584* (constructor's nos 7322-7330 and 7332-7340) and six for No 17(F) *J9585-J9590* (nos 7342-7347). The two remaining aircraft were no 7331, which was fitted with a Jupiter VIA and registered *G-AAHH* on 15 May as a company demonstrator, whilst the other, no 7341 was despatched to the Mitsui Co of Japan.

The second production batch of 46 aircraft followed on immediately, and included five for the Latvian Air Force; two for test and evaluation purposes in the United States; 23 for the RAF squadrons, *K1079-K1101* (nos 7364-7386) between March and June 1930, with nine to No 17(F) and

the remainder to No 54(F) Hornchurch. Export orders continued with two being sold to the Royal Siamese Air Force; eight to the Royal Australian Air Force and three to the Royal Swedish Air Force. Of the remaining three aircraft in the batch, one, no 7399, was built in January 1930 as a test-bed for the Mercury III engine and was fitted with a four-bladed wooden airscrew. It carried the identity marking *R1*, under class 'B' conditions, which meant that it could be flown without a current Certificate of Airworthiness whilst the company was experimenting with its engines. The Mercury engine was changed in May, upon completion of its fifty-hour test schedule, and replaced by a Gnome-Rhone Jupiter VI, whereupon it was registered *G-ABAC* and used as a company demonstrator. Its life was to be short-lived, for T. W. Campbell — a test pilot and Flying School instructor with the company abandoned the aircraft on 4 June after it had sustained damage to its controls whilst he was carrying out aerobatics.

A replacement for *G-ABAC* (no 7403) was subsequently built and demonstrated in Europe before being taken to Chile by Campbell. The Chileans were impressed by its performance and wanted to place an order for forty aircraft, but this did not materialise because the company was not agreeable to the credit terms desired.

The final aircraft of the second batch, *J9591* (no 7397), fitted with a Mercury IV engine, was built to replace the Japanese demonstrator, and now completed the Air Ministry's original order for 25 Service aircraft. *J9591* was loaned back to the company where it was registered *G-AATR* in January 1930, and used for tests by the RAE on various types of drag-reducing ring and helmet cowlings. These cowlings marginally improved performance, but for reasons recorded earlier were not adopted for Service use. These tests were completed by January 1931, and *G-AATR* was then returned to the Air Ministry where it again became *J9591*, and was used as a test-bed for the Mercury IVA engine. It was finally placed back into RAF squadron service in September 1931 as a standard Bulldog Mark II, apart from its engine, which was a Jupiter VIIF.

A third and final production batch of twenty aircraft was completed by August 1930 and included seven further aircraft for Latvia; twelve for the Estonian Air Force; and a mark IIA demonstrator *G-ABBB*, all of which are detailed in later chapters.

* * *

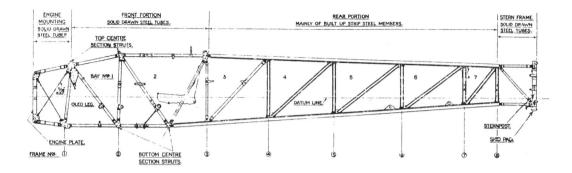

Fig. 1 — Fuselage

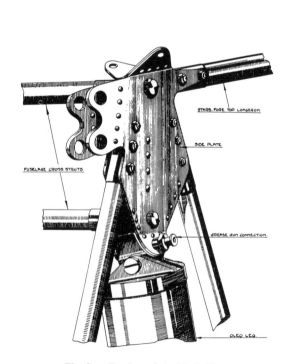

Fig. 2 — Fuselage, Joint No 1, Top

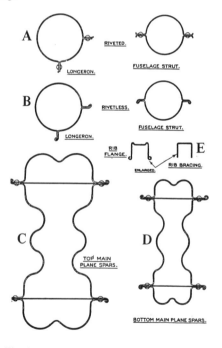

Fig. 3a — Longeron — Riveted

Fig. 3b — Longeron — Wrapped Edge

Fig. 3c — Top Mainplane Spar

Fig. 3d — Bottom Mainplane Spar

Fig. 3e — Rib Flange

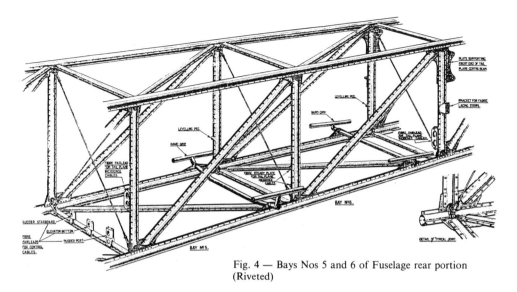

Fig. 4 — Bays Nos 5 and 6 of Fuselage rear portion (Riveted)

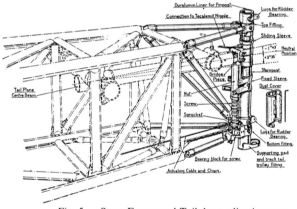

Fig. 5 — Stern Frame and Tailplane adjusting gear

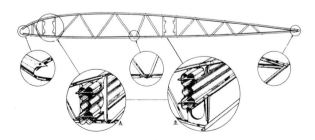

Fig. 7 — Typical Mainplane Rib and details

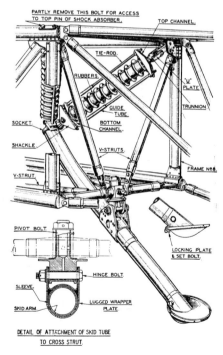

Fig. 6 — Tailskid Assembly

The three production batches, inclusive of the prototype *J9480*, totalled 92 aircraft in all, and their construction is now detailed below.

Airframe

Fuselage

The fuselage (see Fig 1) was built up from four sections comprising:

1. The engine mounting and its fireproof bulkhead.

The mounting and its firewall were connected by four high tensile drawn steel tubes of 1.25 in diameter, each of which was fitted with a machined fork-ended socket secured by taper-pins at each of their ends. At the front their forked-ends were riveted to the four bevelled corners of the square mild steel engine-plate, which was flanged and had a circular aperture cut into it with nine equally-spaced bolt holes for engine installation. At the rear the forked-ends of the tubes were secured by taper-bolts to the four corners of the next section of the fuselage at bay no 1 (see Fig 2). The four side-panels of the engine mounting and its bulkhead were cross-braced by eight 11/32 in BSF tie-rods.

2. The front portion comprising bays no 1 and 2.

This section housed the cockpit area and was largely made up of high tensile drawn steel tubes of 1.25 in diameter, with their tube thicknesses varying from 20 to 26 swg.

Bay no 1 had a single diagonal-strut in each side-panel, whilst bay no 2 had two tubular struts in a vee-configuration. External sleeves fitted over the ends of the longerons and the side-struts at the joints, which were then clamped together by bolts through side-plates. The cross-struts were secured to their longerons by taper-pinned sockets which were bolted at the joint side-plates. The top and bottom panels of bay no 1 were cross-braced by $\frac{1}{4}$ in BSF tie-rods.

3. The rear portion comprising the lower part of bay no 2 and bays no 3 to 7.

This was the largest section of the fuselage and was made up almost entirely by using Pollard's method of rolling two flat strips of high tensile steel into the two halves of tube which, when riveted together, formed a tubular strut or longeron (see Fig 3a).The riveting process soon proved to be too costly and was only used on the first production batch of 26 aircraft to be built. These were 25 for the RAF, *J9567-J9591* (nos 7322-7330 and 7332-7347), and *7331* allocated as a company demonstrator. From there on Pollard used an alternative method of securing the two halves of the tubing by wrapping the edge of the flanged lip of one half around its mating half (see Fig 3b). This dispensed with the use of riveting except at those places where struts were joined by their gusset-plates.

The rear portion of the fuselage was a rigid girder structure, diagonally braced to take loads in compression and tension. Each side of the fuselage was joined by top and bottom cross-struts, with upper and lower diagonal-struts lying in opposite directions (see plan view of Fig 1). Jointing was effected by using gusset-plates which were sandwiched and riveted on the centre-line of each strut-end (see Fig 4) and which were then riveted to the vertical and horizontal flanged lips of the longerons. All transverse frames, except no 8, were braced by 2 and 4BA tie-rods which were secured to the two gusset-plates at each joint.

4. The stern frame portion.

This section carried the tailplane adjusting gear (see Fig 5) as well as the swivelling tailskid assembly (see Fig 6). It comprised eleven high tensile drawn steel tubes of 1 in diameter x 26 swg, each having machined forked-ends, secured by taper-pinning, at each of their ends. Four of these tubes acted as vee-struts, being bolted to top and bottom longerons at one end and meeting at the centre of the bottom cross-strut at the other. The remaining six tubes formed two side panels which were bolted to the 2 in diameter x 18 swg sternpost at one end, and to the rear portion of the fuselage, at frame no 8, at the other end.

The fuselage was given its rounded shape by the addition of steel fairing formers carrying longitudinal stringers which stretched from the tailplane to the back of the cockpit area. At this point they met aluminium panels which continued to the front of the aircraft. The formers, which were used on bays no 3-7, were of a flanged channel section, bent to shape and bolted to brackets which were attached to the longerons. The longitudinal stringers were secured to the formers by set screws and nuts, and then covered with a large single piece of doped fabric. The fabric was joined together by being laced along the underside of the fuselage, and at the rear end of bay no 7; whilst at the front it was laced through eyelets in the aluminium panels. A further small fabric panel, covering the top half of the stern frame portion of the fuselage, was laced to a longitudinal strip on each side of the fuselage underneath the tailplane. These longitudinal strips also received quickly detachable panels beneath the tailplane, which allowed easy access to the tailskid and tailplane adjusting gear during service use.

The 22 swg aluminium sheet covering at the front of the fuselage contained several quickly detachable panels for ease of maintenance. These included all the panels forward of the fireproof bulkhead which gave good access to the engine, and two very large QD panels on either side of the cockpit which, when removed, exposed the flying controls and armament. Two further doors, one on each side of the fuselage and behind the pilot's seat, were removable for access to the wireless equipment. The bigger door of the two was on the port side, which allowed removal and replacement of the wireless crate, whilst the starboard door was only used for access to radio valves.

Tailplane assembly

The tailpane was of cantilever construction, and was made in two halves which were located by their spigot-ends into bearings at the front of the tailplane centre beam. This beam (see Fig 5) was pivoted at the front end of bay no 7 whilst its other end was attached to the tailplane adjusting screw. Each elevator was carried by its bearing in the rear of the centre beam and a bearing at the top of the tailplane spar. The elevators were bolted rigidly to one another by a compound lever in the centre, and actuated by duplicated control cables wholly within the fuselage. The balanced portions of the elevators were shielded, and designed to give light control loads at all flying speeds. Tailplane incidence could be adjusted from -1° 43' to +3° 35' by use of sprocket, chain and cable from a large hand-wheel on the port side of the cockpit.

The fin, which was 3.28 sq ft in area, was offset to balance engine torque, so that the aircraft would sit on its course at cruising speed with little correction from the pilot. It was cantilevered from its fin-post spigot mounting into the top of the sternpost, and carried the top main hinge for the rudder on its fin-post. The rudder, which was 11.5 sq ft in area, including its balanced portion, was hinged in two further places on the sternpost. As in the case of the elevators the balanced portion, or horn, was shielded so that no snatch was felt on the rudder bar as it came into or out of operation. The leading edges of the tailplane were made from sheet aluminium of 22 swg, with spars and ribs from rolled steel sections, whilst the trailing edges of elevators and rudder were made from seamless high tensile steel tube of varying diameters and thicknesses.

The swivelling tailskid (see Fig 6) was made from high tensile steel tube with a cast-iron pad secured to it. The skid pivoted and swivelled at the bottom cross member of frame no 8, and was anchored inside bay no 7 by two shock absorbers in vee-configuration and attached to the top longerons.

Mainplanes

The single-bay biplane configuration comprised two mainplanes, employing a 24.75 in forward stagger, with incidence of 3° and dihedral of 5° to both planes. The top mainplanes had a full span of 33 ft 10 in with a 6 ft 4 in chord, and carried the ailerons; whilst the bottom main planes were reduced in span, and chord, to 27 ft 6 in and 4 ft 9 in respectively.

Each top and bottom mainplane was constructed with two built-up wing spars, connected by four tubular compression struts and braced by tie-rods. The wing spars (see Figs 3c and d) were fabricated from four lengths of corrugated strip steel, with two added horizontal stiffeners, all of which were assembled together by curling over the edges of the web strips. Both spars were of the same section, and were of constant depth until the penultimate wing rib, whereupon extension pieces were attached to reduce the depth down to the plane tip.

The wing ribs were built-up members (see Figs 3e and 7), constructed from thin flat high tensile steel strip formed into open channel sections, with continuous Warren bracing. The ribs were attached to the spars by rib-posts (see 'A' of Fig 7) made from high tensile steel plate, which were themselves riveted to the web flanges of the spars. At the leading edge these ribs were riveted to aluminium sheets which were rolled to the shape of the aerofoil, whilst at the trailing edge they were bolted to clips which were spot-welded to a mild steel tube.

Provision was made on the port bottom mainplane for mounting the W/T generator on a platform over the front spar between ribs nos 3 and 4. A similar arrangement was also made on the starboard plane for mounting the other generator which provided electrical services.

The ailerons, which were fitted to the top plane only, were of the Frise aerodynamically-balanced type giving a light control with good rolling qualities of the aeroplane, but without any appreciable tendency to yaw. Each aileron comprised nine steel ribs, interspersed with nose ribs, built around a single tubular spar of high tensile steel, with duralumin strip at the leading edge and mild steel tubing at the trailing edge. The aileron was pivot-mounted from each end of the tubular spar, with a Ransome and Marles ball-bearing at the inner end, and a plain bearing at the outer end; in addition, there was a centre bearing consisting of two steel half-caps bolted over the spar. All three bearings were lubricated by means of 'Tecalamit' nipples on their undersurfaces. Movement was given to the aileron by cable, chain

Key

1 Starter dog
2 Spinner
3 Two-blade wooden propeller
4 Starboard navigation light
5 Starboard aerial mast
6 Forward-facing fuel vent pipe
7 Starboard fuel tank, capacity 35 Imp Gal (159 l)
8 Bristol Jupiter VIIF or VIIF.P engine
9 Cowling ring
10 Engine mounting plate
11 Cylinder head fairings
12 Cross-bracing
13 Gun synchronising generator (port and starboard)
14 Supercharger
15 Firewall
16 Centre-section support struts
17 Wing centre-section
18 Bracing wire
19 Starboard fuel pipe

20 Oil tank, capacity 7.5 Imp gal (34,1 l)
21 Forward fuselage framework
22 Gun trough
23 Oleo leg attachment
24 Rudder pedals
25 Accumulator (lighting system)
26 Air bottle (high-pressure cylinder)
27 Elevator link tube
28 Aileron rockshaft
29 Ammunition box, capacity 600 rounds (one each gun)
30 Control column
31 Empty case chute
32 Port Vickers 0.303 in (7,7-mm) Mk II or Mk IIIN gun
33 Gun cooling louvres
34 Instrument panel
35 Ring sight (combined with Aldis tube front mounting)
36 Bead sight
37 Windscreen
38 Padded coaming
39 Cockpit
40 Fibre acorns
41 Pilot's adjustable seat

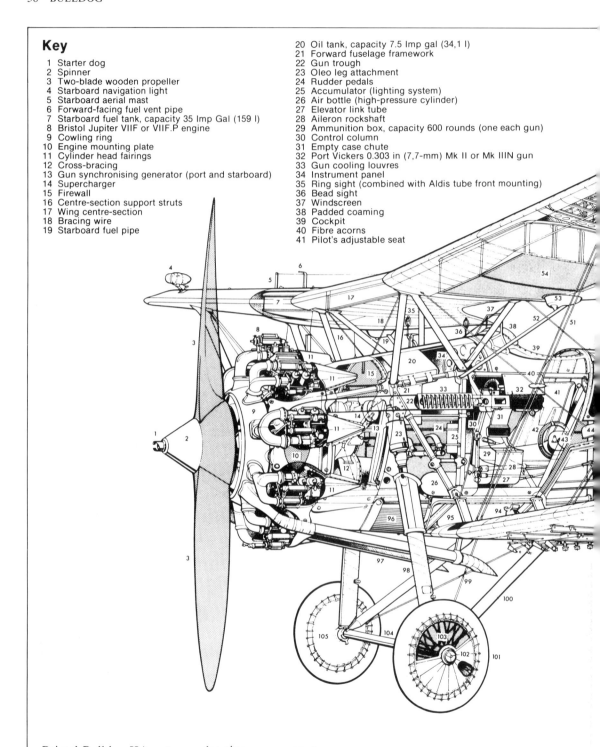

Bristol Bulldog IIA cutaway drawing. (Copyright Pilot Press)

42 Tailplane adjusting wheel
43 Chain and sprocket
44 Handhold/step
45 Elevator cable arm
46 ASI cable on strut leading-edge
47 Fuselage lacing

48 Wireless compartment and crate
49 ASI horn
50 Aerial mast
51 Interplane bracing
52 Port fuel pipe
53 Fuel lead fairing
54 Port fuel tank, capacity
   35 Imp gal (159 l)
55 Front interplane strut
56 Upper mainplane
   leading-edge ribbing
57 Front spar
58 Port navigation light
59 Wing rib
60 Spar strip steel sections
61 Upper mainplane tip
62 Aileron balance
63 Aileron construction
64 Rear spar
65 Aileron cable
66 Rear interplane strut
67 Interplane bracing
68 Aerials
69 Strut cross-bracing
70 Fuselage tubular framework
71 Rudder/tailplane controls
72 Elevator controls
73 Handholds with lifting-bars
   behind

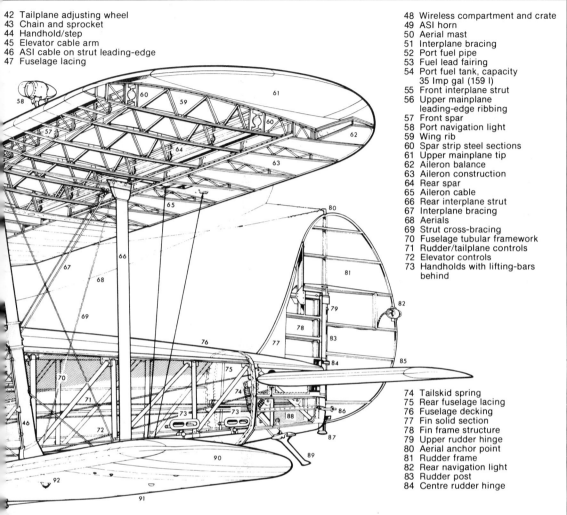

74 Tailskid spring
75 Rear fuselage lacing
76 Fuselage decking
77 Fin solid section
78 Fin frame structure
79 Upper rudder hinge
80 Aerial anchor point
81 Rudder frame
82 Rear navigation light
83 Rudder post
84 Centre rudder hinge

85 Port tailplane
86 Lower rudder hinge
87 Support pad with trolley-fitting track rail
88 Stern frame construction
89 Tailskid
90 Lower mainplane tip
91 Port lower mainplane
92 Tie-down lug
93 Light bomb racks
94 Air-driven generator mounting cradle
95 Centre-section lower frames
96 Oil cooler
97 Exhaust pipes
98 V-strut undercarriage
99 Cross-bracing wires
00 Fixed-length radius rod
01 700 x 100 Palmer Cord Aero Tyre
02 Tyre valve
03 Wheel spokes
04 Axle strut
05 Wheel cover

Bristol Bulldog IIA Specification

Power Plant: One Bristol Jupiter VIIF radial air-cooled nine-cylinder supercharged engine, rated at 440 hp for take-off, 490 hp at 8,000 ft (2 438 m) and 520 hp at 10,000 ft (3 050 m). Two-bladed wooden fixed pitch propeller, 9 ft 1 in (2,77 m) diameter. Fuel capacity 70 Imp gal (318 l).

Performance: Maximum speeds, 178 mph (274 km/h) at 10,000 ft (3 050 m), 162 mph (260 km/h) at 20,000 ft (6 100 m). Time to climb to 20,000 ft (6 100 m), 14.5 min; service ceiling, 29,300 ft (8 930 m). Range, 350 mls (563 km) at 15,000 ft (4 572 m).

Weights: Empty, 2,412 lb (1 094 kg); loaded, 3,530 lb (1 601 kg).

Dimensions: Span, 33 ft 10 in (10,31 m); span (lower wing), 27 ft 6 in (8,38 m); overall length, 25 ft 0 (7,62 m); overall height, 9 ft 10 in (2,99 m), wing area, 306.5 sq ft (28,5 m²); undercarriage track, 5 ft 6 in (1,67 m). Dihedral, 5 deg. Incidence, 3 deg.

Armament: Two Vickers 0.303-in (7,7-mm) machine guns in fuselage sides ahead of cockpit, synchronised to fire through propeller disc; 600 rpg. Provision for four 20 lb (9,07 kg) Mk I HE bombs on wing racks.

The Inspection Room at Filton, circa 1930 *(A. Gregory)*.

and sprocket in the lower mainplane, and connected by streamline wires to a lever which was attached to the aileron spar.

Two 35 gallon (159 litre) fuel tanks were carried, one in each top mainplane, mounted in the bays formed by the second and third compression struts. The ribs surrounding the tank were increased in depth downwards in order to conform to its shape. A tube of high tensile steel, passing from corner to corner through another tube which formed a tunnel in the tank, was used to support the tank and to brace the tank bay. Each tank had its filler cap and forward facing vent pipe located at the front of the tank, near the leading-edge of the wing, and was connected to the engine by fuel pipes which exited through lead fairings on the underside of the wing.

The top centre plane was similar in construction to the mainplanes, except that its two spars were tubular and were joined by three compression struts forming two bays, both of which were cross-braced with tie-rods. The whole section carried ten ribs, interspersed symmetrically with seven nose ribs, all of which were attached to their spars by mild steel rib posts. As in the construction of the mainplanes the leading edge was formed by aluminium strip, and trailing edge by mild steel tube with the usual clips for attachment to the ribs. Provision was made for the mounting of a central navigation lamp, and for an upward identification lamp on the starboard side of the nosing. Camera gun mountings were bolted to wrap fittings on the front spar, and to a pair of tubes connecting the spars between the second and third ribs from the port side. In order to assist the pilot to vacate his seat, particularly in the case of an emergency, two hand grips, formed of spruce blocks covered with sheet aluminium, were arranged about the centre line of the section in the trailing edge. The whole section was attached to the fuselage longerons by two oval sectioned steel 'N' struts with adjustable screwed ends, and braced by means of streamlined wires.

The bottom centre plane similarly had two tubular spars and four compression struts of high tensile steel, the outer struts being at right angles to the spars, whilst the inner pair were arranged in a vee formation. The section carried six ribs, three on each side of the centre line, the two outer ribs on each side being of heavier gauge material than for the mainplanes and the inner pair being of duralumin. These duralumin ribs were shaped at the rear to take a mounting for the downward identification lamp. On the port side, aft of the rear spar, the two outer ribs were stiffened by duralumin sheeting and channels to resist the extra loads imposed by use of the duralumin foot-tread, which was screwed in position between them. Upon assembly the whole section was supported from the fuselage by four high tensile steel tubular struts, front and rear, arranged in an 'M' formation. The upper ends of the struts were attached to the bottom joints of frames no 2 and 3 and in bay no 2 (see Fig 1), whilst the lower ends were secured to the mid-points and ends of the front and rear spars of the section. (Note: Prior to assembly, all steel fittings were protected from corrosion by a paint-dipping and stove-enamelling process.)

The four top and bottom mainplanes were bolted to their centre plane sections and were supported by two pairs of steel interplane struts which were faired with balsa wood into a streamline section. The whole structure was given rigidity by the use of external lift and landing wires of streamline section, running from interplane struts to top and bottom centre section struts, with the customary fibre acorn at the point of intersection in order to lock and prevent chafing. In addition, incidence wires were used within the frame of the interplane struts themselves. Finally, with the aircraft's fuselage placed in position and the undercarriage axle supported so that weight was taken off the oleo legs, a check for correct rigging was made. Incidence was checked by use of a clinometer resting, on a straight edge held up aginst rigging posts which protruded from the wing surfaces. Dihedral was adjusted by using a straight edge placed along the spars of the bottom plane, whilst symmetry and stagger were verified by use of a plumb-line and measure.

Undercarriage

The vee type undercarriage comprised a pair of long travel oleo legs, connected to radius rods of fixed length, and a tubular cross-axle carrying a pair of 'Palmer' 183 (750 x 125 mm) spoked wheels with fabric covers. Landing shocks were absorbed by the oleo-damped legs with rubber buffers in compression, giving a total travel of 7.5 in. The upper ends of the oleo-legs were attached to the top longerons at frame no 1 (see Fig 8) well above the aircraft's centre of gravity, which reduced rolling whilst taxying on the rough grass airfields of its day. The radius rods were attached to the axle (see Fig 9) by a fork fitting and by ball joints at their top end. The radius rod panel was cross-braced by 45 cwt 'Trulay' cables with 'Truloc' end fittings. Balsa and spruce wood fairings were taped to the struts and their links in order to reduce drag.

Cockpit

The cockpit was shielded by a non-symmetrical narrow steel-framed structure carrying two panels of 'Triplex' glass and one panel of sheet steel. The triangular glass panel on the starboard side was larger than the triangular steel panel on the port side, so that full protection was given against the airscrew's slipstream without impeding the pilot's view.

Compared to other fighter aircraft of its period the cockpit was relatively spacious and accommodated an adjustable seat together with its flying controls and instruments. The aluminium seat was contoured to provide for an Irving-type parachute and was adjustable for height by means of a lever on its right-hand side. A push button incorporated in the top of the lever could be used to release the ratchet of its spring-loaded mechanism, allowing nine different positions over a range of 4.25 in. Movement of the seat followed that of the operating lever, so that to raise the seat the lever was pulled upwards and vice-versa. Movement was assisted by two elastic cord 'springs' stretched between a cross tube at the rear of the bottom of the seat, and the top cross fuselage strut of frame no 3. Pilots were warned before vacating the seat to return the operating lever to its highest position, thereby relieving the load on the springs and avoiding the possibility of an accident due to inadvertent release of the lever. The pilot was restrained in the seat by a Sutton harness whose lower straps were attached to the sides of the seat. The shoulder straps were provided with a patented adjusting device and could be locked in any desired position over a fore and aft range of 7 in.

The spade grip control column used its 32° fore and aft range of movement to operate the elevators, by means of a link tube, actuating lever (see Fig 10) and cables, and gave them a 35°

upwards and 20° downwards movement from their neutral position. The control column's lateral movement was restricted to a range of 40° by a limit plate, giving the ailerons a 25° upwards and 25° downwards movement from their neutral position. When the aircraft was left unattended, the control column was restrained in a fixed central position by means of a retractable strap, which was mounted in the cockpit on the upper left-hand longeron.

The rudder bar assembly and its corrugated heel troughs were mounted on transverse bearer tubes, and by means of a rudder bar spindle (see Fig 10) and actuating lever, operated the rudder cables. The rudder bar itself was not directly coupled to the actuating cables but was connected through a lead-screw adjustment gear (see Fig 11). Adjustment to the rudder bar fore-and-aft position, of up to 4 in, by means of the star wheel, did not disturb the rudder cables. This meant that a pilot could adjust the control to suit his requirements even during flight.

The type P3 compass was mounted in the centre of the dashboard with a Schilovsky-Cooke turn-and-bank indicator immediately below it. A combined map case and diagram box was fitted beneath the centre of the dashboard containing twelve map boards in one compartment, and in the other, a folder containing diagrams for erection and maintenance.

The port and starboard running magnetos' double tumbler switch, with its down position for 'off', and up position for 'on', was mounted on the extreme left-hand side of the dashboard and followed by the altimeter, air speed indicator and dimmer-switch. Immediately beneath the ASI were the Holt flare push-buttons for operation of the port and starboard lower wingtip flares. On the extreme right-hand side of the dashboard was the single toggle hand starting magneto switch, followed by Negretti and Zambra oil pressure and temperature gauges, thirty-hour chronometer and rpm indicator. An engraved warning label, headed 'Engine Revolutions' and reading: 'Normal full speed; 1775 — Maximum permissible speed for not more than 5 minutes: 1950' was riveted to the dashboard, at an angle, underneath the rpm indicator.

Cockpit interior of Bulldog II showing instrumentation and controls *(British Aerospace, Filton)*.

An engine priming pump knob lay below and between the two oil gauges, whilst beneath the rpm indicator lay the cranking handle for the hand starting magneto.

In addition, a boost gauge graduated in pounds per square inch (psi) was mounted on a bracket attached to the port side strut of frame no 2, just below and forward of the dashboard, so that the pilot could keep the boost within the prescribed limits. Oil and fuel cocks were mounted beneath the dashboard on each side of the cockpit, whilst the switch and master cock for the gas starter system were attached to the upper part of frame no 2 on the starboard side.

Throttle, altitude and ignition levers were mounted on the port side front diagonal of bay no 2, whilst the tailplane adjusting gear handwheel was behind them on its rear diagonal. The ignition lever was inter-connected to the throttle so that it was automatically retarded as the throttle was closed. The throttle also operated a shutter in part of the air intake, which closed when the throttle closed, and opened above one-third throttle opening.

A 1.5 in Very signal pistol, together with eight cartridges located in clips along the front edge of the seat, was carried for use during emergencies. If a pilot was wise he would make sure that the pistol was well secured before performing aerobatics, for its loss incurred a pay deduction of 37 shillings and sixpence!

Systems

Oil
The oil feed system of the Jupiter VII engine had a working pressure of 60 psi and was not allowed to fall below 50 psi, whilst oil consumption was from eight to fifteen pints per hour, depending upon the throttle opening being used. Oil was fed under pressure to main crankshaft bearings, crankpin, big-end bearing, and cam-sleeve bearing, by oilways passing through the crankshaft assembly. The cylinder walls, pistons and connecting rod wrist pins relied upon splash feed from the crank pin bearing, as did tappets and timing gear from the cam-sleeve bearing. Surplus oil scavenged from the sump was pumped back into the oil tank where it was cooled and re-circulated.

The eight-gallon oil tank (see Fig 12), which had a working capacity of seven gallons, was attached to the fuselage by four round clamp-brackets with wired wing-nuts at the bottom longerons of bay no 1. Its underside was finned for heat dissipation and protruded into the aircraft's slipstream. It incorporated an electrically heated plug, as well as a bypass valve which automatically short-circuited the cooler when the oil was thick. The dipstick, filler neck tube and funnel were located on the starboard side of the fuselage.

Fuel
Petrol was gravity fed from each of the two 35-gallon fuel tanks in the upper wing by two ½ in diameter steel and copper pipes, through a filter, to the carburettor. A contents gauge and emergency fuel cock were located at the rear of each tank, near the trailing edge of the wing, with petrol flowing from them and the front pipes down faired steel tubes into the fuselage. The steel pipes were connected to copper pipes, which incorporated Vickers ½ in BSP two-way cocks, before joining the filter. These cocks could be switched on or off from the cockpit by means of torsion rods connected to operating handles which were situated underneath each side of the dashboard. In addition the fuel system employed an engine priming pump which was situated below and between the two oil gauges on the dashboard. It had two connections for ¼ in copper pipes — one to draw fuel from the petrol filter, and the other to deliver fuel to the engine's priming nozzles. Fuel consumption on the Jupiter VIIF engine, using full throttle at 8,000 ft was 35 gallons per hour.

Engine 'fade-out' was not unknown on Bulldog and was generally attributed to one, or a combination of, three causes:

(a) Accidental closing of the port fuel tank;

(b) Ice formation at the forward facing fuel vent pipes; or

(c) Carburettor icing.

In (a) it was possible for the port fuel tank's emergency cock to be accidentally closed by the parachute harness of the pilot catching on its lever, whilst he was climbing into the cockpit. Warning notices were issued alerting air and ground crews to check for this before flight, after the pilot had taken his seat.

Flight Lieutenant Harry Broadhurst (later to become Air Chief Marshal Sir Harry, GCB, KBE, DSO and Bar, DFC and Bar, AFC), a pilot with No 41 (F) Squadron, relates how he once led his flight on a 'Battle Climb' to maximum operational height through very thick cloud. Upon descending back to the airfield at Northolt the engine of his aircraft stopped and he was forced to make a landing in a ploughed field, the site of which is now London airport! (Service pilots seemed to be quite adept at anticipating the position of future aerodromes for it was the fortuitous forced-landing of a Bulldog, on an evening in May 1934, near Saffron Walden, that was instrumental in the siting of RAF Debden.) The fault was found to be that in (b) where the air vents to the fuel tanks had filled with moisture and then frozen — the mystery was that it did not affect the other two aircraft in his flight. Subsequent ground tests by the RAE, and quite independent of this incident, showed that the time taken for an engine to stop, once the vents had been sealed, was fourteen minutes.

Carburettor icing (c) was quite common in most aircraft of that period, and design measures in the case of Bulldog included oil jacketing of the carburettor, as well as the fitting of an auxiliary deflector plate, directing warm air from the exhaust into the carburettor. However, in spite of these measures an experienced pilot when gliding in from high altitude would occasionally open up the throttle to verify that icing had not taken place, otherwise he might find no response from the engine at the vital point of his landing approach, with disastrous consequences.

Starter

There were three methods used for starting the engine, namely:

(a) Swinging the airscrew by hand;
(b) Use of the 'Hucks' starter; or
(c) Use of RAE Gas starters Mk 1 and 2.

The starting procedure for (a) was for the pilot to make sure that the tumbler switches for the main running magnetos on the port side, and the hand starting magneto on the starboard side, were switched off (ie, in the 'down' position). Fuel, oil and priming cocks would be turned on, and the priming pump used by making a slow stroke for suction and a vigorous stroke for delivery. A member of the ground staff would then turn the airscrew three or four times, in order to charge the engine's cylinders, and then stand clear. The pilot would then turn off the priming pump cock, and open the throttle to $3/16$ in from the stops on the throttle chamber. The hand starting magneto would be switched on, and the hand crank turned rapidly anti-clockwise, whereupon the engine would start. Immediately the main running magnetos would be switched on whilst the hand starting magneto would be switched off.

The Hucks starter, of method (b), was an adaptation whereby a long shaft was supported above and on the longitudinal axis of a service vehicle chassis, such as the model T Ford. The shaft had a starter-dog at its forward end, and was driven by chain and clutch from the vehicle's engine. The driver of the vehicle could align and engage the shaft with a similar starter-dog on the end of the aircraft's airscrew boss. As the clutch was released with the vehicle's engine running, it would spin the airscrew and automatically disengage as the engine fired. In the case of Bulldog it was used with the same sequence of starting operations as that for swinging the airscrew by hand.

The RAE gas starter Mark 2, method (c), used compressed air supplied from a trolley starter, or some other external source, which was stored in a high pressure air bottle carried on the port side of the fuselage between bays no 1 and 2 (see Fig 13). For starting, compressed air released from the bottle, which when fully charged was under a pressure of 200 psi, was passed through a petrol vaporiser to reach the engine gas distributor as compressed petrol-air mixture. The reservoir of the vaporiser was filled, prior to starting, by means of a priming pump, called the auxiliary primer (to distinguish it from the engine priming pump), which drew fuel from the engine's priming pipe system. A drain pipe and cock were fitted to the vaporiser, and the auxiliary primer was operated from outside the aircraft on its port side, until petrol flowed from the drain pipe. The supply of compressed air from the air bottle to the vaporiser was regulated by a master cock and a press cock, the latter being foot-operated, and both under the control of the pilot. Ignition current for starting was supplied only by the hand starting magneto, which had each of its high tension circuits connected to one of the main engine magnetos, the starter magneto switch being kept in the 'off' position.

Oxygen

Just as an engine's efficiency begins to deteriorate in a rarified atmosphere without the benefit of a supercharger, so does that of a pilot without oxygen. Above 12,000 ft a pilot's efficiency begins to deteriorate, until at 20,000 ft his reactions become dangerously slow. Bulldog had a service ceiling of 29,300 ft and so an oxygen system was essential. (It had become apparent from experiences during World War 1 that future air battles would be fought at 20,000 ft plus, where cockpit oxygen supply was essential. A prime example had been that of RNAS pilot Lieutenant S. D. Culley's encounter with the German Zeppelin *L53* on 11 August 1918. Flying a Sopwith Camel, launched from a naval lighter towed by a destroyer, he had engaged *L53* at 19,000 ft (service ceiling of Camel with 110 hp Le Rhone was 21,000 ft) and, with one of this two Vickers guns jammed, had sent it down in flames into the sea. Eleven years later as an RAF Flight Lieutenant at A&AEE he had carried out handling trials on the first production Bulldog II, *J9567*.)

A high pressure oxygen bottle was transversely mounted on the starboard side of the cockpit beneath the rudder bar heel trough. It had external access and was easily withdrawn from its QD cradle through a door on the side of the fuselage. It was connected to a regulator and pressure gauge located on a bracket between the vee tubes of bay no 2, also on the starboard side. From here its supply was carried to a bayonet attachment for the mask, mounted on a starboard longeron in the cockpit. A flowmeter placed in the cockpit fairing, directly in front of the pilot, was connected into the system.

Wireless

A short wave radio-telephony transmitter and receiver, Marconi type T25B and R31B, were installed in the wireless compartment behind the cockpit at the top of bay no 3. The equipment was mounted in a special crate that slid on transverse guides into its compartment from the port side of the aircraft. Access to the compartment was gained by removal of a pair of fabric-covered panels which were secured by cowling clips on each side of the fuselage. The starboard panel, which was quite small, was provided for adjustment of the components fitted on that side and to facilitate fitting the valves to the receiver. The aircraft's structure was bonded and screened to Air Ministry specification GE125 and W/T marking positioned on the covered panel on the port side of the fuselage.

The high and low tension supply for the transmitter was obtained from an air-driven dual-purpose generator carried in a cradle mounted on the upper surface of the port bottom mainplane. The stowage clip for the nine-pin generator plug was provided at the root of the mainplane and covered by a hinged door. The generator had HT and LT outputs of 1,200 volts and 10 volts respectively, but since 6 volt valves were employed in the transmitter, fixed resistances were incorporated in their filament circuits to reduce the generator LT voltage to the correct amount.

A 60-volt HT battery and 2-volt accumulator, carried in the crate, supplied current for the seven-valve receiver which operated on 50-120 metre wavelengths. Provision was also made in the crate for fitting a 4-volt accumulator and a filament resistance for use with certain types of valve installation.

The change-over switch for the transmitter and receiver was remotely controlled from the cockpit whilst a microphone socket and telephone jack-plug socket were readily accessed by the pilot. An ammeter reading from 0-2 amps, and indicating the transmitter aerial current, was mounted on a bracket clipped to the upper part of the rear diagonal strut on the port side of bay no 2.

The copper aerial wire ran from short aerial masts on the outer and upper surface of each top wing, to an anchor point on the top of the rudder frame. Mid-way connections from these two links were taken to the aerial lead-in above the wireless compartment.

Electrical

An air-driven, 12-volt, 500-watt generator was carried in a cradle, mounted on the upper surface of the starboard bottom mainplane, in order to supply power for the aircraft's electrical services. These included heating, cockpit lighting, wingtip flares and identity/navigation lights, with all wiring secured by spring-clips in open channel conduits for ease of maintenance. The circuit's 12-volt, 15-amp/hr accumulator was mounted on a platform located midway along the outside of the diagonal strut of bay no 1 on the starboard side, together with the voltage control and fuse boxes.

Armament
Guns

Two Vickers .303 in Mark 2 guns were mounted, one on each side of the aircraft, between the sides of the fuselage frame and the outer fairings, synchronised to fire through the airscrew's disc. The guns were positioned in stainless-steel troughs riveted to the aluminium cowling, with louvred vents over their muzzles. Their loading mechanisms, located low on each side of the cockpit, and level with a pilot's hips, were easily accessible for clearing the frequent stoppages that occurred with the Vickers. Squadron pilots even carried a special clearance tool, tied to a length of cord around their neck, in order to facilitate this measure. Because both guns were of the same 'hand', the aluminium cowling on the starboard side of the cockpit was bulged out to allow access to its loading handle.

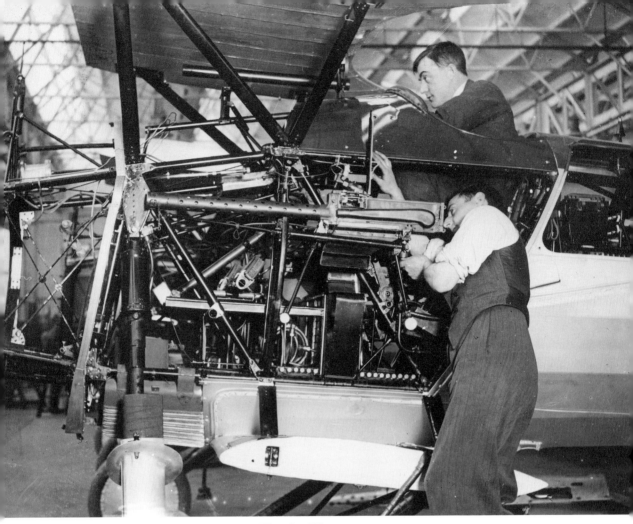

Aligning the Vickers guns on a Mark II at Filton in 1929 *(British Aerospace, Filton).*

A total of 1,200 rounds of belted ammunition, 600 for each gun, was stored in two duralumin magazine boxes which were mounted transversely across the cockpit floor, in front of the rudder heel troughs. These boxes could be loaded in position through their hinged lids, or the boxes could be withdrawn complete through doors in the sides of the fuselage. The guns were fired by the two thumb levers, lying on the centre-line of the spade grip, which were connected by Bowden cable to the Constantinesco synchronising gear, and hence to the guns. Empty cases were ejected out of the aircraft by way of a chute slot on the sides of the fuselage.

The gun sights comprised a 4.5 in diameter ring-and-bead together with an Aldis sight which were rigidly mounted on a fore-and-aft member above the fairing and on either side of the longitudinal axis of the fuselage. The Aldis sight was to the starboard side, and the ring-and-bead to the port side, with a transverse distance of 4.875 in between them.

Provision was also made for the carrying of a G3 aircraft camera gun which was mounted to the port side of the upper surface of the mainplane's top centre section.

Bombs

Four 20 lb high explosive bombs, or four 8·5 lb practice bombs, could be loaded on a light series Mark I carrier situated underneath the port bottom wing. Their release was controlled by the pilot from a lever mechanism situated on the port side of the cockpit and mounted at seat height between the diagonal struts of bay no 2. The bombs could be released either singly, or in a salvo, depending upon the selection made by the pilot.

Engine

The Jupiter series VII, with a power output of 420 hp at rated altitude of 12,000 ft, using full throttle, normal rpm and rated boost of -1·25 lb, was fitted to the airframe. A two-bladed wooden Watts airscrew of 8 ft 10·5 in diameter, and spinner, was fitted as well as valve gear covers over the nine cylinder heads. In order to reduce drag, seven tapered corrugated cylinder head fairings were riveted to the detachable front bulkhead aluminium cowlings, behind the heads of cylinder nos 1 to 4 and 7 to 9. Air intake ducting, behind and below the two bottom cylinders, incorporated shutters which were cable-operated from the cockpit enabling control of the temperature of air to the carburettor. The exhaust collector ring was connected to a pair of exhaust pipes which travelled downwards under the fuselage between the undercarriage legs.

★ ★ ★

No 3 (F) Squadron, Upavon, had been the first, of the ten squadrons to be eventually equipped with Bulldog, to receive the Mark IIs in June 1929. As with any new aircraft, it had its share of teething troubles. The Operations' Record Book for that squadron records that on 22 November 1929 representatives from the company and the Air Ministry, met with Wing Commander C. Maund and Squadron Leader Thompson of HQ Air Defence of Great Britain in order to discuss failures and defects.

Squadron pilots soon found, much to the dismay of the ground staff, that Bulldog was prone to wingtip damage whilst taxying in high winds such as those experienced on exposed airfields like Upavon, and this soon led to the demand for a wider track undercarriage. Bulldog's landing speed was approximately 58 mph, and if on the landing approach the aircraft was not stalled within inches of the ground the nose would fall quite rapidly, necessitating quite heavy application of the elevators. One former Bulldog pilot likened such landings to 'trying to lift a loaded wheelbarrow at arm's length'. No doubt such comment, together with a warning notice issued to riggers that 'after heavy landings the nuts of ball-ended radius rod bolts should be checked for tightness', was to stimulate the company to provide a much strengthened undercarriage on later versions.

Pilots were also quick to notice the extended length of landing run needed on Bulldog when compared to its predecessors Gamecock and Siskin IIIA. This observation was eventually to lead to the fitment of cable-operated Bendix brakes, as well as castoring tailwheels in place of tailskids, with retrospective fitment for all aircraft. Not only did this modification reduce the landing run but it gave far more manoeuvrability whilst taxying. As one former Bulldog pilot records, 'trying to turn a single-engined aircraft down-wind when the wind was strong was always difficult before the days of brakes'. The aircraft were normally flown back to Filton for such retro-fitting to be carried out.

Bulldog's first operational use during the winter of 1930/31 soon produced examples of engine 'fade' as already described, as well as the need for cockpit heating. In January 1931 the three aircraft of 'A' Flight, No 3(F) Squadron, were fitted with kits in which muffs were shrouded around the exhaust pipes, thereby permitting the ducting of uncontaminated hot air into the cockpit. It was noted that 'the smell of enamel paint makes it rather umpleasant when first used'!

A rather testy comment in 3(F)'s ORB dated 5 May 1931, notes that after all the aircraft had been groomed with great care on the eve of the 1st Tactical Exercise, a signal had been received grounding them. Although precise details were not given, evidently modifications were needed to the chain-boxes around the aileron controls in the bottom of the cockpit. It could have only been a very minor modification for six days later the squadron did a 'Battle Climb' with heated clothing and oxygen.

In February 1931 pilots from 111(F) Squadron, Hornchurch, reported that they were experiencing R/T transmission interference which was traced to generator 'noise'. After investigation, testing, and various trials it was successfully eliminated. The generator could be run up on the ground by means of a portable Marconi-Stanley 1 hp engine and flexible drive whilst testing and adjustment was carried out.

In October of the same year a modification was made to the contact-breaker covers of all Watford magnetos fitted to the Jupiter VII engines. Again no precise details are given in the records but the modification obviously did not apply to the more commonly used British Thomson-Houston (BTH) magneto.

Most of the defects and failures recorded were of a minor nature, but more serious, although less frequent, were reported cases of structural failure in the aircraft's mainplane. As more powerful radial and in-line engines came to be used in aircraft of the post-1918 years, so increased speeds, particularly whilst diving, began to highlight problems of elevator or aileron flutter. Although the prototype Bulldog Mark I had survived terminal velocity dives as high as 270 mph, aileron flutter and wing spar failure had occurred in subsequent production aircraft. A Bulldog II (no 7358) had suffered such a failure in November 1929 whilst being dived during evaluation and test trials in the United States — an accident which unfortunately resulted in the death of its pilot. Wing Commander W. G. Easton, an ex-fighter pilot of the time, is quite scathing in his criticism when he recalls being an eye-witness to an incident whilst he was stationed at Calshot:

'I saw the effect of another weak point of the Bulldog whilst I was at Calshot. There had been a dance in the Officers' Mess over the weekend and among the guests were three fighter pilots who had left their Bulldogs at Lee-on-Solent. On the Monday morning after their take-off from Lee they flew across to Calshot to "shoot-up" our HQ. Following a steep dive from about 500 ft with full engine, one of the pilots had started to pull out of the dive when his port lower mainplane crumpled like a piece of aluminium foil and the aircraft plunged straight into the sea killing the pilot.

'It is easy to dismiss such an incident as a foolish attempt by the young pilot to "show off" but it does not say much for a fighter aircraft which folded up when put under strain.'

No doubt deep and searching investigations were made by the company into this serious defect, for revised wing and aileron spars were introduced with the Mark IIA. In fairness it should be borne in mind that design at that time was very largely empirically based and without the benefit of modern test-flight instrumentation. Most fighter biplanes of that period experienced problems with wing flutter, particularly the Gamecock, a fault which it inherited from the Grebe. Easton further recalls that:

'The failure of the lower wings of biplane fighters was not uncommon in those days, for I remember three such incidents involving Siskins whilst I was at North Weald.'

Bulldog did, in its early days, before all its flying characteristics were fully appreciated by the pilots of the newly equipped squadrons, become involved in some dangerous, or near dangerous, accidents. A pilot performing aerobatics at low altitude could, in a manoeuvre such as the roll, end up in a mangled state on the turf, as one famous pilot found to his cost. Whilst Bulldog was light and responsive in its controls, its increase in weight over its predecessors, such as the highly manoeuvrable Gamecock, had always to be borne

in mind. When rolled it needed plenty of speed and power, as well as hard application of the rudder in the vertical plane, and forward elevator whilst inverted, if the nose was to be kept on the horizon. Flight Lieutenant Harry Broadhurst tells of one such similar incident which could well have proved fatal:

'In general I enjoyed my flying on Bulldogs, about 600 hours in all, and in straightforward flying there were usually no problems, but . . . one had to be very careful on carrying out low aerobatics. My one big fright was in a manoeuvre I had performed on many occasions — to go into a half loop from take-off and roll off the top. Of course in those days the engines would not work upside down without position 'G' on the carburettor to keep the petrol flowing (this was to prove a great handicap in World War 2 when fighting the Germans who had fuel injection).

'On this particular occasion, on the top of the loop the aircraft shuddered, indicating that it was about to spin, so I had to continue over the top of the loop until, with the engine running, I had enough speed to roll out — by which time I just clipped the hedge on the boundary of the airfield. Needless to say, the onlookers were most impressed, as indeed was I!'

After a number of such incidents, squadron pilots were strictly forbidden to perform aerobatic manoeuvres in which the aircraft was likely to pass within 1,000 ft of the ground.

Spin recovery had never been Bulldog's strongest feature, as was discovered on the prototype Mark I at Martlesham during its trials in 1927. Bulldog was, according to Pilot Officer W. E. Carr of 56(F) Squadron:

'A charming little aeroplane but with a limited ability to suffer fools, and one which "could" develop a stable nose-up spin.'

The prototype Mark II, *J9480*, had satisfied the A&AEE early in 1928 that its lengthened fuselage had improved spin-recovery, but on 10 December 1928 some difficulty was experienced in recovering from a right-handed spin. Although the aircraft recovered with a burst of the engine it was considered necessary to investigate a little more deeply. On 21 December with Martlesham pilot, Flying Officer S. A. Thorn, at the controls, *J9480* (which had a total all-up weight of 3,210 lb, and the 'x' co-ordinate of its c of g 1 in behind the leading edge of the lower mainplane) was tested. Three right-handed spins were made from a height of 10,000 ft by stalling to the right with the tail adjustment in forward, mid and fully back positions. In each case the aircraft recovered after

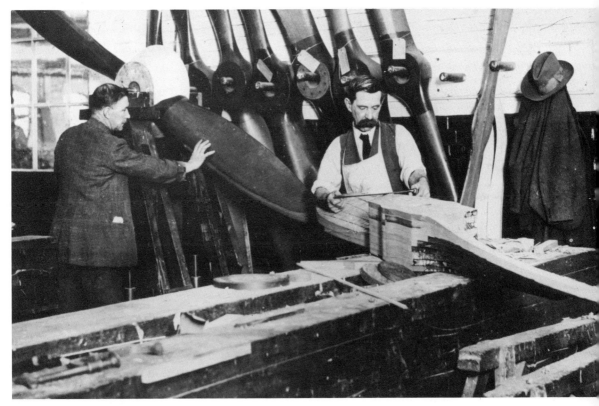

Propellers under construction circa 1927 *(British Aerospace, Filton)*.

being allowed to spin up to ten turns, whereupon opposite rudder and control-column fully forward, brought about recovery within one and a half turns. Total height lost in the three spins varied from 2,000-5,000 ft, depending upon the number of turns the aircraft was allowed to spin. It was concluded that the rate of spin — two seconds per turn — was normal for this type of aircraft and of a gentle character, whilst the variation of the tail adjustment did not appear to have any significance upon the nature of the spin.

One of the earliest records of failure to recover from a spin, and in which a Bulldog was lost, occurred on 9 March 1931 when Sergeant Pilot P. C. Ginn, of 'C' Flight, No 3(F) Squadron, was flying a Mark II near Upavon. He had been carrying out spinning practice and failed to bring *K1079* under control, so that at 2,000 ft he decided to abandon the aircraft. Although he landed safely by parachute he was injured; firstly, when he hit the aircraft upon leaving the cockpit, and again when he was dragged by his parachute upon landing. He was taken to a nearby hospital but his injuries were not serious and within a few weeks he was back on flying duties.

A Court of Inquiry was set up the very next day, conducted by Flight Lieutenant Davey of the Air Ministry's Accident Investigation Branch, whilst a Flight Lieutenant Stainforth carried out spinning tests on an 'A' Flight Bulldog. Ginn was interviewed again on 14 April by Squadron Leader F. E. Hellyer, OBE, also of the AIB, regarding the difficulty that he had experienced upon ejecting from *K1079*. No record exists of any conclusions drawn from the two Inquiries, but Ginn's incident was not an isolated case.

All the defects, including those of a minor as well as a major category, were carefully studied by the company's design office at Filton and considered for possible design modification. They knew that if the aircraft was to be really successful both at home in Service use, as well as overseas, then such modifications must rapidly be incorporated into the Mark IIA version.

* * *

The company received a contract in May 1930 from the Air Ministry for 92 Mark IIAs, *K1603-K1694* (nos 7459-7550), to meet their revised specification F11/29, and immediately planned a batch of 100 aircraft for production. The remaining eight machines were earmarked for the Royal Swedish Air Force who were anxious to place a further order. Two production lines were laid down in order to produce batches of twenty; of the 100 aircraft built, 36 were completed with engines, whilst the remainder were temporarily fitted with an engine and given a short test-flight.

The first of the batch, *K1603*, which was destined for Martlesham in order to gain type approval, was given a fifteen-minute test-flight on 25 September by Uwins, when he reported a failure of the piston of no 6 cylinder of its Jupiter VIIF. Both Jupiter VII and VIIF engines appear to have been suffering a spate of such failures, for no less than

eight entries detailing such occurrences appear in Uwins' flying log-book between the period September 1929 to December 1930. However, deliveries began in October 1930 to nos 54(F) and 111(F) Squadrons, Hornchurch, and no 32(F) Squadron, Kenley, whilst the remainder of the 92 machines were delivered by May 1931. In addition the Royal Danish Air Force had placed an order for four aircraft — designated Type 105D — with Jupiter VIF high compression engines, and these were delivered by March 1931.

The second production batch of aircraft was to fulfil an Air Ministry order for 100 Mark IIAs, *K2135-K2234* (nos 7590-7689), which were delivered, apart from *K2188,* during the period July 1931 to April 1932 to various RAF squadrons including nos 19(F), Duxford, and 41(F), Northolt. *K2188* was converted into a two-seater dual-control version and became the prototype

Assembly of No 3(F) Squadron Mark II Bulldogs on the production line at Filton 1929. Note the large diameter RAF roundels on the wings *(British Aerospace, Filton).*

TM Trainer. Continuation orders for the RAF meant twenty aircraft K2476-K2495 (nos 7691-7710), which were produced during the period April to July, and a further fourteen aircraft K2859-K2872 (nos 7713-7726) following on, with production being completed by the end of the year.

An Air Ministry contract was placed in February 1932 for an aircraft to their specification 11/31, using stainless steel in place of the normally used high tensile steel stove-enamelled finished structure for its airframe. It was allocated serial no K4189 (no 7744) and flown by Bristol's test pilot, C. T. Holmes, on 2 and 4 February 1935. The merits of its construction were outweighed by other factors, and consequently it was never adopted into production but was relegated to be used for static test purposes.

The final batch of 28 aircraft for the RAF, K2946-K2963 and K3504-K3513 (nos 7746-7773), bringing the total of Mark IIAs produced to 268, followed on from a production run of the first batch of TM Trainers and was completed by November 1933.

All the modifications incorporated in the Mark IIA were initiated in two stages; the first affecting mainplane, fuselage, oil system and engine were orginally implemented in the company demonstrator G-ABBB by early 1930, whilst the remainder did not appear until August 1933, when they were incorporated in K3512. Conversion of all aircraft to this standard was completed by the middle of 1934.

The constructional details of the modifications were as follows:

Airframe
Mainplane
Wing and aileron spars were stiffened.

Fuselage
Strengthening of load bearing areas to permit an increase in fully-laden weight, of 3,530 lb, together with provision of a circular hatch, on the underside of the cockpit at bay no 2, in order to permit easier access for maintenance of flying controls.

Oil System
A revised oil system, with a separate Vickers Potts seven-element cooler mounted centrally between the undercarriage legs and fully exposed to the airstream, was used (see Fig 14). The oil tank, now located on the top longerons of bay no 1, and secured as in the Mark II, had a total capacity of 7.5 gallons and a working capacity of 6.5 gallons. The oil filler was readily accessible on the top fairing, whilst its cap carried a dipstick retained by a short length of chain to prevent complete withdrawal and possible loss. A tubular aperture passing longitudinally through the tank facilitated the drive rod of the hand-starting magneto; in addition, provision was made for an electric heater plug on the tank's front face. As in the case of the Mark II a pressure relief valve and bypass system were incorporated for when the oil was cold and thick. A combined oil and fuel cock switch, operating their cocks through a single torsion rod, was grouped together with the starboard fuel tank switch on an indicator plate, situated on the starboard side of the cockpit below the dashboard.

Engine
A Jupiter VIIF with a power output of 490 hp at rated altitude of 8,000 ft using full throttle, normal rpm, and rated boost of zero lb was fitted, together with a Watts airscrew of 9 ft 1 in diameter, but without the spinner. Automatic boost control from the supercharger was a great boon to the pilot, for he no longer had to monitor the boost gauge. The throttle lever was limited by a connection from the ABC, which meant that the boost pressure was maintained right up to the full throttle height.

* * *

Undercarriage
The undercarriage was strengthened and slightly longer oleo legs fitted, in order to provide for the possible fitment of a larger diameter metal airscrew at a later date. The track was increased by 9.5 in to 6 ft 2.5 in and Bendix cable-operated brakes were incorporated in Dunlop disc wheels. Tyres of 19 in diameter, and increased section, maintained at a pressure of 40 to 45 psi, were also fitted.

Brakes
The Bendix cable-operated 13.75 in diameter drum brakes were of the mechanically servo-operated type, using a leading and a trailing brake shoe arrangement, in which the rotation of the wheel contributes toward the braking effort. They were

independently operated from toe-pedals and their bell-cranks on the rudder bar (see Fig 15), with their cables lying in flexible conduits hidden inside the oleo-leg fairings.

Brake torque reaction was effected by two 5/16 in tie-rods attached at one end to the brake back-plate, and at the other end to a lug on the rear spar of the centre-section of the lower mainplane. These rods were adjusted so that a stop on the back-plate, bore against one of the radius rod lugs formed on the axle (see Fig 16). The upper rod prevented the brake from turning with the drum when braking, whilst the lower one prevented the upper one from buckling if the aircraft should move in a rearwards direction with the brakes applied. Brake adjustment was made by rotating the star wheel inside the drum by means of a screwdriver through a slot in the backplate, whilst brake shoe and drum clearance was checked through a feeler-gauge slot.

A secondary hand-operated system was provided to enable the brakes to be applied whilst parking. The hand brake parking gear was constructed from two duralumin tubes, one sliding inside the other. The outer tube was clamped at its top and bottom by hinged clips, bolted to extensions welded to the brackets which held the reservoir of the gun synchronising gear. The inner tube which had extensions at both ends moved along guides within the outer tube. The upper extension of the inner tube was formed into an operating handle, while the lower one was connected through a tie-rod to a compensating link. A rack, formed on a portion of the inner tube, was pressed into engagement with a pawl at the top of the outer tube by a spring-loaded plunger. By this means the parking brake was held on when once applied. The brake was released by pulling the handle downwards so as to withdraw the rack teeth from the pawl by depressing the plunger.

Pilots soon found that their newly acquired brakes needed to be applied with some caution if their aircraft were not to ground loop, or overturn upon landing or during fast taxying. Peter Flint in his book *RAF Kenley* records such an incident occurring when No 3(F) and No 17(F) Squadrons were arriving at their new station from Upavon, in May 1934. Naturally there was a fierce but friendly rivalry between all Bulldog squadrons, but more particularly between these two which shared the same station. Group Captain Edward P. Mackay, at that time a Flight Commander with No 3(F) Squadron, recalls with a certain amount of relish and *schadenfreude* a mishap to one of 17(F)'s aircraft. Squadron Leader F. J. Vincent, DFC, was leading his squadron into a beautiful formation landing under the eyes of No 3(F)'s pilots who had arrived earlier. As they were touching down a Sergeant Pilot to the right of the leader came rather close to his CO who reacted by over-zealous application of his brakes, whereupon his aircraft turned over on to its back, much to the delight of the onlookers from No 3(F) Squadron. No doubt there were one or two wry smiles on the faces of the pilots of No 17(F) Squadron a few weeks later, when on 28 June a young Pilot Officer, T. C. Sanders of No 3(F) Squadron, had landed with his parking brake in the 'on' position, causing his aircraft to flip on to its back as it touched down. Fortunately, neither of the pilots suffered more that a dented ego, and apart from a few bruises were probably all the wiser for the experience.

Tailwheel

The original tailskid had, for a long while, been a source of annoyance to pilots when landing on the rough grass airfields in use at that time. One pilot eloquently described the sound of the skid contacting the grass as, 'just as though you had dropped a bagful of old tin cans'. However, the main reason for changing to a castoring tailwheel was that the tailskid was becoming inadequate as the weight of Bulldog increased to 3,660 lb in its final Mark IIA form. Tyre pressure of the tailwheel was maintained at 20 psi and a revised tail steering arm was issued for handling the aircraft on the ground.

Tailfin

The area of the fin was increased in order to improve directional stability rather than spin recovery, and now had a convex, rather than concave, shape to its leading edge. In addition, the rudder now incorporated an integrally-mounted white navigation lamp on its trailing edge and a longer aerial post on its top surface.

Other Modifications

Sir Frederick Handley Page, together with the assistance of a member of his staff, Dr G. V. Lachman, had designed and patented a safety device which delayed the stalling speed of an aircraft. It consisted of a slat in the form of an aerofoil section, which automatically lifted out from the leading edge of the wing just before normal stall speed. The air flowing through the slot and directed down on to the wing, delayed the break up of airflow on the low-pressure upper

The Fabric Shop, Filton circa 1929 *(RAF Museum)*.

surface of the wing. All the aircraft manufacturers were immediately interested in their idea and Bristol were no exception. On 25 September 1931 Uwins carried out a thirty-minute test flight with RAE 'slots' fitted to Bulldog IIA *K1667*. It had been found that 'slots' were most effective when they extended right out to the wingtip, and as Bulldog's wingtip profile was well rounded it was decided to make the front of the wingtip square. This enabled the slot to be brought to within 7.5 in of the wingtip.

The RAE carried out comparative tests on *K1667,* and on an unslotted Bulldog IIA, *K2476,* whilst permission was given to modify a small number of other Bulldogs in service at the same time. Wing Commander W. G. Easton, at that time a pupil-pilot at No 3 FTS, Grantham, remembers flying one of the experimental Bulldogs equipped with slots as late as 1935, and he recalls:

'. . . it would not spin when stalled, but fell around the sky in a flat slow spiral. We were able to lock the slots closed when spinning practice was required.'

The 'slots' opened at 68-70 mph, which was 12-14 mph before normal stall speed; stability of the aircraft was good below and above the stall speed, but there was a tendency for the left wing to drop immediately before the stall. The conclusions drawn from the tests were that the increase in weight and the impairment of manoeuvrability did not justify their acceptance as a standard fitment to Bulldog. In mock combat the unslotted aircraft was easily able to position itself on the tail of the other; Handley Page slots were also tried, but were no more successful than the RAE type.

The RAE had also been carrying out wind tunnel model tests on a new type of aileron, the Hartshorn, which was known as the twisted-nose type. Basically it was a modification of the Frise-aileron, having a Frise section at its outer tip, whilst its nose was raised progressively from the outer to the inner end (see Fig 17). This enabled the nose of the aileron to emerge progressively from above, or below, the wing contour, as the aileron moved, instead of emerging over its whole length at once, as in the case of the Frise type. Some criticism

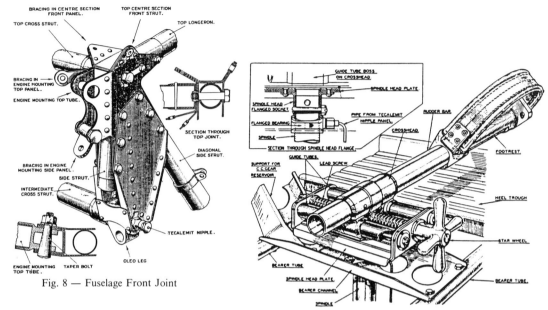

Fig. 8 — Fuselage Front Joint

Fig. 11 — Rudder Bar adjusting gear

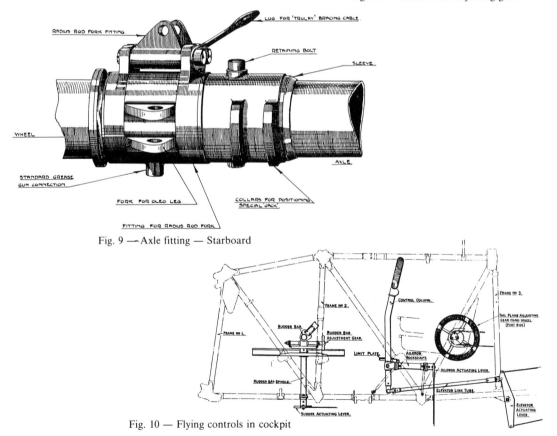

Fig. 9 —Axle fitting — Starboard

Fig. 10 — Flying controls in cockpit

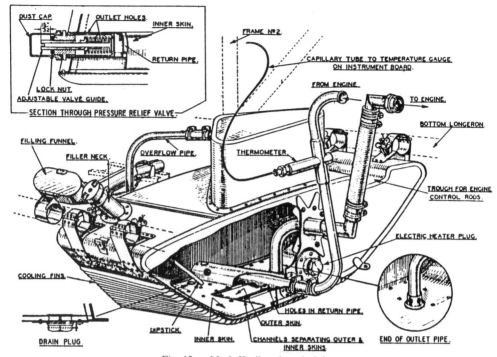

Fig. 12 — Mark II oil tank and piping

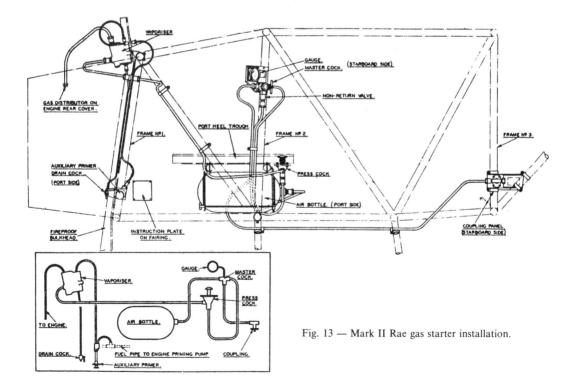

Fig. 13 — Mark II Rae gas starter installation.

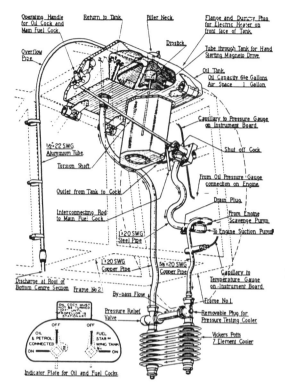

Operating Handle for Oil Cock and Main Fuel Cock.
Return to Tank
Filler Neck.
Flange and Dummy Plug for Electric Heater on front face of Tank.
Dipstick.
Tube through Tank for Hand Starting Magneto Drive.
Overflow Pipe
Oil Tank, Oil Capacity 6¼ Gallons Air Space   1 Gallon
Capillary to Pressure Gauge on Instruments Board.
½"-22 SWG Aluminium Tube.
Torsion Shaft.
Shut off Cock
From Oil Pressure Gauge connection on Engine.
Outlet from Tank to Cock.
Drain Plug.
From Engine Scavenge Pump.
Intercommeng Rod to Main Fuel Cock.
To Engine Suction Pump
1"-20 SWG Steel Pipe
1"-20 SWG Copper Pipe
⅝"-20 SWG Copper Pipe
Capillary to Temperature Gauge on Instrument Board.
Discharge at Roof of Bottom Centre Section
Frame No 2
By-pass Flow
Frame No 1.
OIL COCK MUST NOT BE TURNED UNTIL PROPELLOR IS STATIONARY
OFF   OFF
OIL & PETROL CONNECTED   FUEL STAR WING TANK
ON   ON
Pressure Relief Valve
Removable Plug for Pressure Testing Cooler
Vickers Potts 7 Element Cooler
Indicator Plate for Oil and Fuel Cocks.

Fig. 14 — Mark IIA, oil system.

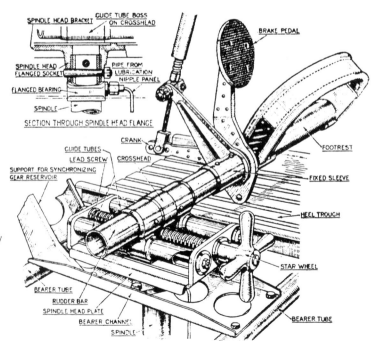

SPINDLE HEAD BRACKET
GUIDE TUBE BOSS ON CROSSHEAD
BRAKE PEDAL
SPINDLE HEAD FLANGED SOCKET
PIPE FROM LUBRICATION NIPPLE PANEL
FLANGED BEARING
SPINDLE
SECTION THROUGH SPINDLE HEAD FLANGE
CRANK
GUIDE TUBES
LEAD SCREW
CROSSHEAD
SUPPORT FOR SYNCHRONIZING GEAR RESERVOIR
FOOTREST
FIXED SLEEVE
HEEL TROUGH
STAR WHEEL
BEARER TUBE
RUDDER BAR
SPINDLE HEAD PLATE
BEARER CHANNEL
SPINDLE
BEARER TUBE

Fig. 15 — Brake Pedal assembly

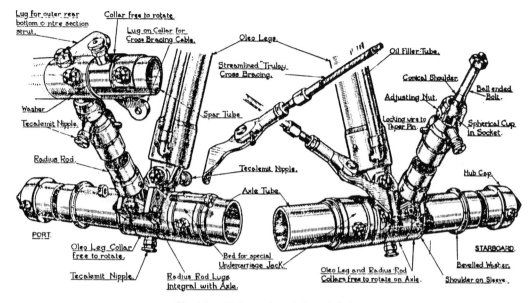

Fig. 16 — Undercarriage Axle and fitting

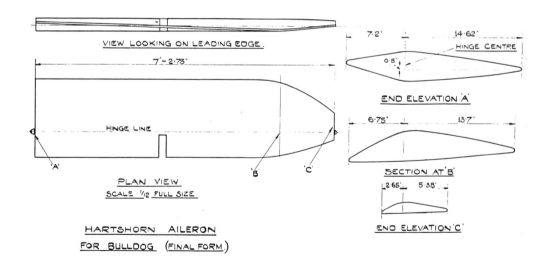

Fig. 17 — Hartshorn Aileron

had been made of the Frise type ailerons which were allegedly susceptible to rigging errors, and it was therefore decided to fit the Hartshorn type to Bulldog IIA, *K2476*. Reports were submitted by the two RAE pilots, who felt that they were an improvement on the Frise type, but with some reservations. One reported 'a slight adverse yaw on application of aileron at low speeds', whilst the other pilot found that 'the rolling effect is less for a given aileron angle than on a good standard Bulldog'. It was decided to let RAF squadron pilots try them out and their concensus was unreservedly in their favour. The RAE's final report concluded that they were an improvement on the Frise type and less sensitive to rigging errors. However, it seems that Uwins had the last word, for in his opinion their yaw characteristics were inferior to the standard fitment, and so the Bristol Aeroplane Co could see no good reason for their implementation.

* * *

Spin recovery problems continued to be reported, even with the Mark IIAs, and were the subject of considerable investigation by the RAE. One of the earliest known cases concerned *K2160* of No 19(F) Squadron, Duxford, which was abandoned near to its airfield in November 1933. This incident was probably the same one as that witnessed by Pilot Officer George C. Lott (later to become an Air Vice-Marshal), who had served as an NCO pilot on Bulldogs with No 19(F). He recalls:

'I well remember that on one occasion when I was flying in the neighbourhood of Duxford from Northolt (I was posted to 41(F) Squadron on commissioning) I actually saw a 19(F) Squadron Bulldog go into a flat spin from which the pilot baled out. I discovered later the name of the pilot, and it was, I believe, Pilot Officer D. Scorgie of "B" Flight.'

George Lott comments further on the incident by giving his own impressions of Bulldog's spinning characteristics:

'The one peculiarity in its performance, as far as I can remember, was its tendency to go into a flat spin off the stall from which it was reluctant to recover. I experimented quite a bit with this problem, and eventually came to the conclusion that the best recovery action was to persuade it into a normal nose down spin with elevator and rudder, and then make a normal recovery which was quite easy.'

The *K2160* incident became the subject of an RAE investigation in which they were requested to perform spinning tests on a similar aircraft from No 19(F) Squadron. Their brief was to ascertain its normal time of recovery from a spin, but more importantly to determine whether an abnormal spin, involving difficult recovery, could be induced by mishandling of the controls. Bulldog IIA *K2141*, complete with camera gun, R/T installation, and navigation lights, which was the standard equipment normally carried by No 19(F) Squadron aircraft, was loaned for the tests. Its 'c of g' was measured and found to be 0.6 in in front of the leading edge of its lower wing. The first part of the test involved a standard spin, with the tailplane adjustment wheel set in its fully back position, and the ailerons in a neutral position, where the control column was brought hard back and full rudder applied. As many as sixteen consecutive turns to the left and the right were made (there were approximately four turns for every 1,000 ft drop in height), with the longest recovery time being recorded as 3.2 seconds in 1.5 turns.

The final part of the test was made in five stages, with different control movements made during the spin, as follows:

1. Ailerons held over and control column back;
2. Ailerons held over and control column forward;
3. Centralisation of all controls after a 4,000 ft spin;
4. Tailplane adjustment and control column fully forward; and
5. A combination of control movements, ie, reversal of rudder, followed by rudder put with spin again; combinations of elevator and rudder movements.

The final report stated that whilst the aircraft had a natural tendency to spin to the left, and right-hand spins gave a marginally slower recovery time, all the spins were of a steady and even nature, and the effect of any given control movement was always consistent. More significantly, under the worst possible handling of the controls, recovery was made without difficulty within 3.5 turns. In retrospect one can only conclude that incidents such as that involving *K2160* were due to the inexperience of the pilot, or carrying out spinning practice with insufficient recovery height.

* * *

By September 1932 nine of the thirteen squadrons comprising Fighting Area (Fighter Command was not formed until July 1936) and based on eight airfields, were fully equipped with Bulldogs. No 23(F), Biggin Hill, was a composite squadron with two flights of Bulldogs and one of Hawker Demon Is, whilst Nos 1(F) and 43(F) at Tangmere, and 25(F) at Hawkinge, were equipped with Hawker Fury Is. Hitler had not yet come to power and the ADGB Air Exercises were being conducted with France seen as the likely enemy in any future war. The Air Staff were by that time well aware that there had been a rapid advance in the performance of day bombers since Bulldog was first introduced in June 1929. Minutes between members of the Department of the Air Member for Supply and Research were, by July 1932, stressing that even when Bulldog was first Service-tested by the ADGB in 1927, its performance was considered to be barely adequate, even for those days. In consequence they had never envisaged a long life for the type, and by August 1933, although pressing for all Bulldogs to be quickly brought up to the final form of modifications for Mark IIA, were arguing that it was an obsolescent type. Bulldog was, after all, a six-year-old design at that time, and lacking the pace of the Hart and Demon two-seaters, which were soon to replace it. The composite squadron of No 23(F), Biggin Hill, had already highlighted this deficiency, for when flying in formation the Demons had to slow down in order for the Bulldogs to keep their position, and by April 1933 the squadron had been fully equipped with the Hawker product.

Barnwell and Fedden were not unaware of the situation, and had already implemented a more powerful Mercury IVA engine into a Bulldog airframe. This engine had been developed during flight testing, as Mercury III and IV, in *R1* and *G-AATR,* already mentioned earlier in the chapter. Bulldog IIIA (no 7560) had been built, again as a private venture, and was first flown, with Uwins at the controls on 17 September 1931 carrying identity marking *R5*.

Wind tunnel tests had established the superiority of the RAF34 section aerofoil over the Bristol 1A from which it had been developed. The RAF34 section also had the added advantage, by virtue of its biconvex form, of accommodating the fuel tanks within its section, unlike its predecessor where the tanks bulged below the upper mainplane surfaces. Wingspan was reduced by 2 in, and the upper and lower wingtip profiles made much squarer, whilst the lower wing chord was reduced by 7 in in order to further improve downwards visibility. Aileron structures were stiffened, and given improved self-aligning ball bearings, in order to cope with the increased speeds resulting from the more powerful engine.

Drag reducing features included integrally-mounted wingtip navigation lights; elimination of the externally-mounted generators which were now driven from the engine; double bracing wires replaced by single wires of improved section, with their attachment points submerged below the wing's surface.

Fuselage modifications included an improved engine mounting, using a steel forging in place of the previously used mild steel flanged fabrication, as well as heavier gauge longerons and a deeper section to the rear end. Improved control was given by an increase in the area of the balancing horn of the elevators. The undercarriage incorporated braked wheels, enclosed by spats which were very much in vogue at the time.

A Mercury IVS2 engine, which was the production version of the series IVA, was installed. It produced 560 hp as against the Jupiter VIIF's 440 hp, and together with a short chord Townend ring brought the all-up weight of the aircraft to 4,000 lb. Improved handling, an increase in rate of climb and service ceiling, together with a 30 mph increase in maximum speed to 208 mph at 15,000 ft were the end results of the modifications.

Although the Mark IIIA lost out to the Gloster SS19B Gauntlet in the Martlesham trials of 1933, the company did not give up. The second Mark IIIA (no 7745) carrying identity marking *R7* became, after some modification in March 1934, prototype Bulldog IV. It was designed to meet Air Ministry specification F7/30 for a four-gun day-and-night fighter, and therefore had provision for the fitment of two further guns under the lower wing. The wheel spats were no longer fitted as they had proved to be quite unsuitable for use on grass airfields, where they could quickly clog with mud, locking the wheels and turning an aircraft on to its back.

In its final form as the Mark IVA, with the 640 hp Mercury VIS2, it was fitted with four ailerons — the top wing ailerons being operated by cables. Although it now had a maximum speed of 224 mph, and an increased service ceiling of 33,400 ft, it was outclassed by the Gloster Gladiator which went into production as the last fighter biplane to be supplied to the RAF. *R7* was subsequently purchased by the Air Ministry and given the serial *K4292* whereupon it was used for flight testing of different types of cowlings. A further Mark IVA (no 7808) was built as a company demonstrator and registered as *G-ACJN* on 16 August 1934, although it only ever carried the identity marking *R8*. It became a test-bed for Bristol's first sleeve valve engine, the Perseus 1A, until it was crashed by Cyril T. Holmes on 17 February 1934. It was rebuilt in the following May, with cockpit heating ducted from muffs shrouding the two exhaust

The last of the initial production batch of 25 Mark IIs, J9591, was retained as a company test-bed for the Mercury IV engine. The aircraft is shown with helmet cowlings *(British Aerospace, Filton).*

pipes, which now extended as far back as the trailing edge of the lower mainplane. A Dowty tailwheel was now fitted, and it carried a large numeral *7* mid-way along the fuselage on its port side. Later in the year it reverted back to its Mercury VIS2 engine with a short chord NACA cowling, and was used for testing the Hamilton variable-pitch three-bladed metal airscrew. Its last public appearance in this form was in 1935, when it appeared at the SBAC trade show. By this time all serious development of the biplane fighter had, within the company and amongst other UK manufacturers, come to an end. An attempt had been made by the company in 1934 with a new design, the Bristol Type 123 single-seat four-gun biplane fighter, using a 600 hp Rolls-Royce Goshawk III, twelve-cylinder, vee-type, steam-

cooled engine. A prototype was built and flown, but it was beset by problems from its power unit's cooling system and the design was abandoned.

The Bulldog Mark IVA, although unsuccessful in obtaining a home contact, did attract overseas buyers, particularly Finland, and an agreement was signed by that country on 24 March 1934 for the supply of seventeen aircraft. A production line was set up and nos 7810-7826 were built and coded *BU59-BU75* before being delivered to Finland between December 1934 and January 1935. Further interest was shown in the Mark IVA by Finland and Australia in 1935 and 1936, but the company was by that time heavily committed to the production of the Blenheim I bomber and the orders were declined.

Chapter 4
Martlesham Heath

Although Cyril Uwins first flew the unmarked prototype Bulldog, designated Mark 1 (constructor's no 7155), on 10 May 1927, its first official test flight was not recorded until seven days later. It looked every inch a fighter, both in the air where it handled well, and on the ground where its short stubby bluff-nosed fuselage gave its canine title a certain aptness. One of Uwins' favourite tricks with the prototype was to come in low over the Filton aerodrome, shielding the aircraft from view, and then to suddenly round the hangar sheds, much to the delight of those who had gathered to watch. The company was not slow to take advantage of the fact that Bulldog had been built as a private venture, and a second unmarked prototype (no 7267) with Bullpup-type wings, was built to attract export orders. It was never flown but put on static display at the Paris *Salon de l'Aéronautique* in June 1928, and at Olympia in July 1929.

One of the aircraft's design features was the excellent visibility for the pilot, who was sat high in the cockpit, shoulders above the coaming, and eyes level with the trailing edge of the upper mainplane. The steep slope of the nose of the aircraft from the windscreen to the engine gave an unobstructed view forward, whilst the lowered top decking of the fuselage, between cockpit and tailplane, gave a good view rearwards. In addition, the deep cut-outs in both mainplanes, particularly the upper one, eliminated blind-spots above and below, an important prerequisite for the fighter pilot. Its aerobatic qualities, assisted by the lightness of the controls, were, according to one pilot, 'delightful' and it was soon to thrill the crowds that gathered every June at Hendon in the early 1930s, making it a great favourite with the public.

The directors of the company had approached the Air Ministry some two months before the private venture prototype had first flown, offering to build a production batch of fifty of the type if some contribution could be made towards development costs. The offer was declined, but the Air Ministry were willing for the prototype to be evaluated and tested by the Aeroplane and Armament Experimental Establishment at

Cyril Frank Uwins, OBE, AFC, FRAeS, Chief Test Pilot, with "Brisfit" in background
(British Aerospace, Filton).

Martlesham Heath, along with other competitors for the Air Ministry's F9/26 day-and-night fighter specification contract. And so, on 15 June 1927, the prototype made a ninety-minute flight to Martlesham where it remained for almost two weeks for its New Type acceptance testing. On the morning of 27 June, Uwins took off quite early at 07:30 intending to make an early cross-country journey back to Filton, but after some twenty minutes' flying time he turned back to the Heath in

From drawing-board to hardware — the Bulldog Mark I prototype in all its glory! Note the distinctive cockpit fairing, later deleted in production *(British Aerospace, Filton).*

order to carry out some adjustments. At 11:00 he again took off and cruised back to Filton, in one hour fifty minutes, this time without incident. Two days later Uwins flew the prototype to Hendon where it remained until 4 July, with great public interest being shown when it appeared in the New Type Park enclosure. It did not return to Martlesham until 23 July where it joined its four competitors, the Armstrong Whitworth Starling, Boulton & Paul Partridge, Gloster Goldfinch and Hawker Hawfinch in their single-seat fighter evaluation trials.

The A&AEE was situated some five miles to the east of Ipswich and was responsible for the evaluation and testing of new ideas and new aircraft types. It comprised two RAF squadrons, nos 15(B) and 22(B) which, although designated bomber squadrons, covered the testing of all military aircraft and their armament, as well as civil aircraft. No 15(B) specialised solely in armament, whilst the three Flights of No 22(B) covered the remaining duties. 'A' Flight covered fighters and light civil aircraft; 'B' Flight dealt with bombers and large passenger civil aircraft; and 'C' Flight dealt with Naval and Army Co-operation aircraft of other categories that were not covered by 'A' and 'B' Flights.

The F9/26 specification had called for a choice of engines which included the Armstrong Siddeley Jaguar V, Bristol Mercury and Orion, as well as the Rolls-Royce Falcon X. Both of the Bristol engines were unavailable at the time of the trials; the Mercury because of delays due to problems in development, and the Orion, (basically a Jupiter VI with RAE turbocharger) which had experienced cooling problems leading to distortion of its turbo casings. The Jupiter VII with its mechanically-driven geared supercharger had superseded the

Orion, and was fitted to all the aircraft in the trial with the exception of the Starling, which used the Jaguar V.

In the original specification, requirements were made for the aircraft to be fitted with exhaust systems suitable for night flying, as well as for radio telephony equipment. As none of the five aircraft at this stage were so equipped it was decided, in order to save time and money, to omit these parts of the tests until a selection was finally made.

The Boulton & Paul entrant — the P33 prototype *J8459,* named Partridge — was a conventional single-bay biplane of 35 ft wingspan with a double strut-braced tailplane. It had a good performance with a maximum speed of 167 mph, but unfortunately it exhibited certain structural defects whilst at Martlesham, which precluded its acceptance.

The Gloster Co had already successfully supplied the RAF with its first generation of post-war fighters in Grebe and Gamecock, and it sought to consolidate its position with the Goldfinch. Their prototype entrant *J7940* was a single-bay biplane of 30 ft span, and like Bulldog used an all-metal structure with fabric covering. Its distinctive feature in appearance was its wide but low fin profile, which extended well past the double cable-braced tailplane and along the top of the fuselage. The Goldfinch, together with the Starling, was eliminated from the competition because of inferior performance in speed, range and payload.

Hawker were anxious to keep their marque to the fore now that the Woodcock was becoming obsolescent, and Sydney Camm's entry, the Hawfinch, was to present tough opposition to the remaining contender, Bulldog. Their entrant *J8776* was a two-bay unequal span biplane of marked stagger, with the distinctive tailplane profile later to be seen on Fury and Hurricane.

The Bulldog prototype remained at Martlesham for approximately two months, but by October the RAF test pilots of the A&AEE had eliminated all but the Bristol and Hawker products from the trial. They found that Bulldog was marginally the faster of the two, and were particularly impressed by its flying qualities, apart from its spin recovery which did not match that of the Hawfinch. It was a criticism which Bulldog was never completely able to shake off, and later during its Service life was to be the subject of further RAE investigation and reports. An increase in fin and rudder area was tried which was effective, but unfortunately it aggravated lateral stability whilst taxiing in cross winds. The A&AEE's final recommendations were that the fuselage should be lengthened and the original fin and rudder retained; additionally, that the undercarriage should be strengthened and the seat height adjusting mechanism be improved. And so in November 1927 the Air Ministry placed an order, subject to these conditions, for a modified Bulldog which could take part in an extension of the trial with the Hawfinch as soon as possible.

The prototype Bulldog Mark II, *J9480* (no 7235) took to the air on 21 January 1928 with Cyril Uwins at the controls, and successfully completed its first ten-minute test flight. Later that same day Uwins gave it further spinning tests, to verify the effects of the modifications recommended by the A&AEE, and was satisfied that its spin recovery had been improved. The fuselage had been considerably lengthened by 26 in, with fewer stringers than its predecesor, and its cockpit fairing — reminiscent of the SE5A — was now removed. Its armament installation had also been modified, and this resulted in a different form of bulge in the starboard aluminium fairing panel, in order to access the gun's loading mechanism.

J9480 was flown to Martlesham early in February to continue its trials with the Hawfinch where its marginal superiority in speed, 178 mph as against 171 mph, was still a source of annoyance to Sydney Camm who claimed that Hawfinch had been given a Jupiter VII of inferior performance. Subsequent perusal of its engine test records showed that such allegations were quite unwarranted. Money had originally been allocated by the Air Ministry in their estimate of costs, for one aircraft from the competition to be issued to No 23(F) Squadron, Kenley. However, because the two prototypes were so closely matched, it was decided that the A&AEE would withhold its verdict until the squadron pilots of 3(F) and 17(F), Upavon; 23(F) and 32(F), Kenley; 29(F) and 56(F), North Weald and 41(F), Northolt (all of whom were equipped with Grebes, Gamecocks, Woodcocks and Siskin IIIas), were consulted. These were the squadrons that were to be equipped with whatever emerged as the final selection from the evaluation trial. The squadron trials continued throughout the first half of 1928, where there was eventually such a diversity of opinion that a decision was finally made in favour of Bulldog because of its easier maintenance.

Comparative tests had been carried out by the A&AEE and it soon became apparent that a great deal of attention had been given in the design of Bulldog to ease of maintenance and upkeep — an important factor in those days of reduced military budgets. Easily detachable panels gave good access to equipment which, combined with the grouping of lubrication points, meant reduced servicing times. The decision finally hinged upon two important factors during service use: Ease of removal and replacement of major components such as fuel tanks and engine; and repairability of structural damage to airframe.

Not only were the Bulldog's wing-mounted fuel tanks of larger capacity than that of the Hawfinch's fuselage tank, thereby giving it greater range, but their removal took two fitters only nineteen minutes as against fifty minutes for that of Hawfinch. Their removal was simply a matter of disconnecting the feed pipe, cutting the fabric away from the underside of the wing, and removing four bolts, whereupon the tank could be lowered from the mainplane. In contrast, withdrawal of its competitor's tank meant removal of the engine top cowling, the two guns, Aldis sight bracket, two side bracing wires of the centre-section, the cockpit control shaft, rev counter drive clip, pipe unions and filler cap before its four holding bolts could be undone. The fuel tank then had to be turned upside down in order to withdraw it from between the centre-section struts.

Under combat conditions any slight bullet damage to the aircraft's airframe, particularly the fuselage, could quickly render it unserviceable. In the case of Bulldog the constructional method, as used by Pollard, enabled 'patches' to be riveted over damaged areas, or whole sections cut out and new replacement sections riveted back. The Hawker method of construction, which used drawn steel tubes, did not lend itself to this kind of quick repair whilst in Service use.

Three further factors that went against the Hawfinch in the maintenance part of the trial were its inferior cockpit instrumentation layout, a gun installation whose access was officially considered to be impracticble, and the added complication of its two-bay wing structure. And so the prototype Bulldog Mark II was purchased by the Air Ministry on 21 August 1928 for a sum of £4,500, and soon after an order for the first production batch of 25 aircraft to specification F17/28, a revision of F9/26, was placed.

* * *

The first production Bulldog Mark II, *J9567* (no 7322), was delivered to Martlesham on 8 May 1929 for acceptance, and was joined by prototype Mark II *J9480* on the 24th of the same month. The reason for *J9480's* delivery was due to an alleged spin recovery problem with the aircraft in the December of the previous year, when it had been the subject of an RAE investigation in which it was exonerated — details being given in the previous chapter. Naturally the A&AEE were very concerned, for they had originally tested and cleared the aircraft for good spin recovery during the second stage of its trial with Hawfinch. However, in order to be absolutely sure before they gave production clearance to the Mark II, they decided to carry out comparative spinning tests, not only with *J9567* and *J9480*, but also with *J9570* delivered on 31 May, and *J9568* delivered on 4 June. No fault could be found with their spinning qualities and the two production aircraft, *J9568* and J9570, were delivered to No 3(F) Squadron at Upavon, whilst *J9567* was retained at Martlesham and prototype *J9480* returned to Filton.

It is interesting to note that *J9567* was given its handling tests by A&AEE test pilot Flight Lieutenant John N. Boothman, who was at that time OC 'A' Flight of No 22(B) Squadron. He was a first-class pilot, having been a Central Flying School instructor during the mid-1920s. As a Flying Officer he had performed at the Hendon Air Displays where he represented CFS in 1925, flying a Gloster Grebe, whilst in 1926, in an Avro 504, he had won the Duke of York's Trophy in a landing competition. He was to distinguish himself when he won the International Schneider Trophy on 12 September 1931 whilst flying the Vickers Supermarine, Rolls-Royce engined, S6B at an average speed of 340.08 mph. He eventually retired

Flight Lieutenant John Boothman after winning the International Schneider Trophy on 12 September 1931 *(Royal Aeronautical Society).*

Bulldog Mark II (no.7399) R-1, with Mercury III engine and four-bladed propeller. It later became company demonstrator G-ABAC and was abandoned in flight by T. W. Campbell on 4 June 1930 *(British Aerospace, Filton)*.

Prototype Bulldog Mark IIIA (no.7560) R-5, with prototype Mercury IVA engine, short-chord Townend cowling, wheel spats, and which first flew on 17 September 1931 *(British Aerospace, Filton)*.

from the RAF in 1956 as Air Chief Marshal Sir John Boothman.

One other test pilot at Martlesham at that time was Flying Officer A. J. 'Bill' Pegg who was no stranger to Bulldog. A&AEE test pilots were often the natural choice of the RAF for performing aerobatics at air displays, because so often they were the only pilots with sufficient experience of new types. It was during the afternoon of Friday 19 May 1933, whilst practising at Martlesham for the forthcoming Hendon Air Display, that he was part of a trio in which his two colleagues Flight Lieutenants J. W. Moir and G. E. Campbell collided. The three aircraft were at the top of a formation loop when two of the aircraft, *K2191* and *K2201,* touched, with disastrous effects for Campbell who was a newcomer to the Flight. Moir baled out, but poor Campbell failed to do so as the two aircraft fell earthwards, one diving straight in and exploding, whilst the other appeared, to Pegg, to gently spin into the ground. Flying Officer Pegg landed safely back at the airfield, much to the relief of his wife who was watching, unsure who was the victim. Nevertheless the event went ahead as planned with Flight Lieutenant Moir, Flying Officers Pegg and Leech performing the smoke trail aerobatics at Hendon on 24 June 1933.

Bill Pegg was to resign his commission with the RAF in December 1935, in order to become a civilian test pilot, and eventually CTP, with the Bristol Aeroplane Co, where he is chiefly remembered for his work on Brabazon and Britannia.

The first production Bulldog Mark IIA, *K1603* (no 7459) was successfully flight-tested by Uwins on 2 October 1930, having earlier suffered trouble with piston failure on its Jupiter VIIF engine. It was delivered to Martlesham later during that month for approval as the Directorate of Technical Development trial installation aircraft and remained at the A&AEE until its disposal in September 1933.

Bulldog Mark IIIA (no.7560) R-5, with Mercury IVS2 engine as used in the service trials during 1932. It was in this aeroplane that Flying Officer J. L. Armstrong was to be killed on 4 January 1933 whilst performing aerobatics *(British Aerospace, Filton)*.

Bulldog Mark IV (no.7745) R-7, with Mercury VIS2 engine and now with rod-operated ailerons on top and bottom mainplanes *(British Aerospace, Filton)*.

Bulldog Mark IVA (no.7808) R-8, was originally fitted with the Mercury IVS2 but is seen here with the sleeve-valve Perseus 1A engine for the June 1934 SBAC Show. In its final form it used the Mercury VIS2 *(British Aerospace, Filton).*

J9567 was used at Martlesham during 1932 for the flight testing of the Townend cowling ring, as well as testing the larger fin which was eventually fitted to the Mark IIA. Boothman's flying-log records a forced landing on 27 February 1932 at Bidleston whilst carrying out a terminal velocity dive. The trouble must have been of a minor nature for he managed to take-off again from the landing area. Tailwheel tests were also carried out on the last production IIA, *K3513* (no 7773) during early February 1934, again by Boothman. Subsequently tailwheels were fitted to all Mark IIAs.

* * *

The prototype Mark IIIA Bulldog (no 7560) fitted with the prototype Mercury IVA engine and a Townend short-chord cowling, first flew at Filton on 17 September 1931. It carried the identity marking *R5* as well as RAF roundels when it made its first test flight of ten minutes' duration with Uwins at the controls. After he had made 22 further test flights, varying in length between five and seventy minutes, and totalling 9 hours 55 minutes, it was delivered to Martlesham on 7 December 1931. It is interesting to note Uwins' comments at about this time, for on 31 October he recorded:

'This aircraft *(R5)* is to proceed to Martlesham as soon as possible . . . there is no position for storing the inertia starter handle. The handle has to be stowed after the engine has been started.'

Again, on 24 November he recorded:

'The aircraft is extremely easy and untiring to fly; at cruising speed it may be flown for considerable periods with hands and feet off the controls. Take-off and landing are very easy and both runs are short. Brakes of Bendix pattern, pedal-operated and developed on the Mark IIA are fitted and have proved very satisfactory both for steering and retardation after landing.'

The Air Ministry were looking for a successor to the now obsolescent Bulldog Mark IIA, and had issued a new specification F7/30 for a day-and-night fighter carrying an armament of four fixed guns. At last the biplane was moving away from its twin-Vickers gun armament of First World War standard with which officialdom had for so long been satisfied. The two aircraft against which *R5* was to compete in the evaluation trials, were the Armstrong Whitworth AW16 designated *A2*, which was the first to arrive at Martlesham in October 1931, and the Gloster SS19A serial no *J9125,* which arrived during the following month.

The AW16, which came from the drawing-board of Armstrong Whitworth's chief designer John Lloyd, originator of the Siskin, was a derivative of the AW14 'Starling' which had unsuccessfully competed with Bulldog Mark I in the latter part of 1927. The prototype AW16, serial no *S1591,* had been built to conform to Air Ministry specification N21/26 as a Fleet fighter. It had first flown in December 1930 and after much modification was delivered to Martlesham in April 1931, where it exhibited overheating of its supercharged Panther III engine and some problem with directional control. A second AW16, carrying identity marking *A2,* was built as a private venture and first flew early in 1931 where it displayed similar problems to that of the prototype *S1591.* It was a good looking conventional single-bay biplane of 33 ft wingspan, with 'N' type interplane struts, wheel spats and a Townend ring cowled engine.

The Gloster SS19A was conceived by chief designer H. P. Folland, the former British Nieuport designer who had already established his reputation with Nighthawk, Grebe and Gamecock. SS19A was derived from the prototype SS18, serial no *J9125,* which was designed to meet specification F9/26. It subsequently flew as a Jupiter VIIF-engined SS18A in 1929, and a year later as SS18B, when Panther III and IIIA engines were installed. In 1931 *J9125* reappeared as the heavily armed six-gun SS19 with Jupiter VIIFP engine. Four Lewis guns, one on the underside of each upper and lower wings, fired outside the airscrew disc, whilst two synchronised Vickers guns were mounted on the sides of the fuselage. The heavy armament was dispensed with in SS19A, in favour of the twin-Vickers and provision for only two wing-mounted guns, and modifications were made to improve lateral control. The Gloster product was a 32 ft 9 in wingspan, two-bay biplane, with a performance of 204 mph at 10,000 ft, which was a considerable improvement over the similarly-engined Bulldog IIA which it sought to replace. Boothman's log records a thirty-minute handling flight of *R5* on 4 January 1932, as well as a ninety-minute test flight three days later, when he carried out 'partials at full boost height of 12,000 ft'. By February *R5* had been returned to Filton for installation of the Mercury IVS2 engine, which was the production version of the prototype Mercury IVA previously installed. After a 25-minute test flight on 4 March 1932 Uwins reported:

'On the last diving test the highest speed recorded was 250 mph, whilst on this test the machine was dived to a speed of 270 mph indicated, at 12,000 ft. Recovery had to be made owing to the presence of clouds at 8,000 ft. The aircraft was generally steady, although there was slight vibration in the wing bracing . . . the Townend ring and wheel fairings have proved steady up to this speed.'

It was given four test flights by Uwins totalling two hours twenty minutes between 27 February and 5 March, when it made a 65-minute flight back to Martlesham. Apart from an appearance at the SBAC Trade Show at Hendon on 27 June, and a brief period at Filton during the early part of July, *R5* continued with its trials along with its competitors throughout that summer at Martlesham.

In October 1932 the Service Trials of two of the three aircraft began when RAF pilots from No 41(F), Northolt, collected *R5* and AW16 from Martlesham on the 20th of that month. Delivery of the Gloster SS19A was delayed by several weeks

Cyril Uwins "rounding the hangar" in the prototype Bulldog 1927 *(British Aerospace, Filton).*

Cyril T. Holmes *(British Aerospace, Filton).*

owing to trouble with its Jupiter VIIFP engine. Flight Lieutenant Harry Broadhurst was flying *R5* on 2 November and he records:

'. . . whilst pulling out of a dive for an upward roll the box-rib in the starboard aileron collapsed. After a somewhat hairy ride I managed to get *R5* back on to the airfield without breaking it.'

New wings were despatched from Filton and the old ones returned for examination and investigation, where it was found that the aileron spar had buckled in several places. Overall, the pilots of No 41(F) preferred the SS19A, and although *R5* had a better performance than AW16, which was suffering from engine trouble, this incident did not exactly endear it to them. Broadhurst flew *R5* again on 25 November after it had been repaired, and again he experienced aileron flutter in a dive, but this time without damage. He records that:

'On 4 January of the following year (1933) three pilots arrived from No 111(F) Squadron, Hornchurch, to collect the three experimental aircraft. I specifically warned them of my experience in *R5* whilst diving at high speed, but whilst to the north of Hornchurch they dived and pulled up into a Prince of Wales feather. In the process *R5* disintegrated and the pilot, Flying Officer J. L. Armstrong, was killed . . .'

This incident must surely have seriously undermined the Bristol product, both in the eyes of the Air Ministry and amongst RAF pilots who were subsequently to be engaged in the Service trials. A replacement was soon found for *R5* in Bulldog Mark IIIA (no 7745), which was flown from Filton to Martlesham carrying the identity marking *R7* on 12 May. This aircraft had originally been registered as *G-ABZW* on 3 October 1932, and was exhibited at the Paris Salon in November of that year. Even on the delivery flight of *R7* on 12 May fate seemed to be against Bristol's entry for Uwins records:

'After forty minutes' flight at 1,950 rpm a smell of burning rubber was noticed, and shortly afterwards small flames were seen near the cut-out; these subsided after a few seconds. A landing was made at Halton (Buckinghamshire) where it was found that one of the wires which normally run to the accumulator, and now connected to a terminal above the cut-out, had burnt away. The flight was continued to Martlesham . . . without further incident. It should be pointed out that the generator was switched off when the fire occurred — in fact the switch had been in the 'off' position throughout the flight.

'The behaviour of the Townend ring is still not satisfactory; it still distorts badly when the engine is hot and the vibration of the leading edge is bad. A modification to stiffen the leading edge is considered absolutely necessary.'

R7 joined the other two aircraft at Martlesham. In the meantime the SS19A had been fitted with a Mercury VIS engine giving 536 hp at take-off, and 'spatted' tailwheel, becoming SS19B, whilst the AW16's Panther IIIA engine had been replaced by a Panther VII with Townend ring. As in 1932, trials were again interrupted in order to allow the manufacturers to display their new aircraft at the Hendon Air Display and SBAC event. It was whilst *R7* was being flown back from Hendon on the evening of 26 June, with Flight Lieutenant M. Ward at the controls, that it suffered engine failure. It landed heavily in a field suffering severe damage, but it was quickly repaired, for on 24 July the aircraft, now a Mark IV and fitted with ailerons on its top and bottom mainplanes, was delivered back to Martlesham by Uwins.

The Service trials continued with all three aircraft being delivered to No 17(F) Squadron, Upavon, in July 1933, where Flying Officer Jeffrey Quill, later to become a famous test pilot, recalls that the SS19B was by far the most popular of the trio. He remembers that he found the AW16 an exciting aeroplane to fly although disappointing in its performance, whilst *R7* was more cumbersome than its Mark IIA predecessor, he welcomed the advantages of cockpit heating and wheel brakes. In his opinion the outcome of the trial was a *fait accompli*, and it was just a case of enabling RAF pilots to gain some experience of operating the types within a squadron environment. It is recorded that 17(F)'s CO was unimpressed by any of the three aircraft which he flew, deeming them to be little in advance of present equipment. Another

senior officer of the squadron criticised the AW16 for being a poor gun-platform, owing to its over-sensitivity in control response at speeds above 200 mph. Upon completion of the Service trials at Upavon, the aircraft were flown to No 32(F) Squadron, Biggin Hill, in August, where the general opinion was that the SS19B was marginally better in performance.

The final decision was made in favour of the SS19B, the prototype *J9125* having achieved a maximum speed of 215 mph at 16,500 ft, when fitted with the 560 hp Mercury IVS2 engine. The first production version of the SS19B, which was known as Gauntlet I, first flew in December 1934, and was fitted with a more powerful Mercury VIS2 engine giving it a maximum speed of 230 mph at 15,800 ft. Production orders followed, and by early 1935 it was beginning to displace Bulldog IIA in the squadrons. It was to be the last open-cockpit biplane fighter used by the RAF, and it continued

T. W. "Jock" Campbell *(British Aerospace, Filton).*

in service until June 1939, with No 17(F) Squadron being the last to use it.

Bulldog Mark IV *R7* was returned to Filton in March 1934, in order to be prepared for the next round of competition of the F7/30 specification. After modifications to its fin and rudder, and installation of a Mercury VIS2 engine, it became the Mark IVA. In this its final form, Bulldog had a maximum speed of 224 mph, some 25 mph slower than its main competitor the Gloster Gladiator — a true four-gun fighter — which went on to succeed in the F7/30 competition. The unsuccessful contender *R7* was purchased by the Air Ministry on 26 July 1934, being given the serial no *K4292,* and subsequently used for flight testing various arrangements of cowling on the Mercury engine.

The Bristol Aeroplane Co made two further unsuccessful attempts in 1934 on the F7/30 specification, with their single-seat biplane fighter Type 123 and their monoplane fighter Type 133, both of which are detailed in other chapters.

Chapter 5
Kennelmates

The concept of Bullpup — the diminutive kennelmate of Bulldog — really began in May 1924 when the Air Ministry issued its specification F17/24 for a single-seat, fast-climbing, high altitude interceptor fighter using a Rolls-Royce Falcon V12 in-line engine (later to be developed as the Kestrel). As has already been recorded, the engine requirement dampened Bristol's enthusiasm for a submission, because as a company they were fully committed to radial air-cooled engines. The specification's *raison d'être* was primarily for a fast-climbing interceptor, unencumbered by the carrying of radio equipment as used in the then present standing patrols of day-and-night fighters. Such a fighter would be used to meet any possible threat from high flying foreign bombers targetting Britain over its southern and eastern borders. Whether the enemy would be aircraft of France's *Armée de l'Air*, or those of a resurgent Germany, was not clearly established, but the arrival of the Fairey Fox in 1925 certainly highlighted Britain's vulnerability.

The specification was updated some three years later as the F20/27, whereupon a fresh interest was shown by the company and a design, Type 107, was prepared to meet its requirements using a Mercury III engine. It was to be a single-bay biplane, with wings of unequal span (upper 30 ft; lower 24 ft) and an unequal chord (upper 5 ft 6 in; lower 4 ft), and with square cut profiles to the wing tips. Top and bottom wings of Bristol Type IA and Clark YH type aerofoils respectively, were connected by inverted 'N' type interplane struts, with provision made for mounting a Lewis .303 in machine-gun under each wing as well as synchronised twin-Vickers .303 ins on the fuselage sides. A total loaded weight of 2,850 lb (inclusive of oxygen apparatus, ammunition, fuel and pilot) together

Prototype Bullpup, Type 107, in skeletal form with small rudder *(British Aerospace, Filton)*.

Bullpup, *J9051*, with Mercury IIA as flown in the F20/27 competition at Martlesham in 1929
(British Aerospace, Filton).

with a total wing surface area of 229.9 sq ft gave it a wing loading of 12.4 lb/sq ft, whilst the proposed Mercury engine gave a power loading of 5.28 lb/bph. A square profile large rudder in the original layout, was changed to that of a smaller pointed rudder which appeared on the prototype *J9051* (no 7178).

The design was accepted by the Air Ministry and an order was placed for a prototype aircraft to compete with other manufacturers' aircraft in evaluation trials. Owing to long delays in the development of the 450 hp Mercury II engine,

Bullpup did not fly until almost a year after the Bulldog prototype, and even then with a Jupiter VI engine taken from Type 101. Captain Cyril Uwins took the prototype *J9051* into the air for the very first time on 26 April 1928, where he deemed it to be a more pleasant and faster aircraft to fly than Bulldog. Eventually a 480 hp Mercury IIA engine was fitted and Bullpup was flown to Martlesham on 12 September 1929 where its main competitor was Hawker's Jupiter VII-engined biplane entry. Although it put up a creditable performance it failed to obtain a production order, that privilege

Bullpup, *J9051*, with Mercury IIA and Townend cowling ring, Filton, May 1929 *(British Aerospace, Filton).*

Bullpup, *J9051*, with short stroke Mercury engine and long chord cowling at Filton, July 1931
(British Aerospace, Filton).

eventually going to Hawker's entry which, after exchanging its Jupiter VII for a Mercury VI, finally went into production with a Rolls-Royce Kestrel engine as the Fury.

There is every possibility that had there not been inordinate delays in the development of the Mercury engine then Bullpup, rather than Bulldog, might well have been the main Bristol product at that time. Certainly it had great potential as a four-gun fighter, well before the issue of the F7/30 specification and the Gladiator which was developed from it. Only the one prototype Bullpup was ever built, and apart from a reversion back to the larger rudder after its first flight and the installation of various engines and cowlings, it hardly changed. A short chord Townend ring was fitted over its Mercury IIA in order to improve performance and subsequently it was installed with a Jupiter VII for demonstration at the 1930 Hendon Air Display. It appeared again in the following year at the same event, this time acting as a test-bed for Fedden's 400 hp short-stroke Mercury, complete with close-fitting long chord cowl. It was last seen in public at the 1935 SBAC show, fitted with a modified Dowty undercarriage, and where the flamboyant Bristol test pilot, Chris Washer, impressed the crowds as Bullpup performed with its subdued sounding Aquila I sleeve valve engine.

* * *

The Bristol Bulldog had created quite an interest, both at home and abroad, when it appeared in public for the first time at the Hendon Air Display

in June 1927. Barnwell and Fedden were, during those lean years of the late 1920s, anxious to enhance the reputation of Bulldog and its Jupiter engine in any record breaking attempt that might bring in good publicity. To this end they persuaded the directors of the company that an attempt on the world's altitude record, with a modified high-altitude Bulldog, would be no bad thing. And so it was decided to modify the prototype Bulldog Mark I (no 7155) upon its return from Martlesham Heath in October 1927, in order to make such an attempt.

Cyril Uwins took the 50 ft wingspan H.A. Bulldog into the air for its first brief test flight on 7 November 1927, before it was sent to Farnborough. Its wings, now spaced 6 ft apart, were of wooden construction with ailerons operating on the lower wing only. A single fuel tank in the top wing centre section now had a wind-driven fuel pump mounted on the starboard upper wing, to assist gravity feed for when it would be literally hanging on its propeller, as it aimed for a ceiling of 40,000 ft. A supercharged Jupiter VII engine powered the aircraft, and heater muffs were incorporated in the exhaust system in order to provide adequate cockpit heating.

Test flights and stress checks of the aircraft's wing structure showed the need for four smaller span ailerons, rather than the original two. In December the Italians raised the world's altitude record to 38,800 ft, and this fact combined with the need for aileron modifications, brought about delays in the attempt until finally there was a loss of interest by the company. Flight Lieutenant John A. Gray (later to become an Air Vice-Marshal, CB, CBE, DFC, GM), a former Martlesham pilot, was OC Engine Flight at the RAE Farnborough at the time and recalls:

'There was some talk of a Bulldog designed for high altitude coming to the RAE for trials. As the Engine Flight had been doing some testing on exhaust-driven superchargers, involving flying at some 30,000 ft, it seemed likely that we should have to do the flight trials. The Press got wind of this, and an article did appear in the *News Chronicle* giving my name as the likely pilot.'

The event never did take place, and at the end of 1929 Flight Lieutenant Gray left the RAE upon being posted to No 55(B) Squadron, Iraq.

Although the Bristol Aeroplane Co, and their design teams, were to be denied the privilege of an attempt on the world's altitude record with Bulldog, they were to succeed with another aircraft some five years later. On 16 September 1932 Cyril Uwins, clothed in an electrically-heated flying suit and using oxygen equipment, took the open-cockpit Pegasus-engined Vickers Vespa biplane *G-ABIL* to a record-breaking height of 43,976 ft.

* * *

The prototype Bulldog TM (Training Machine), two-seat, dual-control trainer variant of the single-seat fighter, first flew at Filton on 7 December 1931, when it was given a thirty-minute test flight by Cyril Uwins. Given the RAF serial number *K2188* (no.7643), and Bristol designation Type 124, it had been built to meet the nascent Air Ministry specification T12/32 for evaluation by the Central Flying School. The concept was following the pattern set by the RAF's Snipe and Siskin two-seat instructional trainers, and was destined to be supplied not only to the CFS, but also to the Flying Training Schools, and to squadrons operating Bulldog fighters.

The design had been drawn up in October 1931, and differed very little in its constructional detail from that of its fighter counterpart. The main differences were in a $3\frac{1}{2}°$ sweep-back of its top and bottom wings, which increased the wingspan by 4 in to 34 ft 2 in, and a positioning of the VIFH engine (it was 75 lb lighter than the VIIF) some 5 in further forward. These features were intended to compensate for the additional weight of the occupant of the rear cockpit, and to aid spin recovery — an aspect which was to cause some concern in the TM. Radio equipment was not carried, this space being occupied by the rear cockpit, but a small locker, with access door on the port side of the fuselage behind the rear cockpit, was provided for carrying light articles. Provision was made for the carrying of six lead ballast weights, which were located into canvas sockets attached to the underside of the fuselage, three on each side, beneath the rear cockpit. These weights were only added when the aircraft was flown with the rear seat unoccupied. Two fairly major modifications were made during the course of the TM's Service life, namely an increase in track from 5 ft 6 in to 6 ft, and the fitment of a larger area angular shaped rudder. Communication between instructor and pupil pilot was made by use of Gosport tubes which were standard equipment on RAF trainers at the time. It was a very simple, non-electrical piece of equipment, in which rubber mouthpieces connected by flexible tubes running from front to rear cockpit, and vice-versa, enabled communication once headphone sockets had been plugged in. Armament was dispensed with, although brackets for camera guns on the port side of the top mainplane section were retained. Whilst the prototype TM, *K2188,* was fitted with a Jupiter VIIF engine, the production TMs used the VIFH series engine which gave a maximum speed of 168 mph, some 10 mph less than the fighter version. Paint finish consisted of standard silver doped fabric, with olive green anti-glare decking along the whole length of the top of the fuselage.

K2188 was flown from Filton to Martlesham Heath by Cyril Uwins on 30 December 1931 for testing, but not before he had taken Frank Barnwell up, two weeks earlier, for a ten-minute flight. This was in all probability Barnwell's first trip in a Bulldog, for although he was a qualified pilot, such was his flying record that it is highly unlikely that the company would have ever permitted him to fly the single-seat fighter. The outcome of the evaluation of TM was successful and it gained the approval of the A&AEE, whereupon it was returned to Filton in time to be exhibited at the SBAC trade show in June 1932. It was flown to Hendon on 26 June and back again on the next day. Bristol were always keen to market their products abroad and had gained some interest in the TM from the Italian military, for two days later, at Filton, one of their representatives was given a brief demonstration flight in *K2188* by Uwins.

After a brief test flight on 30 August, *K2188* was loaned to the CFS in order for them to carry out an evaluation of the aircraft's suitability as a fighter trainer. They approved its use and as a consequence a production order for seventeen aircraft, *K3170-K3186* (nos 7727-7743), was placed with the company. The first of the batch, *K3170,* was flight-tested by Uwins on 8 December, and on the following day it was demonstrated to the Chief Flying Instructor of the CFS, Squadron Leader

The 50ft wingspan high altitude Bulldog Mark I prototype with large rudder which was first flown on 7 November 1927 *(British Aerospace, Filton)*.

Richard Harrison, DFC, AFC, at Filton. The RAF Squadron Leader was quite familiar with Bulldog for he had, prior to his appointment as CFI with the CFS in November 1931, been the CO of No 17(F) Squadron at Upavon. All of the TMs were delivered over the next three months with Nos 17, 19, 32, 41, 56 and 111 Squadrons each receiving one; five were placed into store, minus their engines, at RAF Kenley whilst the remaining six were equally divided between the CFS at Wittering and No 1 FTS at Leuchars, Scotland.

A further final production order for 42 aircraft was placed by the Air Ministry in 1933, with the first of the batch, *K3923,* being test flown on 7

October. Of the initial 31 aircraft, *K3923-K3953* (nos 7777-7807), eighteen were shared between the RAF College at Cranwell, No 3 FTS at Grantham and No 5 FTS at Sealand, near Chester, whilst the remaining thirteen airframes went into store in January 1934. The final eleven TMs, *K4566-4576* (nos 7827-7837), which were built to Air Ministry specification T13/34, an up-date of T12/32, were fitted with reconditioned Jupiter engines and also went into storage between July and December 1934. An allocation was subsequently made, from the aircraft in store, to No 4 FTS at Abu Sueir in Egypt, where they were reportedly in Service use until as late as 1939.

The prototype Bulldog TM, *K2188*, dual-seat trainer *(British Aerospace, Filton)*.

A military air force is no better than the men who fly its combat aircraft, and consequently the training of its pilots must always be a crucial factor in its overall efficiency. The RAF has, during its relatively brief history, established for itself a reputation for flying standards that is second to none and no doubt a large part of the credit must go to its CFS. That institution has been described, without exaggeration, as the birthplace of Britain's air power, and at the time of Bulldog that realisation had been clearly understood, even by those outside of the UK. Foreign nationals from Europe and many other parts of the world, as well as RAF pilots, were trained in the valuable art of instruction. In addition, refresher courses were given to those men who had been deskbound on office duties, and who needed to be brought up to date with flying techniques.

The three Bulldog TMs allocated to CFS arrived at Wittering late in December 1932, where two were added to the 34 existing aircraft already in use, and one to seventeen aircraft already held in reserve. The other aircraft included 24 Avro 504N primary trainers and then two each of the following: Armstrong Whitworth Siskin IIIA and Atlas, Bulldog IIA and Hawker Hart. In addition, there was a single Hawker Fury and Tomtit (Avro Tutors did not arrive until later in 1933). The station was manned by approximately thirty officers, a third of whom were instructors, and 160 airmen all under the command of Group Captain P. C. Maltby, DSO, AFC.

One very well known pilot to be posted to the CFS on a four-week refresher course late in September 1932 was Pilot Officer Douglas Bader who had, some ten months previously, lost both legs when he crashed Bulldog *K1676* at Woodley, near Reading. He had, after careful nursing and intensive rehabilitation, been passed by the Central Medical Board at Kingsway earlier in the month, as fit to fly as a 'pilot under supervision'. Naturally he was very anxious to re-establish himself as a competent pilot and was particularly encouraged by Squadron Leader Ferdinand West, VC, a former World War 1 pilot who had lost a leg and yet continued to fly solo. His first flight at the CFS was dual in an Avro 504N, and then after three days he was passed on for dual in the Bulldog TM.

One cannot but help reflect upon exactly what was passing through Bader's mind as he gripped that familiar spade-grip column, and heard the Jupiter crashing away up front, as he flew Bulldog once again. This was the aeroplane, this was the beast, that he had not quite tamed, and one which had inflicted such a harsh and severe punishment upon him in the loss of both legs. How would he

View of cockpits of Bulldog TM *(British Aerospace, Filton).*

control the memory of that cold December day a year ago. The realisation that he was not going to complete that roll without ploughing into the ground. The sound of tearing fabric, the crunching of steel tubes, the dust, the interminable slide before the silence. No doubt he reacted with the combined determination and aggression that he was to show to the Heinkel 111s and their Me 109 escorts over the Thames estuary in later years — 'here was an enemy to defeat'. Confidence returned and grew, as he performed all the old aerobatics from his repertoire, the ones learned in No 23(F)'s Gamecocks and Bulldogs. There was little that the CFI at Wittering could do, other than recommend his return to first-line flying, but sadly he was to be defeated by the rule book, for King's Regulations admitted no such precedent as a legless pilot.

Fortunately for Bader the outbreak of World War 2, some seven years later, was to bring him back to the CFS (necessity knows no bounds), which had, in the meantime, moved to Upavon in Wiltshire. He returned in October 1939 for re-assessment of his flying capabilities, and was given his first flight in a North American Harvard dual-trainer. Confronted, but undaunted by, the complexity of variable-pitch propeller, retractable undercarriage, wing flaps and the unfamiliar cockpit enclosure — all unknown on Bulldog — he mastered all the controls except the foot-operated brakes. The last aspect was not considered to be a serious impediment because all the operational types that he was likely to fly, such as the Miles Master trainer, Hurricane and Spitfire, used a hand control lever operating from the control column. He evidently satisfied the CFS that he was capable of re-establishing himself as an operational pilot, for within a few weeks he was back at Upavon on a refresher course. On 27 November he soloed in a CFS Avro Tutor biplane trainer, and this time one does not have to speculate on his feelings. The old irrepressible spirit of Bader returned, if it had ever left him, and he was observed, much to the chagrin of the CFI Wing Commander H. J. Pringle (who was himself flying in the area), in inverted flight at 600 ft, not far from the airfield. The CFI had at one time been with 'B' Flight of No 3(F) Squadron, Kenley, operating Bulldogs, and this fact no doubt mellowed the admonition that was given to the 'new boy' when he was duly warned. The rest of the story is history — if not legend!

Pilots' flying impressions of the Bulldog trainer, although not numerous, do throw some suspicion upon the aircraft's spin recovery. Wing Commander W. G. Easton, former pupil pilot at No 3 FTS, Grantham in 1935, briefly recalls:

'The dual-control Bulldog was more sluggish than its fighter counterpart and we were emphatically instructed never to let the aircraft spin more than one turn'.

Another former Bulldog pilot, Group Captain Eddie Glennie-Carr, recalls his experience with No 56(F) Squadron's TM, stating:

'. . it *could* develop a stable nose-up spin. . .' implying that it was an aircraft that needed handling with some caution.

Finally, Air Vice-Marshal John K. Rotherham, CB, CBE, former 17(F) Squadron Bulldog pilot, recalls his experience with the type:

'I had my first flight in a Bulldog Trainer at No 5 FTS Sealand on 29 December 1933, my previous training having been on Siskins, Atlas and Bristol Fighters. The dual Bulldog at that time had a reputation of being difficult to recover from a spin and my log book shows that this was the first exercise we carried out (my instructor was Flight Lieutenant Macallum). I was fairly apprehensive at first, but soon found

Prototype Bulldog TM, *K2188*, used as a test-bed for the AS Cheetah IX engine at Farnborough in May 1937 *(Imperial War Museum)*.

Bulldog TM, *K3183*, with Napier Rapier I engine at Farnborough in April 1937 *(Imperial War Museum).*

out that with a little care there was really no great problem. After approximately twenty hours on the TM I was posted to Upavon . . .'

Certainly complaints were made by the CFS to the manufacturers, with respect to *K3171* and other machines of the type, about its spinning characteristics and the aircraft became the subject of an RAE investigation at Farnborough. The allegation was made that the aircraft would fall into a very uneven right-handed spin, when stalled with rudder central and stick hard back. It was claimed that the nose of the aircraft would rise intermittently during the spin, from a steep to a flat position, level with the horizon, and that such was the violence of the manoeuvre, the occupants of the cockpits were thrown about from side to side.

Consultation took place between representatives of the RAE and the company, and it was agreed that the fin area be increased by stages until the spinning characteristics were improved. This procedure was carried out, until in its final stage three square feet of surface area had been added to the fin, bringing its total area to 6.12 sq ft. Cyril Uwins was responsible for the tests at Filton, where he found that although the increases in fin area lessened the violence of the spin, it did not eliminate it completely. Further tests with the normal area of fin, but with extra surface added to the lower part of the rudder, gave the best results. It gave a reduced level of disturbance in the spin and provided a more powerful rudder for spin

recovery. *K3171* was returned in this its final form to the RAE in July, where tests were made on behalf of the CFS who were loathe to recommend the placing of a further contract for TMs, until the problem was satisfactorily resolved.

The tests were carried out by the RAE with the centre of gravity of *K3171* in three different positions; normal at 6.1 in behind the lower leading edge of the wing; fully back and fully forward, a variation of 2 in either side of normal. These differences were obtained by a combination of subtracting or adding ballast weights and passenger. Two types of induced spin were used in the tests; firstly, the standard spin by application of full rudder with stick hard back, ailerons neutral and TPA set back; secondly, the uneven spin by neutral rudder and stick hard back. In addition deliberate mishandling of the controls by various movements were made during the spins in order to see if the spin recovery was made any more difficult. Measurements were taken of the rate of turn, incidence of turn and rate of descent, as well as the number of turns for recovery and height loss. The results did not show any cause for concern and were deemed to be acceptable. In standard spins the rate of turn varied between 2.43 and 2.95 seconds, with a 40° angle of incidence. Rate of descent varied between 125 and 131 ft/sec, with never more than a single turn for recovery and height loss between 800 and 1,000 ft. In an induced uneven spin there was some jerkiness, but not to any alarming degree, recovery being possible at most phases of the motion within one turn of spin. The most critical condition, caused by pushing the stick forward with simultaneous full left rudder, demanded two or three recovery turns. The forward centre of gravity positions could cause a fast steep spin during which the propeller stopped but recovery was still easy. The remedial modification was accepted and drawing amendments were made at Filton on 27 August 1933, with subsequent production of the final batch of 42 aircraft incorporating the revised fin and angular rudder.

In spite of this shadow of doubt being cast upon the TM's spinning qualities there were, unlike the fighter, surprisingly few accidents recorded with the type. This fact is an eloquent testimony to the high calibre of the RAF's Flying Instructors who must take their share of the credit.

An RAF College Bulldog Trainer, *K3928,* was involved in a mid-air collision with one of their Hart Trainers, *K3152,* in the Cranwell area on 1 May 1934, causing the death of both instructors, Flying Officers D. J. Douthwaite and J. S. Tanner as well as their pupils. Nine days later, Flight Cadet F. R. Foster was slightly injured when he undershot on his landing approach in *K3926,* and struck a wall on the edge of the aerodrome at Cranwell. The only other recorded accident with a TM occurred on 4 January 1936, when LAC J. M. Gwillym, who was making a solo flight in *K3936* from No 3 FTS, experienced engine failure. He made a successful forced-landing but hit a wall at the far end of the run, and although he was uninjured the aircraft was a write-off.

Two TMs, the prototype *K2188* and *K3183,* went

An RAF College Cranwell Bulldog dual seat trainer with Flying Officer H. V. Satterly (later to become an Air Vice-Marshal) in the rear cockpit. The numeral "3" is in blue and outlined in black; note the absence of wheel disc covers *(MoD).*

on to be eventually used by the RAE as test-beds for various engine manufacturers. *K2188,* after it left the CFS, was fitted with the Armstrong Siddeley Cheetah IX and appeared at Farnborough in May 1937 powered by this engine. Over 37,200 Cheetah engines were to be built by ASM in all its series, with the last, the 425 hp version, being installed in Avro Ansons. *K3183*'s Jupiter was exchanged for the 340 hp Napier Rapier I, a sixteen-cylinder air-cooled engine of 'H' configuration designed by Frank Halford. The aircraft was used for wind-tunnel and flight development tests of the engine and appeared in this form at the RAE in April 1937. A year later *K3183* was loaned by the Air Ministry to Airspeed Ltd, at Portsmouth, for the installation of the prototype 450 hp Alvis Leonides nine-cylinder radial engine during its flight testing. During one such test flight, with Flight Lieutenant George B. S. Errington at its controls, the Leonides-engined Bulldog with its healthy-sounding exhaust note attracted the ears and eyes of the works' staff as it roared over the factory at Coventry, having made the flight from Portsmouth in forty minutes. *K3183* was also used as a test-bed for the Alvis Pelides engine, a Gnôme-Rhône product made under licence, before finally being scrapped on 7 May 1940.

The C in C of the ADGB, Air Marshal Sir Robert Brooke-Popham, used the Bulldog Trainer *K3172* when he made a tour of stations involved in the Coastal Defence Exercises on 22/23 September 1933. In later years, after September 1937, when they had fulfilled their role as trainers in the UK and been declared as obsolete, they became a great favourite with senior RAF officers who used the aircraft as a personal means of transport.

Unfortunately, no examples of the Bulldog Trainer exist today, the last known survivor being *K3932* which was in existence until 1953. The only opportunity one now has of seeing the type, is by watching out for a Channel 4 repeat of one of George Formby's old films, *It's in the Air,* where, if you can keep awake, one can be seen making a brief appearance!

Chapter 6
The Squadrons

The period during which Bulldog was to re-equip ten of the thirteen fighter squadrons of ADGB's Fighting Area, was one in which the Royal Air Force was beginning to rise like a scorched phoenix from the ashes of its post-war emasculation. Lord Trenchard, that great architect of British air power, was to compare its post-war demise, where its wartime strength of 30,000 officers and 300,000 men fell within two years of the Armistice to less than a tenth of that number, with that of Jonah's gourd. Here for a season in the necessities of war, and then to quickly wither away with the clamour for the economies of peace. Admittedly it was still a time when the political outlook was one of financial stringency and disarmament, but for the RAF the tide was beginning to turn. It had all really begun in 1924 when, as Chief of Air Staff, Trenchard, and Secretary of State for Air, Sir Samuel Hoare, laid plans for an expansion of the RAF that was to slowly materialise over the years. The plans included the establishment of the Auxiliary Air Force which came into being on 9 October 1924. This was a force of civilian volunteers raised on a territorial basis and allocated to a particular squadron, where they received regular training so that they could be quickly absorbed into the RAF in time of emergency. In addition, a new Directorate of Technical Development was established in 1924, so that a greater emphasis could be placed upon the integrity of the equipment supplied to the RAF. This meant that the DTD were responsible for not only the development of a complete fighter such as Bulldog, but for every component used, even down to a split cotter-pin. Trenchard also laid great emphasis upon training, with the establishment of a Cadet College, Navigation School, Flying Instructor's School, an Administrative and Technical School for Officers, a Wireless and Electrical Training School, a School of Photography, a School of Naval Co-operation, a Balloon School, an Airship School, and Schools of Technical Training for boys (at Halton) and men (at Manston). Trenchard was, some years later, to recall that his plans for expansion were comparable to the laying of the foundation for a

Flight Lieutenant Harry Broadhurst — 19(F) Squadron *(Sir Harry Broadhurst).*

castle, for even if only a cottage were to be built on it, then at least it would be a very good cottage!

As Trenchard's plans came to fruition, so the junior Service gathered up its lost confidence, and by 1925 the RAF comprised 54 squadrons, deployed both at home and overseas, including those squadrons of the FAA and Coastal Defence. At home the defence force of the ADGB had been established in April 1924 with HQ at Uxbridge, and comprising some eighteen squadrons (ten of them classified as Fighter) shared between the three Commands of Fighting Area, Bombing Area and the Special Reserve which included AAF, all under the command of Air Marshal Sir John Salmond. Overseas Commands included Middle East, India, Palestine, and Iraq where a policy of 'control without occupation' was the order of the day. The late 1920s and early 1930s, have been described as 'the golden era' of aviation, for it was a time of great pioneering flights when the eyes of the world were focused upon pilots such as Alan

Sergeant Pilot W. John Rye — 19(F) Squadron
(W. J. Rye).

year when an RAF formation of Southampton flying boats, under the command of Group Captain H. M. Cave-Browne-Cave, DSO, DFC, left Plymouth on 17 October to fly on a 23,000-mile cruise to Singapore, with Egypt, India, Hong Kong, Australia and Japan being visited en route. Truly the RAF was now firmly established as a world force, and although not yet the veritable castle that it was later to become in the 1939/1945 period, at least it was something of a king-sized cottage!

The technology of aircraft design, now aided by the DTD, was slowly changing as Service aircraft began to use the development of ideas pioneered during World War 1. The parachute, once limited for use from the balloon, was by 1929, in either its seat or chest-type versions, standard equipment in all Service aeroplanes except sea-going craft. After a limited use of the Calthrop type, the Irving and GQ parachutes became the standard issue to the squadrons from the Test Centre at Henlow, where the life history of each one was monitored with its own record card. Air communication had, during its infancy, primarily been limited to messages either dropped from the air in a weighted bag with streamer, or to their pick up when slung between poles on the ground. Marconi had taken out patents on wireless telegraphy (W/T) as early as 1896 when he first arrived in England. Subsequent

Cobham, Charles Lindbergh, Bert Hinkler, Amy Johnson and Amelia Earhart, to name a few. They aroused a new interest in a public which was quickly becoming air-minded as they attended the now familiar air displays, and where the chance of a five-shilling flight was within their reach. Grebe, Gamecock and Siskin fighters became familiar sights at the annual Hendon Air Displays, where their aerobatic prowess fascinated an ever-growing number of spectators. The Air Ministry were quick to realise the value of such public relations exercises and did not confine them to the UK, for they encouraged a series of long-distance flights with Service aircraft in order to wave the flag abroad. In 1926, Wing Commander G. W. H. Pulford was to lead a flight of Fairey IIIDs from England, via Cairo, to the Cape and back; whilst on 26 December of that year, Secretary of State for Air, Sir Samuel Hoare, left Croydon for a flight to Delhi that was to take fourteen days to complete. In January 1927 the RAF spread its wings further afield by establishing a Command known as RAF China, with a base at Kai Tak airfield, Hong Kong, together with FAA aircraft based on board the aircraft carriers *Hermes* and *Argos* as well as warships HMS *Vindictive* and *Enterprise*. Another notable event was to take place during that same

Corporal/Fitter making final adjustments to the Jupiter engine of a 17(F) Bulldog *(Flight).*

demonstrations by him at the turn of the century had shown that it had practical implications, not only on land and sea, but also in the air. By 1910 W/T had been used with a morse buzzer from an aeroplane in flight to give air-to-ground communication. With the outbreak of war in 1914 its potential was quickly exploited for artillery spotting and although only effective over a ten-mile range it proved to be a very useful piece of equipment. The real breakthrough, however, came nearer the end of the war, when wireless telephony (R/T — radio being used as the prefix instead of wireless, in order to give an unambiguous abbreviation), using speech and not morse as the medium of communication, was developed. It now gave not only air-to-ground and ground-to-air, but more importantly air-to-air communication, and was in this form demonstrated, at St Omer, to Trenchard and officers of the Air Staff in the summer of 1917. During the post-war period development work on radio equipment continued under the guidance of the staff of the Controller of Communication in the Department of Civil Aviation. Marconi transmitters and receivers, installed on Grebe, Gamecock and Siskin fighters, showed that much development was needed if they were to be used in fighter direction. Speech was

Pilot Officer W. E. Carr — 56(F) Squadron
(E. Glennie-Carr).

Flying Officer I. C. "Blondie" Bird — 56(F) Squadron
(E. Glennie-Carr).

often unintelligible over anything other than close range, often being distorted by electrical interference from wind-driven generators and ignition.

As complexity in design increased, so too did the demands made upon the skills of those who serviced the aircraft, but such was Trenchard's foresight in establishing excellent Schools of Technical Training, they were well able to provide the necessary expertise. The economic background of the country at that time of depression and joblessness made recruitment, for any of the three Services, relatively easy, as was selecting those with the necessary educational ability. Pay was paltry, ten shillings (fifty pence) a week for a Boy Apprentice with a deduction of five shillings to be paid at leave time; men with no particular skills received only fourteen shillings a week — but free accommodation and food, plus good training, were not to be lightly disregarded! Trenchard's plan for a technical elite concentrated on the Boy Apprenticeship scheme, which came to provide the bulk of ground staff, or 'erks', as they were commonly known during the RAF's post-war years. Once trained and enlisted on a twelve-year engagement, most remained as technical tradesmen, carrying out duties such as Fitter-Aero

Engines, Fitter-Motor Transport, Fitter-Armourers, or Riggers. Moreover, encouragement was given to suitable applicants to volunteer on a five-year basis for flying duties, and by the end of 1927 there were 256 NCO pilots within the squadrons. At the end of the five-year period they either reverted back to their trade, or were invited to stay on as pilots, some even being commissioned. One such example of boy apprentice to officer pilot, was A. J. 'Bill' Pegg, who became an RAF test pilot at the A&AEE Martlesham Heath and later CTP of the Bristol Aeroplane Co. It was whilst serving as an eighteen-year-old LAC Fitter, at No 9(B) Squadron, Manston, having completed his apprenticeship, that he was invited to volunteer for flying duties, whereupon he was posted to No 43(F) Squadron, Henlow, in 1925 as a 'pupil pilot'. Although it was customary for flying training to be carried out at one of the Flying Training Schools, there was at that time a move to speed up the training of NCO pilots by delegating the duty to an existing fighter squadron. As a consequence, after twelve months' training, during which time he soloed in six hours twenty minutes under the guidance of Flying Officer Tommy Rose, he took his final flying test in the squadron's dual Snipe, which eventually enabled him to proudly wear the brevet and three stripes of a Sergeant Pilot. A small number of NCO pilots, never more than two or three a year, were invited to apply for a commission, and after three years as a fighter pilot at Tangmere, on Gamecocks, he was to make a successful application.

The total amount spent on the RAF was, under the Air Estimates for 1929/30, a miserly £19,645,000 (in 1925 it had been £21,319,000) which meant that money needed to be spent prudently if Trenchard's plan for an elite force capable of rapid expansion was to be fulfilled. In order to ensure an adequate reservoir of officer pilots, to supplement the small core of permanently commissioned men, a Short-Service Commission scheme had been inaugurated, in which men were invited to serve for a five-year period only. Upon completion of such a period, they either returned to civilian employment — not always a welcome prospect — or were invited to stay on for an additional five years, in what was known as a Medium-Service Commission. During, or at the end of, a MSC a select few were offered Permanent Commissions. It was against the background of this highly trained cadre that the RAF was slowly resuscitated to become once more an efficient fighting force that was to be without equal.

On 23 May 1929 Flight Lieutenant H. W. Taylor in a factory-fresh J series Bulldog Mark II, starkly displaying its No 3(F) Squadron green stripe markings against its silver-doped fabric, came in to land at RAF Upavon after making the short hop from Filton. It was the first Bulldog to be supplied to an RAF squadron and was, over the next four months, to be joined by eleven further single deliveries, thereby completely replacing the existing Gloster Gamecock Is. The squadron, one of the oldest in the RAF, had firmly established its reputation as a fighter squadron when equipped with the highly successful Sopwith Camel, in the autumn of 1917, in France. Given a ground strafing role in the Battle of Cambrai, in March 1918, it was also to be pitched into fierce air battles with Richthofen's *Jastas* as it flew on offensive patrols along the Western front. After being disbanded and re-formed on two occasions after the war, it was finally brought back to its role as a fighter squadron when equipped with Sopwith Snipes, at Manston, in April 1924. Later in that same month, it moved to Upavon, where it now became a day-and-night fighter squadron flying Hawker Woodcock IIs. These aircraft were grounded in August 1928 during an investigation into an accident which cast a doubt upon their

Pilot Officer George Lott of 41(F) Squadron, Northolt 1933 *(C. G. Lott)*.

safety, and temporarily, they were replaced by the Gloster product until the arrival of the Bulldogs.

The airfield at Upavon lies some two miles to the south-east of the village, on the northern edge of the Salisbury Plain, and was the oldest active airfield in use, having been originally opened in 1912 as the home of the CFS. Although there had been plenty of ideal ground on the plain itself, Upavon had been purposely chosen for its remoteness. The War Office had felt that its covert position would discourage the prying eyes of the Press, who might seek to sensationalise the accidents that are inevitable with flying training. It was far from being the ideal location for an airfield, for it was virtually on top of a hill — C. G. Grey had, during its CFS days, described it as the 'school on a mountain'. Apart from being windswept, it was also the victim of its own local geographical features, with a 200 ft escarpment along its northern edge and the Avon valley on its western side. Northern winds would, according to one pilot, send upward currents that could be felt at 3,000 ft, whilst the valley, combined with a dip in the middle of the area, produced their own vortexes. Not surprisingly these were to test the skill of the neophyte and to catch out more than a few!

During those transitional summer months of 1929 both pilots and ground crew of No 3(F), under the command of Squadron Leader E. Digby-Johnson, AFC, were familiarising themselves with their new Bulldog fighter replacements. Envious and inquisitive eyes were being cast over the unfamiliar aircraft by the members of No 17(F) Squadron, who shared the station at Upavon with them. The No 3(F) motto, 'Tertius primus erit' ('The third shall be first'), had a literal meaning when it came to being re-equipped, for No 17(F) were still using their well-worn Siskin IIIA's whilst awaiting their Bulldog replacements. A friendly, but distinct rivalry, existed between the two squadrons, with No 3(F) overshadowing their neighbours by virtue of their wartime record. The younger squadron's more modest battle honours had been acquired whilst cast in the mundane role of reconnaissance and bombing in the Middle East during the 1915-1918 period, rather than in aerial combat as a fighter squadron on the Western Front.

On 16 September 1929 No 3(F) flew to No 3 Armament Training Camp at Sutton Bridge, in Lincolnshire, for its annual two weeks at the Air Firing practice camp, with the ground crews following on by road. It was one of three annual events on a Fighter Station that broke the monotony of daily routine for both pilots and

Air Vice-Marshal Don Bennett CB CBE DSO, former Bulldog Pilot, with 29(F) Squadron, North Weald. *(RAF Museum)*

ground staff — the other two being the Hendon Air Display in June, and the ADGB Air Exercises which normally took place in July or later. Although the pilots gained a certain amount of experience by practising with live ammunition against ground target-flags on their home airfields, it was only at Sutton Bridge that they had the chance to shoot at aerial targets, albeit only a drogue towed by an anxious tug aircraft. Preparation for the annual event inevitably became a busy time for squadron armourers. LAC E. A. Robins recalls his time as an armourer at Upavon when he was posted to No 17(F) in 1931.

'I joined the RAF as a nineteen-year-old in 1929 and completed my six months' training as an armourer at the Air Armament School, Eastchurch, the following year. My pay in those days was fourteen shillings per week until I had passed the course.

'We wore brown overalls for everyday work, over our working uniform, and best blue for parades. For walking out, when we frequented one or two pubs in Devizes (the names of which I can no longer remember), we wore our "cheesecutter" peaked caps, button-up dog-

Sergeant Pilot Leslie S. Holman — 56(F) Squadron
(L. S. Holman).

collar tunic with pantaloons, puttees and boots
. . .'

'Bullets used for firing at the target drogues during Armament Training Camps were tipped with various coloured dyes. This process would take place in a separate shed which housed long wooden benches upon which were placed metal tubs, each filled to a depth of one inch with their own particular colour of dye, mainly red, yellow and blue. Belts of ammunition, holding 200 rounds, were then placed so that the tips of the bullets were immersed for a depth of half an inch into the dye, and then taken out and left to dry. Evidence of those bullets hitting the drogue target could then be clearly seen by the dye marking.'

Firing at drogue targets was not always the simple thing that it was supposed to be, for whilst the tug aircraft flew a course along the Wash so that bullets finished up in the sea, accidents did occur. Tug pilots and winch-operators were not regarded as the safest of occupations within the RAF, and if live ammunition did come unacceptably close then the miscreant would be promptly warned off by a burst of red Very lights. Not only was the tug aircraft vulnerable, but so too

was the 'attacker', for it was not unknown for those whose enthusiasm or aggression caused them to come in really close before opening fire, to hit the drogue with aircraft as well as bullet! Group Captain Glennie-Carr recalls a drogue incident with the wry comment:

'Flight Lieutenant Harry Broadhurst was my gunnery instructor at the practice camp at Sutton Bridge and took me up in a dual-seat trainer Bulldog to do my air firing on a towed drogue. I learned NOTHING as my eyes were firmly closed long before he considered we were near enough to open fire!'

Former 17(F) Bulldog pilot Jeffrey Quill records, in his excellent book *Spitfire*, how he worked out a successful technique for drogue firing practice. This consisted of a relatively slow and deliberate approach, thereby enabling a long burst to be fired; secondly, to keep the engine rpm low because of the nature of the interrupter gear, and lastly to judge the approach angle with precision and come in close. He admits, on one occasion, to damaging a wingtip after colliding with the weighted leading edge spar of a towed flag as he broke away from his attack. Flying Officer Bernard Matson of 'B' Flight No 19(F) Squadron had a similar fright when, on 20 September 1932, he hit the drogue whilst flying Bulldog *K2160* on gunnery practice over the Sutton Bridge area. The accident record card states:

'Flew into the drogue when he misjudged the speed of approach of the towing aircraft which was coming at a more acute angle than he allowed for'.

It was usual for only two squadrons from Fighting Area to be in attendance at Sutton Bridge at any one time during the Annual Air Gunnery and Bombing practice. The event was conducted on a competitive basis which meant that it took several weeks before the results could be announced, and in the case of the 1929 event, No 3(F) finished up in a creditable third position with an average of 50.64 per cent hits. The squadron's ORB records that

'. . . it was the highest score yet, in spite of considerable teething troubles with the Bulldog!'.

By the time No 3(F) had returned to their home base on 4 October, the first of No 17(F)'s replacement Bulldogs, complete with their black double zig-zag markings, were beginning to be shuttled in from nearby Filton. Deliveries continued until, by the spring of 1930, Upavon was fully equipped as a Bulldog station. Pilots' flying-log entries and ORBs give a good indication of this period of high activity, as both pilots and ground crews came to terms with their new equipment. The two squadrons were anxious to show off their new fighters, and on 13 January 1930 a demonstration was given by 3(F) at nearby Old Sarum, home of No 16 Army Co-operation Squadron, to a group of Army Liaison Officers. Quite naturally the Air Council and the AOC of ADGB were taking a great deal of interest at this time in the two Bulldog squadrons, who were being relied upon to give a feedback on an aircraft that was soon to equip ten out of the thirteen fighter squadrons comprising the Fighting Area Command. And so, on 1 April 1930, the AOC of the ADGB, Air Vice-Marshal Sir Edward Ellington, visited Upavon for an inspection and squadron flypast. Both squadrons were anxious to become fully operational as soon as possible and Flight Lieutenant John Oliver, OC 'B' Flight No 3(F), records a whole range of activities in his flying log during the early part of 1930 reflecting this desire. These included many R/T tests, aerobatics, flight formation, bombing practice, visits to the firing butts in order to check the correct operation of armament, as well as a day's visit, with 'B' Flight, to Eastchurch for air firing practice.

Meanwhile, 17(F)'s pilots were obviously similarly engaged, for the first recorded accident involving Bulldogs was reported on 6 March when a mid-air collision occurred during close formation flying practice over the airfield. Maybe the incident is evidence of the strong upward air currents encountered over Upavon, for it was reported that Pilot Officer C. A. Watt's *J9588* had hit a 'bump' which threw it towards, and into the slipstream of, *J9586* being flown by Sergeant Pilot W. C. Maher. Fortunately no serious damage was done and both aircraft landed safely.

Activity on the ground was no less hectic than in the air, with fitters, armourers and electricians busy in the hangars bringing the aircraft up to date with respect to engines and R/T equipment. It had soon been realised, after initial Service use, that the greater all-up weight of the Bulldog, over its Gamecock and Siskin predecessors, demanded a greater output from its engine. This extra power, as much as 60 hp, was to be found in the VIIF which was now coming off the production line at Patchway. This improved engine used a drop-forged duralumin cylinder head, screwed and shrunk into position (hence the suffix 'F'), rather than the VII's cast aluminium bolted cylinder head. It is not always realised that engine changes involved armourers, as well as fitters, as LAC Robins recalls.

'An armourer was responsible for four aircraft in those days, and whenever an engine change was made a check would be carried out for the correct setting of the Constantinesco

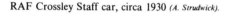

RAF Crossley Staff car, circa 1930 *(A. Strudwick).*

RAF Trojan van, circa 1930 *(A. Strudwick).*

interrupter gear which timed the firing of the Vickers gun through the propeller. Synchronisation was accomplished by means of a small plate, fitted with two cams, connected to the extreme rear of the engine shaft, which enabled the correct timing of oil-pulsation to the firing mechanism of the gun. The setting of the mechanism, which included a bleeding of the hydraulic system, was carried out in the hangar with the aircraft positioned on trestles so that it was in the flying position. Once adjusted, the pilot would then taxy the aircraft to the Stop Butts, with the armourer in attendance, where, with the engine running, a series of short bursts would be fired. If everything went off without a hitch, as it usually did, the exercise was duly noted on the F700.'

A further busy time for the hardworking ground staff was during dusk or night flying exercises which were to become a regular activity at Upavon. LAC Arthur Strudwick was posted to RAF Upavon in September 1931 as an MT driver (it was an occupation, he recalls, considered to be 'the lowest form of animal life next to an ACH'). His time at Upavon as a jack-of-all-trades driver varied from General Transport, Ambulance and Fuel Tanker duties. One of the less pleasant tasks, particularly during the winter months, was when assigned to the Flare Path Duty for monthly night

flying exercises. Air Traffic Control was extremely primitive in 1931 and merely consisted of the Aldis signalling lamp, operated by the Ground Duty Officer, allied to a flare path in the form of a letter 'T'. The flares were known as 'Goosenecks' and resembled large (five-gallon) watering cans but with their spouts stuffed with a porous asbestos wick material. Arthur Strudwick's job was to collect the GDO and six-man duty crew in his solid-tyred Leyland tender (it was never called a lorry in those days), having previously loaded six paraffin-filled flares on to a trailer, whereupon he was directed across the bumpy grass airfield to the appointed location. The GDO would then see that each 'erk was positioned with his flare, so that the head of the 'T' was at right angles to the wind's direction. Once lit, the flares would enable the Bulldogs to taxy out, position into wind, then take off on the right hand side of the four flares forming the stem of the 'T'. From then on it was the GDO's responsibility not only to signal the aircraft when to land, but also to re-align the flare path if there should be a change in the direction of the wind during the night. Such repositioning meant six cussing, unhappy airmen trundling across the airfield in the dark with their foul smelling bonfires — not a happy event! Apart from the tedium, inhalation of black smoke, paraffin-soaked trouser legs and bitter cold, there was always the hazard of being run over by a wayward 1½ ton fighter approaching at 60-70 mph.

Pilot Officer (later Air Vice-Marshal) J. K. Rotherham joined No 17(F) Squadron at Upavon in February 1934, having completed his flying training at No 5 FTS Sealand. He recalls:

'On another occasion at Upavon I was the Ground Control Officer under instruction for night flying. The flare path was laid out so that aircraft would be approaching over the road to the west of the hangars, and at this point there is quite a high bank between the road and the landing area. Several aircraft had landed successfully then one came in low and hit the bank wiping off the undercarriage and finishing on its nose. We rushed over only to find that the cockpit was empty and no sign of the pilot anywhere. Shortly a figure appeared staggering up the road, muttering "Where am I, what's happened?" The pilot, whose name I will not reveal, was unhurt but temporarily stunned and disorientated. There was still one aircraft in the air, so we moved the flare path to a new position and signalled it into land. This aircraft also came in rather low and with the same disastrous result. Two wrecked Bulldogs in half an hour may be a squadron record, but not one to be proud of.'

The night flying mishaps were not confined to No 17(F) for some fairly heavy landings were made by the pilots of their fellow squadron. On 12 December 1930 Sergeant Pilot L. G. James of 'C' Flight No 3(F) Squadron was making a dusk landing in *J9578* when he misjudged his height and broke the main axle of his Bulldog. The subsequent career of this pilot is worth noting, for his aerobatic skill was such that he was nominated to participate in the 'Air Combat' event at the 1933 Hendon Air Display with fellow pilots Flight Lieutenant B. W. Knox and Flying Officer D. P. A. Boitel-Gill. James had originally volunteered for flying duties in 1929 whilst serving as an LAC Carpenter/Rigger. No 3(F)'s ORB records that on 1 November 1934, after completing his five-year term as a pilot, he was remustered back to his basic trade and posted to No 65 Squadron, RAF Hornchurch. One can only conjecture how he made the adjustment back to life in the hangar, making rigging checks, after tasting the freedom to be found in roaming the skies of England's southern counties. Another victim of the Wiltshire darkness was to be Flight Lieutenant John Oliver, who was by no means a novice for he had over 2,500 hours' solo flying time in his log by the evening of 22 January 1931. It was on his second flight of that night from Upavon when he too made

a heavy landing, breaking not only the axle on Bulldog *J9570*, but, as recorded in the ORB, 'breaking a life record also'.

MT driver Arthur Strudwick was fairly typical of those men recruited into the RAF in the early 1930s, and a brief *résumé* of his background will enable the reader to gain some impression of the era in which the Bristol Bulldog became 'the' fighter aeroplane of Britain's defence. Born and bred in the tiny West Sussex village of Wisborough Green, he had, since leaving school, worked on a local farm where he regularly drove tractors and farm vehicles as part of his farm labouring duties. Life was hard but pleasant, apart from one thing — he rarely, if ever, had a day off, even at weekends. A chance meeting with an RAF driver from nearby Tangmere airfield, smartly bedecked in peaked cap, tunic, breeches, puttees and swagger stick of the time, convinced him that he could do better for himself. And so on a cold December day in 1930, an apprehensive eighteen-year-old alighted from the steam train at Victoria station and quickly made his way across London to Gwydyr House, Whitehall, where he joined 34 other anxious applicants. After many hours spent taking written aptitude tests, followed by an interview and a lengthy wait, he was summoned into a room to be told 'you are one of the lucky ones', for only nine out of the 35 had been chosen. A few weeks elapsed before he was told to report to the Reception Centre at West Drayton where he was hurriedly sworn in, allocated a never-to-be-forgotten Service number, and taken to the nearby RAF Depot at Uxbridge. He remembers that as a country lad the noise of an adjoining railway yard, combined with the lumpy firmness of biscuit mattresses on a standard issue Macdonald iron bed, were not exactly conducive to a good night's sleep. Accommodation of new recruits at the depot was made in a series of recently erected monolithic two-storey buildings, each one named after some First World War battle such as Mons, Ypres, Somme, etc. It was in this stronghold that the new recruits were kitted out and put through a three months' stint of 'square-bashing', which included the customary drilling by numbers, arms drill, bayonet-fixing and the weekly ritual of kit inspection. Contrary to all popular belief the food was plentiful, if not of a very high quality, for Arthur found that his weight had increased by over two stone by the time he left Uxbridge in April 1931. He recalls that during this twelve weeks' training, there was an outbreak of meningitis causing the deaths of thirteen of his young colleagues. As a consequence all recruits were given throat swab tests, and although relieved to

19(F) Squadron Leader's Bulldog, *K2159*, complete with drogue pennants *(RAF Museum).*

find that he was clear of the infection, it did mean extra fatigue duties to compensate for the depletion in numbers caused by those found to be carrying the germ.

Weight gained at Uxbridge was soon to be lost at Manston's 2nd School of Technical Training, for not even the sparrows' droppings, aimed from the rafters of the station's canteen, could compensate for the lack of quantity or quality. As a consequence there was an unwelcome drain on an airman's limited financial resources by the NAAFI, where their rock cakes and cups of tea (both equally priced at a penny) were purchased in order to supplement the meagre fare. Young AC2 Strudwick had requested the trade of Carpenter/Rigger upon joining the RAF, but owing to little demand for that particular occupation as all-metal aircraft became mandatory, he was forced to accept his second choice of MT driver. His life at Manston, at that time also the home of No 2(AC) and No 9(B) Squadrons, now revolved around First World War Crossley and Leyland tenders with their acetylene lamps and solid tyred wheels, Trojan two-strokes with their chain-driven back axles, Hucks starters

on Model T Ford chassis and P and M motorcycles.

Upon passing out as a qualified driver, which meant a bonus on pay of 3d per day, he was posted to RAF Upavon, in September 1931. He recalls that soon after arriving there the yo-yo craze was in full swing amongst the airmen. This innovation was a hand-held novelty which comprised of a pair of brightly coloured discs, some 2.5 in in diameter by ½ in wide, and rigidly spaced, ¼ in apart, on an axle, much like a narrow span cotton reel. A string approximately 30 in long, with one end attached to the spindle and the other end looped to go around the operator's finger, enabled the yo-yo to be oscillated to the length of the string and back into the hand — all great fun. It had become a very popular toy throughout the country, but one of the 'erks decided to go a stage further and build a giant one, of some 10 in diameter. Obviously it needed to be operated from quite a height, for it had a 15 ft length of cord assembled around it. The practical joker decided that the most suitable place to operate it from would be the walkway along the hangar roof. Unfortunately, he timed the trial run at an inopportune moment for the Flight Sergeant was covertly observing and the culprit was placed on a charge for endangering life. Strudwick recalls with some glee that the charge sheet read, 'Airman disciplined for playing yo-yo from the hangar roof'.

The majority of Arthur Strudwick's time at Upavon was spent on ambulance duties when he would be required during times of flying to be at the ready with his vehicle outside the Sick Bay. Two indicator lamps were installed above the building's entrance to signal an ambulance to an accident, for at the time of Bulldog there were two airfields in use at Upavon, one on the north side of the A342 Upavon to Andover road and the other, as used by the two squadrons, to the south. Considering the number of flying hours being logged by the two fighter squadrons, which could during the summer months amount to a combined total of 700 hours, accidents were not that frequent. The first Bulldog to be lost in an accident was that of Pilot Officer M. A. Douglas-Hamilton from No 3(F) whilst participating in an ADGB training flight on 12 June 1930 with Hawker Horsleys from No 100(B) Squadron, Bicester. The

young Bulldog pilot dived on his 'enemy' in a simulated camera-gun attack, misjudged his speed and collided with the bomber. Douglas-Hamilton parachuted to safety, but poor Sergeant Pilot O'Mears in attempting to bale out was caught on the aircraft's gun mounting, trapped, and taken to his death with the descending Horsley.

Arthur Strudwick recalls one or two sad memories from his early days at Upavon in which No 17(F) were to lose pilots under tragic circumstances. One was to involve the squadron's newly arrived CO, Squadron Leader L. M. Elworthy, who was killed during a parachute drop at the Andover Air Display on 7 June 1932. Evidently he jumped awkwardly from the Boulton and Paul Sidestrand bomber, colliding with part of the aircraft's structure as he went and knocking himself out, with the inevitable result of not being able to operate the 'chute.

The following year three more pilots met their death; one during a take-off accident and two during a mid-air collision. The first accident was to occur whilst 17(F)'s 'A' Flight was on detachment at Imber Clump, on Salisbury Plain, whilst co-

32(F)'s Bulldog IIAs from Biggin Hill. How many aircraft — three or four? *(RAF Museum)*.

operating with the Army during the Southern Command Exercises. The Flight was made up by officer pilots Reggie Pyne (Flight Commander), Jeffrey Quill and NCO pilot 'Spot' Little. They were just taking-off in a Vic formation during the late afternoon of 22 September 1933, when Little hit the top of a haystack. He was pulled from the wreckage of his Bulldog by his distressed colleagues and, although still alive, he died in the ambulance on the way to hospital. He was sorely missed at Upavon, for he was a popular figure renowned for his devotion to his Bugatti sports car, a passion which engendered much good humoured leg-pulling by virtue of the fact that his pride and joy was more often in pieces that on the road.

Later during the year, on 4 December, ambulance driver Strudwick was summoned to the scene of a crash which had occurred at Milton Lilbourne some two miles to the east of Pewsey, near the B3087 Burbage road, when the aircraft of Pilot Officer G. O. Llewellyn and Sergeant Pilot J. C. Hopkins collided. The wreckage of the two aircraft had fallen, not so very far from some houses, on to farmland owned by racehorse trainer Cliff Richards, brother of the famous jockey Sir Gordon Richards. Hopkins baled out and for some unknown reason — it may have been injury on egress, or just insufficient height — his parachute failed to open. Llewellyn was also killed on impact and Strudwick remembers that he had to be extricated from the wreckage of the cockpit — a very sad day indeed for 17(F) Squadron.

Squadron Leader Elworthy's successor was to be Squadron Leader F. J. Vincent, DFC, who took over as CO of 17(F) on 20 November 1932 and was to remain with the squadron right up until its Kenley days. Originally he had served with the Royal Marines during World War 1 before transferring to the RFC where he was to distinguish himself as a pilot on combat duties. Retired Air Vice-Marshal J. K. Rotherham recalls his impressions of the man thus:

'The Squadron Commander was Squadron Leader F. J. Vincent, a strict disciplinarian and a fine pilot, he was feared and greatly respected by the whole squadron. One of my early encounters with him made a lasting impression and gives some indication of his quality as a leader. At that time (early 1934) the Bulldog IIA had a tailskid and no brakes and as the Upavon aerodrome is situated on top of a hill it was essential not only to avoid overshooting but also to use a lot of rudder to keep straight, failure to do so could result in a violent swing and the wingtip hitting the ground.

'It was not long before I found myself taxiing in with a bent wingtip and being ordered to report to the Commanding Officer. I had no idea what terrible punishment was in store for me. Squadron Leader Vincent, however, was most kind and sympathetic and then said: "My aircraft is out on the tarmac, take it now and do a couple of landings".

'I managed those two landings successfully, but what an ordeal and I really learnt my lesson. Fortunately, shortly after this incident our Bulldogs were fitted with brakes and a tailwheel and there was no longer any problem in keeping straight or coming to a stop on downhill slope.'

No doubt Pilot Officer Rotherham's apprehension was increased by the sight of those billowing black and white drogue pennants that would be very noticeable on that particular Bulldog, for it was the custom of a Squadron Leader and Flight Commander's aircraft to fly them. They resembled miniature windsocks, being some six inches in diameter by two feet in length, and in the case of a Squadron Leader's machine were flown from the trailing edge of the lower wing, one on each side, some 3.5 feet inboard of the wingtip, and, in addition, from a mid-way position along the rear edge of the rudder. In the case of a Flight Commander's aircraft, only a single pennant would be flown from the rudder. The use of drogue pennants, combined with the brightly coloured wheel discs and spinners of the squadron Bulldogs, must have evoked more than a little magic as they roared overhead in formation at the air displays of the 1930s. How very reminiscent of the heraldry of the mediaeval knights as they charged into battle, but now with the roar of Jupiters supplanting that of hoofbeats, and threat of twin-Vickers for that of jutting lances. The vulnerability of the pennant to the increasing speeds of more modern aircraft was to soon bring about its demise, but their use reminds us of the narrow concepts of military thinking still prevalent in those days, where the use of the aeroplane as a military machine was still thought to be merely an extension of the cavalry of earlier wars. Like the wearing of breeches and riding boots, and carrying of canes by officer pilots, they were the very last vestigial remains of a bygone era which were soon to be swept aside.

On the evening of 4 October 1930 the ill-fated airship *R101* left its mooring-mast at Cardington on the first leg of its ill-advised trip to India. Political expediency had, in spite of design criticisms, unsatisfactory trials and poor weather conditions, determined its departure from England, and within seven hours 47 of its 54 passengers were to be killed as it fell in flames at

Beauvais, in northern France. Amongst those killed were to be the Secretary of State for Air, Lord Thomson, as well as Air Vice-Marshal Sir Sefton Brancker and many other notables whose bodies were to be brought back to Bedford for burial a few days later.

On 10 October Flight Lieutenant John Oliver was detailed to fly with No 3(F) Squadron to Duxford, where they stayed overnight before being led the next day in a farewell flypast at the burial ceremony at Cardington. This same officer was to pilot the squadron's DH Moth *K1206* with the Station's Commander, Wing Commander Norton, as passenger to Tangmere on 28 April 1931 in order to attend the funeral of Air Vice-Marshal Holt. The AVM had been tragically killed when a Siskin fighter had collided with his aircraft whilst visiting the station. A study of John Oliver's flying-log during the 1930-1931 period reveals a whole range of training exercises being carried out by the squadron. These included practices for aerobatic competitions; Andover and Hendon Air Displays; 'Battle Climbs' with his Flight to 20,000 ft when

oxygen and heated clothing would be used; searchlight exercises with the 1st Air Defence Brigade at Farnborough; camera gun attacks on ground targets; flight attacks on Hawker Harts during Affiliation Exercises; leading a squadron attack on RAF Manston; monthly slow flying and spinning tests; forced-landing training exercises for new pilots as well as their instruction in the station's dual Siskin.

It was not all work and no play, for Wednesday afternoons on a pre-war RAF Fighter Station were given over to sports activities, with the normal cricket, tennis, football and rugby matches backed up by golf, squash and the annual boxing tournament. Weekends allowed the relaxation of wearing civilian clothing for those not on duty, with blazers, or sports jackets and flannels being the vogue. This concession was particularly a welcome relief for the 'erk, who was more than grateful for being able to dispense with the breath-restricting button-up dog collar tunic. Personal transport, for those rich enough to afford it, took the form of sports cars and motor cycles which

32 (F)'s Bulldog IIAs from Kenley. Note the exhaust heater muffs and white-lined coloured elevators of the lead aircraft, *K1617 (RAF Museum)*.

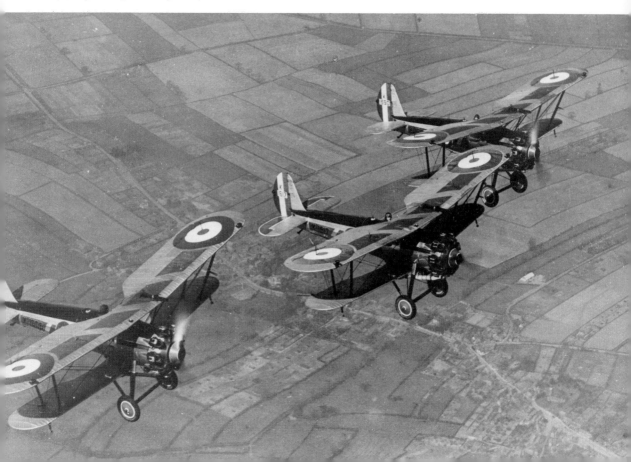

were used for trips home on weekend leave. For those less wealthy, it meant a trip to one of the two public houses in Upavon or a visit to the cinema in Devizes.

Ostensibly the pay of even the most junior of officers — an Acting Pilot Officer — at 14/10d a day seemed quite attractive, but out of this sum there could be quite large deductions. Although messing fees were officially only a shilling a day, the sum could vary by as much as four times this amount on any particular station, depending upon how well its officers decided to live. Attendance at dinner in the Mess was compulsory on four occasions during the week and entailed a strictly observed protocol. This included the wearing of mess uniform, punctilious arrival in the ante-room where one's senior officers were greeted in the manner of a parade, and the ritualistic downing of a glass of sherry before going in to dine. Further to this quite heavy expense there was the payment of one's batman, as well as the maintenance and upkeep of uniforms. The large majority of young officers remained single, for the marriage allowance was not paid to those below the age of thirty. To marry below this age was interpreted by one's senior officers as showing a lack of commitment to one's career, and it could therefore go against a young officer in being offered a permanent commission — a much sought-after prize in those days.

In spite of such minor infringements of personal liberty the fighter pilot was, in those somnolent pre-war days, in fact a member of a very elite club indeed. Where else could a young man pursue a career in which he was not only admired and respected but where he was paid for carrying out duties that he thoroughly enjoyed. The RAF was described by some 'as the finest flying club in the world'. A pilot knew that he belonged to a closely knit community for frequent visits between the eight stations of Fighting Area created a warm camaraderie and *esprit de corps* that was to vindicate the plans laid earlier by Trenchard. A former Bulldog pilot of the period recalls:

'I put in 350 hours flying in Bulldogs and in retrospect it must rank as my most favourite aeroplane. Finally my time in 17 Squadron was perhaps my happiest and undoubtedly my most carefree in 36 years' service with the Royal Air Force.'

No 3(F) and 17(F) Squadrons were to leave Upavon for Kenley in Surrey, on 10 May 1934, after it had been decided that the Wiltshire station should become a FAA shore base. The move was a popular one with both pilots and ground crew, for it now meant that they would be nearer to the entertainment provided by London itself. The airfield was some five miles south of Croydon and had previously been the home of Bulldog squadrons 23(F) and 32(F) who had vacated it in September 1932 when it was due for reconstruction. The squadrons were, soon after arrival, to be busily engaged in practice for the 1934 Hendon Air Display in June and the ADGB Command Exercises in the following month. The ADGB exercises, which usually lasted for a period of three days, were primarily meant to simulate attacks by 'enemy' bombers, consisting of Fairey Gordons and Hawker Harts, attacking south-eastern England by day, and Vickers Virginias, Handley-Page Hinaidis and Boulton and Paul Sidestrands by night. Equipment for directing the fighters on to their bomber targets was more than a trifle primitive for it was in the days before radar, or even its precursor RDF (radio direction finding) which was still some three years away. Total reliance was made upon Observer Corps posts strategically positioned around southern England which were in direct telephone link with both the HQ of ADGB at Uxbridge, as well as the operations rooms of the fighter stations at Kenley, Biggin Hill, Tangmere, Hawkinge, Northolt, North Weald, Duxford and Hornchurch. Once scrambled and in the air the fighters were vectored by R/T from the plotting table of their station, with map references being given. It was all rather a hit and miss affair but it was all that there was. Camera guns were used to record a hit on an 'enemy' bomber by day and the searchlights of AA ground defence units of the Territorial Army were used by night for assisting the fighters to their nocturnal targets. Wing Commander W. G. Easton recalls with some scepticism the ADGB exercises at that time.

'I well remember in 1934 when I navigated a formation of nine Fairey Gordons of No 207(B) Bircham Newton to attack London, via Lee-on-Solent. During our flight, which lasted three hours, we were ordered to fly at 120 mph "to enable the fighters to overtake us" . . . I never saw a single fighter. So much for the Air Defence of Great Britain and this at a time when Labour and Liberal politicians were screaming for disarmament, much the same as they are doing today.'

Not all such attempts at interception were as abortive as the one recorded above by any means, for No 3(F) had, during the 1931 exercises, recorded twenty night patrols by individual aircraft during which 28 'enemy' bombers had been attacked. The exercises did no doubt lay the foundation for a system which, some six years later with the timely assistance of radar, was to prove itself highly successful in war. John Rotherham has quite vivid memories of navigation at that particular time.

'Early in May 1934 the squadron moved to Kenley, a much better airfield and within easy reach of the bright lights of London. Life was fun and training not too arduous, navigation exercises mostly involved flying to one of the other fighter stations for lunch and return in the afternoon. The standard of navigation was not very high, there were no radio aids and no radar, it all had to be done by dead reckoning, while the only aids for blind flying were the turn and bank indicator and the magnetic compass. I remember on one occasion setting off for Lydd ranges for a firing practice in a flight of three aircraft led by my Flight Commander, then Flight Lieutenant G. P. Chamberlain, who subsequently commanded the squadron. We took off from Kenley and climbed up through a thin layer of cloud; we cruised along very pleasantly in the sunlight, while the Flight Commander, his head in the cockpit, was busily working out his course and ETA. In due course he gave the thumbs-up signal and pointed downwards. We dived through the clouds and came out at about 2,000 ft with good visibility all round but with nothing but sea below us and no land in sight in any direction. In this instance we had to fly in a northerly direction for quite a long time before we sighted the South Coast.

'I remember this incident particularly well because there was an occasion when one of the pilots set off for a station on the East Coast and neither he nor his aircraft were ever seen again. He could possibly have lost control in cloud or had engine failure and come down over the North Sea.'

The summer of 1935 was to be a busy time for the two Bulldog squadrons at Kenley, for apart from being involved in the usual practices for the June Hendon Air Display, there was also participation in King George V's first formal review of the Royal Air Force at Mildenhall and Duxford on 6 July. The event had been planned as part of the King's Silver Jubilee celebrations and was a mammoth exercise, needing several weeks' practice, and involving the 365 aircraft of the ADGB's 38 squadrons together with their pilots and ground crews. The serried ranks of highly polished fighters and bombers glistened in the sunshine as they formed a four group crescent around the four hangars of the recently opened Mildenhall airfield. Ground crews in best blue, together with their white-clad pilots, stood smartly to attention as the

King, in Marshal of the Royal Air Force uniform, slowly made his tour of inspection from an open-topped Rolls-Royce landau. At the end of the inspection the customary order for removal of head dress and three cheers for His Majesty was given, before the King and his entourage, which included the Prince of Wales and the Duke of York dressed in the uniforms of Air Chief Marshal and Air Vice-Marshal respectively, departed for the forty-minute drive to Duxford.

The peace of Mildenhall was slowly but determinedly broken as Kestrels and Jupiters, coughed into life and the aircraft taxied across the airfield into position for their take-off before an expectant crowd of some 25,000 spectators. The first wave of aircraft into the air were the ungainly, wheelspatted Heyford heavy bombers of 99(B) and 10(B), led by the CO of RAF Mildenhall, Wing Commander Linnell. Following on at an interval carefully timed to give a two mile distance of air space, were the more sprightly Hawker Hart light bombers followed by Audaxes and Demons of 23(F) Squadron. Then came the six proud Bulldog squadrons, 3, 17, 32, 54, 56 and 111(F) — all that now remained of the original ten squadrons — followed by the Furies and Duxford's own Gauntlets of 19(F) to complete the nine-mile-long column of aircraft heading for the Cambridgeshire airfield.

In the meantime the Royal party had arrived at Duxford some eighty minutes earlier, having been cheered on their way along the route by an estimated crowd of 100,000 people. The carefully planned schedule gave time for the most honoured guests to be entertained in the Officers' Mess, the party including the Lord Lieutenant of Cambridgeshire, the Chief of Air Staff, Sir Edward Ellington, Lord Trenchard and the Maharajah of Kashmir. Less important guests were given a buffet lunch served in one of the squadron hangars which had been tastefully decorated, not only with tables and chairs, but also with the prototype Gloster Gladiator *K5200* arranged at one end as a focal point.

It took just over five minutes for the 182 aircraft to make the initial flypast — the largest that the world had ever seen — with the King taking the salute from the dais of the covered pavilion. The Gauntlets of 19(F) Squadron were the only machines to break away from the main body of aircraft, whereupon they carried out a series of drill manoeuvres much to the delight of the 60,000 in attendance. Meanwhile, seventeen of the twenty squadrons engaged in the flypast had made a wide circling turn over Duxford ready for the return, this time in wing formation at 1,200 ft to complete

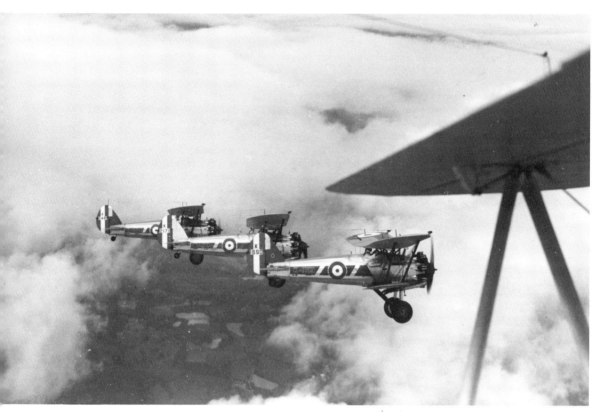

32(F)'s Bulldogs above the clouds. Note the nearest aircraft has *K1690* on the rudder and K1619 on the fuselage
(RAF Museum).

the spectacle. It is rather interesting to note that every one of the aircraft participating on that day was of a biplane configuration. It was to be a further two years before more modern monoplane aircraft, both fighters and bombers such as the Hawker Hurricane I, Handley-Page Harrow, Vickers Wellesley and Wellington, Bristol Blenheim I or Fairey Battle, came into squadron use.

Later during the September of that same year the Abyssinian crisis was to mean the hurried despatch of No 3(F) to the heat of the Sudan, where they were to spend almost a year abroad acting as watchdogs. They returned to Kenley in August 1936, and within a few months they learned that they were to be re-equipped with Gloster Gladiator Is. On 8 March 1937, by which time the faster and more heavily armed biplane fighters were already beginning to arrive, the personnel of 'B' Flight 3(F) were detailed to form the nucleus of No 80(F) Squadron. The Bulldogs lingered on during this transitional period until they were finally phased

out in the July as obsolete, having served with the squadron for just over eight years. Similarly, in August 1936, the pilots of their companion and rival squadron, 17(F), were to take-off from Kenley for the last time in their well-worn black zig-zag marked Bulldogs and head towards the storage unit at Waddington, for they too were to be re-equipped with a Gloster product — the Gauntlet II.

* * *

The Cambridgeshire airfield of Duxford became the home of No 19(F) Squadron on 1 April 1923, when it re-formed as a fighter flight attached to No 2 FTS after being disbanded in 1919. The squadron was originally formed at Castle Bromwich in September 1915 and later served with distinction in France where it was successively equipped with the

BE12, Spad VII and Sopwith Dolphin. The Snipes, Grebes and Siskins of the post-war period finally gave way to the arrival of the blue and white chequerboard marked Bulldog IIAs, and by September 1931 19(F) was fully equipped with its new fighters. The Fighter Squadron was not the sole occupant of Duxford, for they shared it with the Meteorological Flight and the Station Flight. The Met Flight primarily consisted of two Flying Officer pilots and their Siskin IIIAs, which made morning and afternoon flights daily to altitudes varying between 18,000 and 25,000 ft. Their task was to record temperature and humidity readings, as well as the height of cloud base and its type, together with general weather conditions. The Station Flight, which was equipped with Avro 504Ns and some eight instructors, provided flying training to the Cambridge University Air Squadron; it was also responsible for the administration of the Met Flight.

Sergeant Pilot W. John Rye (later to become a Wing Commander, AFC) was posted to 19(F) at Duxford in 1932, having joined the RAF as a seventeen-year-old apprentice at Halton in 1925. He had volunteered for a five-year period on flying duties and had been sent to RAF Sealand, where he recalls that his course was the first to take their six months' primary training on DH60Xs before going on to Siskins. He recollects that the Siskin was very prone to drop a wing upon landing, this tendency being exacerbated by the then-current RAF practice of making gliding landing approaches without 'so much as a wisp of engine being allowed'. The philosophy behind the practice had been formulated in the days when engines were not as reliable as they might have been, so therefore the making of forced-landings was still thought to be all-important. Rye found little difficulty in making the transition from Siskin to Bulldog and refuses to believe that an aircraft had vices — merely flying characteristics that had to be mastered. Spin recovery in Bulldog — a type in which he was to log 511 hours — was never a problem as far as he was concerned. He does, however, believe that it did have characteristics not unlike the monoplane designs that were to follow it, inasmuch as it required more than merely the centralising of controls. Many of his senior officers had been taught in the early days that such neutralising of the controls was all that was necessary to recover from a spin, whereas Bulldog did require full opposite rudder and stick hard forward.

John Rye has several vivid memories of his time with 19(F) on Bulldogs, one such being the regular ADGB exercise of 'Battle Climbs'. Every squadron in Fighting Area was required to designate, on a weekly basis, one flight known as 'Battle Flight', which was responsible for the daily interception of an 'enemy bomber' over its particular sector. It meant that the three aircraft had to be outside the hangar on the tarmac from the crack of dawn with engines already warmed up at the ready, and with their guns loaded, depending upon whether the firing ranges were open or not. At a given signal received from ADGB's HQ at Uxbridge, which could occur at any time during daylight hours — lunchtime being a favourite time — the 'Battle Flight' was scrambled to intercept the invader. Once in the air they would receive a heading; and climb (the height was restricted to 16,000 ft if oxygen equipment was not installed) to find the target aircraft. Camera gun verification of an interception was rarely considered necessary, for the RAF bomber usually contained some high ranking HQ officer from ADGB as a passenger. Once interception, or failure to intercept, was signalled back over the R/T to the station's ops room, instructions would be received either to return direct to base, or to proceed to the firing ranges at Sutton Bridge or Lydd, use up ammunition and return.

John Rye recalls that during one particular 'Battle Flight' he had opened his map case, which was situated centrally on the dashboard below the compass, and was showered with hot oil. It transpired that the aircraft's oil-tank had been overfilled, with the result that it had frothed out of the oil filler and back into the compartment used for holding maps and diagrams.

The highlight of John Rye's time with 19(F) was, without doubt, the squadron's participation in the Hendon Air Displays of 1933 and 1934. The 1933 event was carried out on 24 June under bad weather conditions, with the three A&AEE pilots from Martlesham Heath, Flight Lieutenant J. Moir, Flying Officer Leech and Flying Officer A. J. Pegg, performing the smoke evolutions with Bulldogs. 19(F)'s aircraft took part in the 'Set Piece' event, where they were cast in the role of the defending force whose job was to protect the airfield, complete with dummy huts, from enemy attack. The Bulldogs were painted a ghastly reddish orange colour and during the attack on the Sidestrand bomber were all deemed to have been shot down. This meant that they could not return to Hendon and the plan was that they should fly back to their station at Duxford. Somewhere between Baldock and Royston the exuberant young pilots of 19(F) decided to fire off the remainder of their blank ammunition. It caused something of a panic to the unsuspecting residents living along the route below, who quickly telephoned the police that some strangely painted foreign fighters, without national markings, were shooting up the towns and villages of Hertfordshire! It took quite a bit of explaining to the Station Commander later during that afternoon.

The 1934 Hendon Air Display saw 19(F) become the first RAF squadron to perform synchronised flight formation aerobatics with smoke. Much argument has raged around who was first with this event, but Rye is quite adamant that other squadrons had performed smoke evolutions, but not in flight formation. Five Bulldogs led by Flight Lieutenant Harry Broadhurst took part in this particular event, the remaining pilots being Flying Officer S. F. Godden, Sergeant Pilots J. S. W. Bignal, R. Parr and W. J. Rye. Much hard practice was to precede the day of the event, with 'Broadie' working out each and every manoeuvre to the split second. Rye is full of admiration for the man who led them and recalls:

'He was an "ace" pilot in every sense of the word, a superb marksman who taught us how to shoot, an absolute born leader of men, well liked and not afraid to cut out red tape.

'Flying in formation with him was just like flying solo — it was so smooth — for he had a wonderful understanding of exactly what each pilot had to do in whatever position he was in. He took the trouble to try out those positions for himself, which meant that in a very steep turn he knew that the man on the inside would not be going very fast, so he would speed up. Going into a loop and coming out at the top in a piston engine aircraft one has to throttle back, otherwise you will overspeed . . . other leaders couldn't cope with that, and by the time they got over the top we were fifty yards behind. He wasn't like that, he knew how to keep the boys together.'

Their *pièce de résistance* was the 'Lovers Knot', in which the five aircraft would fly line abreast diving across the aerodrome, with Bignal and Rye out on each wing, and Godden, Broadhurst and Parr in the middle. The inner three would then go up into a tight loop belching red, white and blue smoke trails, as the two wingmen fanned out into an exaggerated winnow, smoke on, up and through the loop from each side in perfect timing. As Rye and Bignal passed each other they would count, 'one, two, three-smoke off', thus leaving the five ribbon strands of the nuptial knot for all to admire. John Rye recalls that the blue used by Broadhurst had to be chosen very carefully, for if it were a true blue it would not be all that visible against the sky.

The final choice was a turquoise peacock colour, slightly verging on the green, but sufficiently blue to have a patriotic flavour.

The smoke equipment consisted of a streamline fifteen-gallon tank strapped underneath the fuselage, with its contents being force fed at 15 psi, by means of a wind-driven pump, into each of the engine's exhausts. The supply was controlled from the cockpit and its contents monitored by a small gauge, which Rye remembers was not too easy to see because of its awkwardly placed position. The whole apparatus was supplied and fitted by a character known as Major Jack Savage of 'Skywriting' who was a familiar figure at Hendon. He used an old Rolls-Royce saloon kitted out as a mobile workshop and carrying every conceivable gadget and tool that he could get in it.

Sir Harry Broadhurst recalls those days and the part 19(F) played in the 1934 event:

'At the beginning of 1934, I was posted to 19 Squadron, to command 'A' Flight also equipped with Bulldogs. Whilst there I led the Flight in Flight Aerobatics for the Hendon Air Display — also did Solo Aerobatics in the same thing. The most spectacular combination was leading a flight of five, demonstrating aerobatics with smoke. Incidentally, making smoke in those days was not quite the happy procedure that it is today, when the Red Arrows pump the liquid into their jets and exude it behind them. In my day you pumped the stuff into the exhaust and the smoke came out on each side of the aircraft, just ahead of the cockpit, so that when you landed you were beautifully stained red, white or blue, depending on which colour you had been operating.'

All the manoeuvres for the displays, including a slow roll by three of the squadron Bulldogs in formation, were carried out within the confines of quite a small airfield, which meant a lot of hard concentrated practising in the weeks preceding the event itself. Radio reception using R/T equipment varied considerably in the early 1930s (the use of VHF did not come until some years later) and as a consequence the manoeuvres were practised with and without the use of an air-to-air radio link.

Once the Hendon event was over, Rye recalls that the squadron would be detailed to participate in Affiliation Exercises, which for 19(F) often meant flying north to Scotland. Here at Renfrew, home of No 602 'City of Glasgow' Squadron, or at Turnhouse where No 603 'City of Edinburgh' Squadron was stationed, the Bulldog men would spend a fortnight's summer camp. It was an enjoyable time joining together with the weekend

Bulldog Mark II, *J9574,* of No 3(F) Squadron with stick hard back and plenty of revs being led out of the line at Hendon in 1929. Note the valve covers on the engine *(MoD).*

civilian volunteer pilots of the AAF, in conducting what were in effect 'mini ADGB exercises', complete with mock dog-fighting and armament practice. Later in the year came the usual two weeks under canvas at Sutton Bridge on air firing practice, and it was whilst attending the 1934 camp that John Rye experienced his one and only mishap in a Bulldog.

Detailed to firing at an aerial target, he took off and soon had the drogue nicely positioned in his gun sights. As his thumbs pressed the two gun triggers and the Vickers guns sprang into life, he felt a splash of hot oil on his goggles. His first thoughts were that the hydraulic system of *K2158's* Constantinesco interrupter gear was leaking, and so, releasing the gun triggers, he instinctively pulled his goggles from his face. Much to his surprise he found that, unlike the fluid in the interrupter system, the oil was thick and that he was being blinded. With scarcely any time to ponder on a suitable landing place, he selected a large triangular shaped field, and came in for what might have been a perfect landing nicely into wind. Unfortunately, it was a potato field and its furrows were at right angles to the direction in which he was forced to land. As the Bulldog's wheels touched down the aircraft bounced, hit the next furrow and

turned over breaking its back in the process. Hanging from the straps dazed and bruised, the pilot released the pin holding his Sutton harness and slowly slid out head first and scrambled clear, only to return to the cockpit a moment later when he remembered that the guns were still loaded. The aircraft was a 'write-off' and later post-mortem investigation revealed that the return pipe from the engine's scavenge pump to the oil tank had fractured and caused the accident.

January 1935 saw the Bulldogs being replaced by the Gloster Gauntlet I, No 19(F) being the first RAF squadron to be equipped with the new fighter (it was also to be the first squadron to use that most famous of fighters — the Spitfire I — in June 1938). Rye recalls that the Gauntlet, although faster and more powerful than contemporary RAF fighters — it was 53 mph faster than Bulldog and could outclimb the Fury — did suffer with vibrational problems from its Mercury VIS2 engine. On one occasion when performing an exercise that needed a stop watch, he placed it, before take-off between the rubber head bump pad and the Aldis sight rubber. Once in flight and needing to refer to the instrument, he found that such was the vibration that the dial had become a blur and the seconds hand was going backwards!

The Bulldogs continued to be used at Duxford alongside the newly arrived Gauntlets, but now only as part of Met Flight, where they superseded the old Siskin IIIAs. The last recorded incident at Duxford occurred on 22 September 1936, when Pilot Officer P. Hutchinson was forced to make a very heavy forced-landing outside the fog-bound home airfield whilst flying *K2963*. The aircraft was a write-off but fortunately the pilot was not reported as having suffered any injury.

* * *

No 23 Fighter Squadron was re-formed as part of the peacetime Royal Air Force with Sopwith Snipes, on 1 July 1925 at Henlow having been disbanded in March 1919 after war service in France. It was the first squadron to be equipped with the venerable Gloster Gamecock I, an aeroplane that was to be long remembered for its agility and manoeuvrability, qualities which it so ably demonstrated during the early Hendon Air Pageants. The short stubby Gamecocks, with their gaily coloured squadron markings of red and blue check and large national insignia roundels, were the last all-wooden fighters to be ordered by the RAF and were to remain in service at Henlow, and later Kenley, for just over five years.

The Gamecocks of 23(F) were to be phased out by July 1931 when the first of the heavier, faster, all-metal Bristol Bulldog IIAs began to arrive at Kenley in April of that year. Here they were to join with the Bulldogs of No 32(F) Squadron who had also received the new fighter in January of that same year. This was to be the first meeting of the two squadrons since they had fought together in northern France during March 1917. No 23(F) was destined never to be fully equipped with Bulldogs for it had been decided by way of an experiment, to make it a composite squadron by the addition of a Flight of Hawker Hart (F) two-seat fighters (later to be known as Demon I). The first of the Hart (F)s were to arrive at Kenley by 10 July and by September the remaining three. In spite of the addition of a rear gunner and Lewis gun, the Hawker fighter was to prove itself faster than the Bulldog, owing much of this success to the installation of its 485 hp Rolls-Royce Kestrel IIS engine. It did not go into production as the Demon I until 1932 when it was designed to meet Air

"Factory fresh" Bulldogs of 41(F) Squadron, Northolt, with drogue pennants of the Squadron Leader's aircraft nearest the camera *(RAF Museum)*.

Ministry specification 6/32. In its final form, as the Turret-Demon, it was equipped with a 584 hp Kestrel VDR engine and a Frazer-Nash hydraulically-operated gun turret, complete with a folding-segment shield for the gunner.

The motto of 23(F) Squadron, 'Semper Agressus', an aircraft named Bulldog and Douglas R. S. Bader, complement each other like King Saul, David and Goliath, so closely are their histories inextricably woven. Bader was posted to the squadron at Kenley on 25 August 1930 as a permanently commissioned Pilot Officer, having completed his two years as a Flight Cadet at Cranwell. It was to be the beginning of a career that would leave its mark not only on the squadron but on the Service itself, for not even the senior officer's statement 'Plucky, capable, headstrong . . .' could presage just how much an understatement this was to prove. Posted to 'B' Flight, he was soon in the air in a nimble Gamecock which responded to all that he had learned on Avro 504Ns and Siskins — and more! The CO of No 23(F), Squadron Leader A. W. Woollett, DSO, MC, had chosen 'C' Flight Commander, Flight Lieutenant Harry Day (a pilot in his early thirties who had fought in the First World War), to select and train two pilots to accompany him in the forthcoming Hendon Air Display. Bader trained hard to be selected, as did many others, and was eventually chosen to partner Day in an aerobatic double, with close friend and colleague, Pilot Officer Geoffrey Stephenson, held as reserve. Day had worked out new routines of synchronised aerobatics for the 1931 event which meant that the three pilots were required to practice assiduously, for such closely spaced mirror manoeuvres demanded absolute concentration. *The Times* was not only to report Day and Bader's contribution as 'the event of the day' but that the Gamecock pair had 'provided the most thrilling spectacle ever seen in exhibition flying' before an estimated crowd of 175,000 spectators, not only inside the Hendon aerodrome but many more thousands watching in bright sunshine from the surrounding fields and hillsides outside.

For Douglas Bader life at pre-war RAF Kenley was a dream come true and he found himself to be completely fulfilled, for if flying was his first love then sport ran it a very close second. Not only was he to play cricket for the RAF at the Oval in June, but also later, in November, to be selected to play for the Combined Services rugby team as a fly-half. His irrepressible spirit caused him to constantly reach out and test the boundaries of his abilities, and in no less a dangerous place than in the air. It

was whilst returning from an aerobatic display in the north-east, at Cramlington, that he had broken formation, descended, and spent an hour tree skimming and hedge-hopping, much to the displeasure of his Flight Commander Harry Day. Maybe in hindsight the administering of a mere verbal warning on the dangers of undisciplined flying was not severe enough, for it was soon dismissed from the mind of this exuberant 21-year-old. It was not long before Bader was allocated Bristol Bulldog IIA *K1676*, an aeroplane some 600 lb heavier and less forgiving that the Gloster Gamecock that he had flown for the past twelve months. Within a very short time, two of 23(F)'s pilots had been killed whilst performing aerobatics at low altitudes in Bulldogs. This seemed to have very little effect upon Bader, for in the November he was reported for carrying out low level aerobatics and making low level passes across the Kenley airfield. An admonition for showing off was to be reinforced again in December when Day, now acting as CO, was to call all the squadron pilots together in order to read them the riot act. Day made it quite clear that HM Government was not in the business of investing considerable sums of taxpayers' income in the purchase of valuable aircraft, and the training of young fighter pilots, with such poor return for its investment. The pilots were firmly ordered to obey Fighting Area's instruction that aircraft must not be aerobatically manoeuvred from a height of less than 2,000 ft.

Monthly slow flying and spinning tests had already been deliberately introduced into the curriculum of each squadron's flying training during the middle of 1931, in order to emphasise the need for correct speed so that pilots would not be caught out and spin into the ground — Day reminded them of this aspect too.

On Saturday, 5 December, Bader had played his heart out for the Combined Services team against the Springboks, so much so that he had sustained a broken nose. Quitting was not a word to be found in his vocabulary, especially as he knew that he was under surveillance for a possible England cap, and so he played on. The following Saturday however, now back with his regular team — the Harlequins — he played badly. Maybe he had overtrained and was stale, or maybe it was just that the after effects of the nose injury were worrying him, but he knew that he was not on form. Climbing into the cockpit of *K1676* on the morning of Monday, 14 December 1931, no doubt quickly dispelled all thoughts of gloom from the weekend. A quick check over the flying controls; engine primed by engine fitter; the hesitant movement of the Watts propeller as the gas starter wheezed its rich mixture into the nine hungry cylinders of the radial; a cough of blue oil smoke and the valve-clattering Jupiter burst into life. Peaked capped, brown overalled fitter and rigger, one at each wingtip, guiding the forward-blind fighter across the tarmac and out on to the dew-laden grass airfield. A fast, wing-rocking, taxying run across the bumpy turf before turning into wind for take-off; oil-pressure check, tailplane adjuster trimmed, goggles down, throttle forward, slight rudder to correct engine torque, stick gently forward, more speed and then stick back as the fighter climbed into the cold crisp clear Surrey air. After he had put the Bulldog through its paces with a brief spell of aerobatics just outside the confines of the airfield, he noticed the two aircraft of colleagues George Phillips and Geoffrey Stephenson, glinting in the light of the weak winter morning sun as they climbed into the sky. The sight of the two Bulldogs reminded him that they were off to Woodley aerodrome, to visit George's brother who was an instructor at the Aero club there, and Bader quickly decided to join them. Visiting a neighbouring airfield for lunch was a pleasurable and not unusual task and was considered to be part of the navigation exercises in what was essentially a 'fair weather' Air Force. It improved cross-country navigation and at the same time fostered a building of relationships with what was to become a fairly close-knit company of men known as Fighting Area.

Lunch was enjoyed with, and followed by, the usual banter and shop talk that is common amongst men of any highly trained profession. No doubt the young Bader was the centre of questioning with respect to aerobatics during that lunchtime, for his reputation after the Hendon event with Day assured it. What is in doubt is whether he was actually goaded into performing what was a dangerous and foolish beat up of Woodley airfield, or whether he did it merely to impress. He had only logged just over 33 hours in Bulldogs by the time of that fateful day and was therefore relatively inexperienced in the handling of the fighter. The three 23(F) fighters took off, closely watched by a small group that had gathered outside of the clubhouse, and climbed with Phillips leading the Vic formation and with Bader on his port side. In the distance the group could see Bader's aircraft making a banking turn and dive towards the clubhouse, gathering speed as it came towards them at no more than roof top height. The Bulldog began its clockwise roll at 125 mph, fast enough at exhibition altitude but insufficient at the height Bader was now attempting. The aircraft's starboard wing was at right angles to the airfield with marginal clearance, on to its back but losing

height, and with the manoeuvre almost completed the port wingtip clipped the grass. The engine was torn from its bearers as the cartwheeling Bulldog careered towards the clubhouse in a cloud of dust and flying debris and finished up in a crumpled heap. Fortunately the fighter did not catch fire and Bader was soon extricated from the cockpit, but with both legs badly damaged. The subsequent double amputation, recovery and eventual rehabilitation of Bader as a fighter pilot is another story. However, the news of his injury evidently soon spread around the stations of Fighting Area, for Flight Lieutenant John Oliver's flying log records that he made the 45-minute flight in *J9571* from Upavon to the scene of the accident, with the entry '14.12.1931 — Woodley; Bader's crash'. The two men had struck up a friendship earlier in the year when they had met at Hendon, for Oliver had represented 3(F) in the 'Fighter Wing Evolutions' event.

The training of pilots on ADGB's Fighter Stations followed a pattern, whereby three periods throughout the year were used to concentrate on the development of individual, flight and squadron skills. October to February would be set aside for an emphasis on individual skills, for freshly trained officer pilots from Cranwell and NCO pilots from the FTSs would arrive at the end of the summer. Initially they would be given dual-instruction by their Flight Commander in the station's Moth, Siskin or (from 1932 onwards) Bulldog TM, and then be detailed to aerobatics, cross-country dusk or night flying exercises. From February until April there would be flight formation exercises, in which the Flight Commander would endeavour to co-ordinate their skills into that of a whole entity. Finally from April to the end of the summer months would come the time for squadron training. This involved a series of training events which regularly included Affiliation Exercises, the Hendon Air Display, ADGB Exercises and the traditional fortnight at Sutton Bridge for air firing practice. For 23(F) in 1932 this meant a fortnight at Upper Heyford affiliating with 18(B) Squadron and where the Bulldog and Demon fighters were scrambled to intercept and carry out camera-gun attacks on the Hart bombers. In the June four of the Demons participated in the Hendon event, making mock dog-fights with Tangmere's Furies.

Finally came the ADGB exercises, in which 23(F)'s fighters' task was to intercept and 'destroy' the enemy Hinaidi bombers of 10(B) Squadron which were flying from Boscombe Down in simulated daylight raids on the capital. Night interceptions were also carried out later in the year in co-operation with the 51st and 52nd Anti-

Aircraft Brigades of the Royal Artillery, and the 26th AA Battalion of the Royal Engineers, all of which were stationed at Chelsea. This entailed 23(F)'s fighters flying at 6,000 ft over the capital on a triangular course, taking in Marble Arch, Hammersmith Bridge and Tower Bridge, whilst the guns and searchlights sought to track them. Night interceptions between fighters and bombers would mean the attacking aircraft flying in reasonably close to the enemy and then firing a Very light flare to confirm the 'kill'. Primitive as the exercise might sound in retrospect, they did pave the way for the aerial defence of London and other major cities during the *Luftwaffe's* night bombing campaign in the early 1940s.

The first of the Bulldog IIAs of 32(F) Squadron, with their blue broken-striped markings along the fuselage sides and top mainplane, began to arrive at RAF Kenley in October 1930 and by 3 January 1931 the squadron was completely re-equipped with its new fighters. They were to replace the obsolescent Siskin IIIAs which were at that time under the command of Squadron Leader B. E. Baker, DSO, MC. Although junior in length of service to their 23(F) Kenley companions by some four months, 32(F) had similarly been formed, during the early part of World War 1, in response to the national outcry over the massacre of RFC pilots and their aircraft by Germany's Fokker *Eindeckers*. After a working up period at Netheravon it was moved to France where it saw action when equipped with the DH2, DH5 and finally the SE5a. Disbanded at Croydon on 29 December 1919, it was not re-formed until 1 April 1923 at Kenley, where it was successively issued with Snipes, Grebes, Gamecocks and Siskins.

Very little is recorded in the squadron's ORB of its time at Kenley during the early Bulldog period apart from the list of officers and NCO pilots. The squadron did, however, visit Upper Heyford on 26 March 1931 for the annual map reading competition of the Sir Philip Sassoon trophy where it tied for first place with 23(F) and 29(F) Squadron from North Weald.

The reconstruction of Kenley airfield was planned to commence in the autumn of 1932, which meant that both of the Kenley fighter squadrons were to be relocated at the Kent airfield of Biggin Hill, or as it was more commonly known 'Biggin on the Bump'. Originally sought in 1916 as a new site for the RFC's Wireless Testing Park unit who were anxious to vacate the fog-prone and often waterlogged airfield of Joyce Green, the airfield was situated on top of the North Downs overlooking the Weald of Kent. There is a large valley to the west of the airfield and it is recorded

that one mischievous pupil, making his first solo in a 504, used it to disappear from the view of his anxious instructor, turning east climbing over the Downs to land safely from the other side of the aerodrome. By the time he had landed a party had gone out to look for the wreckage and were puzzled by not being able to find any trace of him!

Although Biggin was chosen more for its receptivity to radio signals than for its strategic position, it was well placed for the interception of enemy aircraft attacking the capital. The Kent airfield had itself been the object of considerable reconstruction during the 1929-1932 period, and by the time the Bulldogs and Demons arrived on 17 and 21 September respectively the builders had not long since departed. Such was the financial stringency of those days that the original order for new furnishings were overruled by the Air Ministry and the old equipment including furniture, bedding, linen, cutlery, etc, was transported across from Kenley. The move was closely watched and little time was given to the station's 300 RAF residents to settle in before the customary visit and inspection of a new station took place, with high ranking officers from the HQ of ADGB arriving in the October.

By April 1933 the Bulldogs of 23(F) had been phased out, their use in this squadron being the briefest of any of the ten squadrons so equipped. The faster Demons, Gauntlets and Gladiators were to eventually replace all of the Bulldogs within the Fighter Stations but 32(F) was to continue with their use until July 1936. Of the few remaining ARCs (Form 1180) on 32(F) Squadron during the period of Bulldog, it appears that close formation flying and the fitment of brakes were causing some problems. Two minor mid-air collisions were to occur over the airfield, one involving Flight Lieutenant Barrow in *K2147* and Sergeant Pilot Rumble in *K1623* on 25 September 1933, and another on 31 March 1936 involving Sergeant Pilot Adams in *K2963* and a pilot (name indecipherable) in *K2493*. In neither case does it appear that any of the four aircraft were prevented from making a safe landing, although there is no doubt that there were a few ashen faces and grey hairs at the time. Two aircraft, *K2155* and *K1619*, were written off during landing accidents in the early part of 1936, when their pilots made over-zealous application of the brakes, but with neither of the men being injured.

Quite naturally the spirit of healthy rivalry and competition between the two squadrons was heightened when 23(F) was fully equipped with Demons. However, the desire for supremacy was not confined solely to activities in the air, for during the summer of 1934 the ground crews at Biggin Hill stripped and reassembled various components from their Bulldogs and Demons against the stop-watch; meanwhile MT personnel were engaged in convoy exercises between the stations in Fighting Area. The RAF might well admit to being a small fighting force but it was determined to be an efficient one. Doubts in the wisdom of pacifist policies were beginning to be voiced early in 1934, and by June it had been decided that home squadrons would be increased from 52 to 75 squadrons. This expansion of the RAF was given further impetus by Italy's incursion into Abyssinia in 1935, as well as by Hitler's harangues in Germany before swastika-carrying stormtroopers demanding *lebensraum* in Europe.

The last appearance in public of 32(F)'s Bulldogs was to be on 27 June 1936, when the nine aircraft of the squadron carried out a low flying attack at the Hendon Air Display. A few days later they were to fly from the Kent airfield for the last time, for by July they had been replaced by the Gloster Gauntlet IIs.

* * *

No 41(F) Squadron was formed on 14 July 1916 at Gosport, and after a three-month period of training was sent to France equipped with the Royal Aircraft Factory's FE8 pusher scout biplane. Even from the time of its arrival on the Somme, in 1916, the FE8 was considered to be an outdated design and consequently was relegated to ground-attack duties. In spite of the remaining FE8 squadrons being re-equipped with more modern aircraft in the early part of 1917, 41(F) continued to use the type until they were replaced by DH5s in July of that year. Again the squadron was to be put into a ground strafing role, this time because of the new fighter's relatively poor performance at high altitude. By November the DH5s had been withdrawn in favour of the SE5a, and it was with this successful fighter that the squadron eventually scored daily victories in 1918 during the final air battles of the war. After the Armistice the unit returned to England and was finally disbanded at Croydon on 31 December 1919.

The squadron was to be re-formed on 1 April 1923 at Northolt aerodrome some six miles south-west of Hendon. It was to be the home of 41(F) for the next twelve years, during which time it was successively equipped with Sopwith Snipes and Siskins before finally being supplied with Bulldogs

in October 1931. The first of the squadron's red striped Bulldogs flew across the west London suburbs from the Bristol factory to land at Northolt on 19 October, and by 30 November 41(F) was fully equipped with its new fighters.

The squadron's first CO at the time of Bulldog was Squadron Leader (later to become Air Vice-Marshal) S. F. Vincent, AFC, a former First World War pilot. J. W. Taylor in his superb book *CFS – Birthplace of Air Power* relates an amusing incident involving Vincent and Lieutenant Colonel Robert Smith-Barry, founder of Gosport's School of Special Flying. Smith-Barry was very conscious of the need to quickly restore the confidence and morale of any of his pupils who might become involved in an air accident whilst at Gosport. One such recipient of his attention was the young Captain Vincent, whose Avro 504 had broken up in the air with the result that he lay unconscious for four days in hospital, with his anxious parents by his bedside. Smith-Barry's cheerful friendliness and optimism for the young pilot's recovery encouraged the parents, especially when he remarked, 'Let me know of anything he wants — anything that the hospital says he mustn't have — and I'll get it for him at once'. Some seven months later when Vincent was up and about, he went to see 'SB' who greeted him with the words 'You must want to fly again — take any aeroplane you like and go and enjoy yourself'. Needless to say Vincent chose an Avro, similar to the one he had crashed earlier, and it was not long before he was in the air regaining his confidence.

Whilst the Bulldog provided excellent all round visibility for a pilot when once in the air, its lack of forward visibility when taxying was, like so many aircraft of its time, inclined to be a source of danger. There was a real need for a member of the ground staff positioned at each wingtip when taxying, particularly before the advent of wheel brakes and when taxying near to other aircraft. This aspect was to be highlighted at Northolt on 10 June 1932, when 41(F)'s Sergeant Pilot B. J. Marsden was taxying *K2178* quite close to other stationary Bulldogs after a practice flight for the Hendon display; his aircraft swung around and hit *K2182* causing considerable damage to it.

June was a busy time for air displays and 1932 was no exception, for on the 17th 'A' Flight flew to Andover where it took part in a mock attack on an RAF Sidestrand bomber. The following week saw the squadron represented at Hendon by Flight Sergeant Pilot Boucher performing aerobatics. Four of the pilots stationed at Northolt at this time were to leave their imprint on history. The station commander, Wing Commander Keith Park (later

Air Marshal), was eventually to command brilliantly the vital 11 Group in the Battle of Britain, whilst fellow New Zealander Pilot Officer T. G. Lovell-Gregg was to lead 87 Squadron's Hurricanes from Exeter in the same battle. Pilot Officer Donald Finlay will long be remembered not only for the part he played in Britain's defence during that summer of 1940, but also for his athletic records. In 1936 he set up not only the British and English Native record of 14.6 seconds for the 120-yd hurdle event at the AAA in White City, but he also represented his country in that year's Olympics. It was in Berlin in the 110 metres hurdles that he split the American pair Towns and Pollard, being narrowly beaten into second place by gold medallist Forrest Towns with a time of 14.2 seconds.

Finlay joined the squadron at Northolt in the August of 1933 and soon settled into the routine of training as a fighter pilot. Flying over the London conurbation, particularly in the winter, presented its own peculiar hazards for it was not the smoke-free zone that it is today. Open coal fires from houses and factories all contributed to the annual 'peasouper' fogs that were a regular feature of pre-war London and made cross-country navigation exercises quite difficult. Added to the pollution hazard were the icing problems that Bulldog had experienced with their fuel tank vent pipes, particularly when engaged on 'Battle Climbs' over the capital. Small wonder that on 2 November 1933, whilst on a cross country flight across the south of London, Donald Finlay had the dubious honour of landing his Bulldog on Streatham Common. No doubt the incident produced its share of mirth and leg-pulling in the Officers' Mess during that evening, but this was as nothing compared to the hilarity that greeted the arrival of

19(F)'s Bulldogs performing their "Prince of Wales feather" over Hendon in 1934 *(RAF Museum)*.

The Royal Review at Mildenhall on 6 July 1935 with Hawker Furies in front rank and Bulldogs in second *(MoD)*.

the London evening newspapers some four weeks later. A formation of 41(F)'s Bulldogs were over the capital on 11 December, with ground mist and fog below them, when suddenly Pilot Officer F. G. L. Smith's aircraft experienced engine failure. Anxious colleagues watched as the silent Bulldog descended into the murk below them. With little time to spare the young pilot looked for a suitable open space, saw what appeared to be a large park, and commendably put the Bulldog down in a perfect three-pointer without hurting any member of the public. One wonders exactly how Smith was greeted in the middle of Hyde Park, but it certainly gave Londoners a close up view of the RAF's new fighter!

The country's early warning system for the tracking of possible incoming enemy aircraft before the advent of RDF, was, in 1933, limited to the use of acoustical devices known as sound locators. They took the form of large circular concrete 'mirrors', of some twenty feet in diameter, strategically placed around the country which, with a range of ten to twenty miles, were used in an attempt to track an aircraft's speed, height and direction. The research for these devices was controlled by the Acoustical Section of the Royal Engineers, and plans were made for a whole system

of circular and strip locators around the south coast but the whole idea was overtaken by the implementation of RDF. During the later part of October 1933, however, 41(F)'s pilots were detailed to the tedium of flying their Bulldogs on a pre-set course around the capital, over a three-day period, so that the 1st AA Brigade could pick up their sound 'signatures'.

The squadron's ORB for 1934, the last year in which 41(F)'s Bulldogs were to be operational, has few entries; sadly it records the death of Sergeant Pilot F. Baker, who was killed on 18 May when his aircraft dived into a towed flag target whilst carrying out an air firing practice. Although the Bulldogs were to be phased out in July and August, it was thought worthwhile to update the aircraft, and, during the period 11 June to 17 July, certain of the fighters were flown back to Filton for the fitting of tailwheels and revised tailfins. The last entry before the arrival of the Hawker Demon two-seat fighters reads, somewhat humorously, *17.7.1934 – Demonstration to the South Bucks Mother's Union.*

* * *

No 29(F) Squadron was formed at Gosport, on 7 November 1915, from a surplus of 23(F) Squadron's personnel and flew to France in March 1916 equipped with DH2 pusher scouts. A small number of FE8s were added from May, the squadron being the first to be chosen to operate this particular aircraft, and they flew alongside the DH2s in offensive patrols over the Somme during the summer of that year. Both types of aircraft were in constant use right up until March 1917 when they were replaced by Nieuports which were kept in operational use, mainly in a ground strafing role, including dangerous sorties against usually well-defended enemy observation balloons, until the Spring of 1918. The squadron was then equipped with the SE5a, and used this type until the Armistice by which time they had destroyed a total of more than 200 enemy aircraft.

Re-formed at Duxford on 1 April 1924, the squadron was equipped successively with Snipes and Grebes, whereupon in April 1928 it moved with its Siskins to join 56(F) Squadron, similarly equipped and already resident at North Weald. By 29 June 1932 the Siskins of 29(F) had been completely phased out in favour of the newly arrived Bulldog IIAs, whilst their companions of 56(F) continued with their ageing fighters for a further three months. The first public appearance of the red XX marked Bulldogs of 29(F), as recorded within the pages of its ORB, was to be on 1 July 1933 when the squadron flew north to RAF Sealand, near Chester. It was to be from this station that they were to act as an escort for the Secretary of State for Air, the Marquess of Londonderry, KG, MVO, when he opened Speke aerodrome nearby. Upon their return to their Essex base and during the rest of that month each pilot averaged some 31 hours flying time, with 2.5 hours of that period in night exercises.

One prominent landmark during night exercises, apart from the nearby town of Epping to the south-west, was the Marconi Wireless Station's radio masts to the east, near Chelmsford, which were lit up at night. It is worth noting that Bulldog was equipped with magnesium Holt flares which could be operated electrically from the cockpit in case of a forced landing at night. Allen Wheeler, in his autobiography *Flying between the Wars*, recalls that once fired they burned for approximately three minutes and would have been effective in providing illumination if forced to land in a field at night. However, some pilots held the view that such a landing would be dangerous enough in itself, without the additional hazard of carrying a bonfire under each wingtip!

The only fire involving a Bulldog at North

Weald was totally unconnected with night flying, and occurred on 25 April 1933 when *K2215* caught fire whilst being refuelled. Details on the ARC are brief, only recording that the aircraft was damaged, which is not very surprising when one considers that the Bulldog was fabric covered.

The programme for the 1934 Hendon Air Display, which took place on 30 June, reveals that 29(F)'s Bulldogs played quite a prominent role in two of that year's events. The first of the two commenced at 14:00 with Event E, 'Air Gunnery Training', in which the method by which pilots were trained in firing against an aerial target was demonstrated. A Fairey Gordon, from No 3 Armament Training Camp, Sutton Bridge, was flown across the airfield towing a drogue and then the three Bulldogs flown by Flight Lieutenant S. L. Blunt, Flying Officers R. B. Lees (later to be Air Marshal Sir Ronald) and S. Keane made a simulated attack upon it firing blank ammunition. The target was subsequently dropped and the 'hits' counted. The second Event F, 'Air Combat — Overstrand v Bulldogs', followed on with Hendon's traditional promptness at 14:10 when three of 29(F)'s fighters, flown by Flight Lieutenant J. B. Lynch, Flying Officer J. G. Bigelow and Pilot Officer R. R. Fairweather attacked the bomber. (Bigelow was to be tragically killed two months later when he crashed *K2866* whilst carrying out a low level 'attack' on troops along the Kent coast during Army Co-operation exercises.)

Two pilots on the strength of 29(F) at the time of Bulldog are worthy of particular note, Flight Lieutenant J. W. F. Merer and Australian Pilot Officer D. C. T. Bennett (later Air Vice-Marshal, CB, CBE, DSO). The former, once an Adjutant of the RAF College, Cranwell, had been responsible for the writing of the RAF's Drill Manual, whilst the latter, who is on record as having described Bulldog as 'an aircraft without vice', was to achieve fame in two spheres. Firstly, as an Imperial Airways pilot he achieved the distinction of flying the *Mercury* pick-a-back seaplane when it was launched from its mother flying boat *Maia*, whilst later his expert knowledge of astro-navigation was put to good use when he became, in 1943, the leader of Pathfinder Force.

If the pilots and ground staff of 29(F) were proud of their history, then their companion Bulldog squadron at North Weald was more so. Sergeant Pilot Leslie Holman, who was at North Weald from 1931 to 1936 and was to log almost 600 hours in the red and white chequerboard marked Bulldogs of 56(F) Squadron, recalls that such was the squadron's illustrious history — the award of

Cranwell cadet Douglas Bader in 1929 *(P. B. Lucas).*

two VCs in World War 1 — that the names of
Albert Ball and James McCudden were almost
remembered in one's morning prayers (their dinner
jackets were prominently displayed in a glass case
and proudly shown to all visitors). 56(F)
Squadron, although late on the scene in France in
April 1917, where it was to be the first RFC
squadron to be equipped with Farnborough's new
fighter the SE5, was soon to make its mark on the
air war. The squadron was disbanded at Bircham
Newton in January 1920 and, apart from a spell of
duty in the Middle East as part of Nos 80 and 208
Squadrons, was not re-formed until 1 November
1922 at Hawkinge.

As part of the RAF's new, but truncated, post-
war defence force 56(F) was equipped with Snipes
and moved to Biggin Hill in May 1923, where it
successively   received   Grebe   and   Siskin
replacements. The squadron then moved to North
Weald where it had been in residence for almost
five years when the first of the Bulldog IIAs flew in
from Henlow, piloted by the CO, Squadron Leader
G. E. Wilson, on 17 August 1932. The remainder of
the new fighters arrived in the next few days and
finally, in January 1933, a Bulldog TM two-seater
was also collected from Filton. The squadron's
ORB for 1933 records a variety of exercises carried

out including the evening of 20 April spent co-
operating with the RE's 'listeners' over Hackney
Residential School, Brentwood; three weeks at No
3 ATC Sutton Bridge for Annual Air Firing in the
period late June early July; three days from 17 to
20 July on ADGB Exercises which involved night
as well as day flying; twelve days under canvas at
Mount Batten on Affiliation Exercises with No 204
(Flying Boat) Squadron early in October; and
finally a visit from the AOC of ADGB, Air
Marshal Sir Robert Brooke-Popham, KCB, CMG,
DSO, AFC, on 29 November.

By the mid-1930s Britain's scientists had come to
the conclusion that the only future for a viable D/F
system lay with the use of radio rather than sound
waves. Flight Lieutenant E. M. Grundy (later to
become Air Marshal Sir Edouard, KBE, OBE, CB)
was stationed at North Weald from 1933-36 and
recalls the part that the Bristol Bulldog fighter
played in the development of such a system.

'I had been a pilot in 56 Squadron back in
1928-29 when they were equipped with Siskins;
I left on posting to HMS *Hermes* in the Far East
(Flycatchers) whence I returned to endure the
Long Signals Course at Cranwell in 1932-1933.
At the end of the course I went to Biggin Hill,
where we flew Wapitis in an effort to develop a
"sound locator" which was all the rage before
RDF (later radar) sunk it without trace.
Subsequently I was transferred, as Station
Signals Officer, to the brand new station at
North Weald, occupied by 56 and 29 Squadrons
and equipped with Bulldogs. This was just at
the beginning of the metamorphosis of Fighting
Area ADGB into what finally became Fighter
Command. My function was to oversee the
local North Weald installation of the Sector
plotting and communications system, the
equipment of the Bulldogs of 56 and 29
Squadrons with the new TR9 HF airborne
"voice" wireless sets, and the siting and
installation of our sector's share of the HF D/F
stations upon which we hoped to depend for
vectoring. For the airborne side of this work I
used the Bulldogs of 56 Squadron.

'In due course we got all this worked up to the
point where our Sector exercises, tied into 11
Group, became what, with hindsight, were
recognisable as the primitive beginnings of the
ultimate Fighter Command defence system. I
say primitive because radar was missing, and we
depended upon the Observer Corps and our
eyeballs for final interception — I was engaged
on this job from early 1935 to mid-1937.

'All this meant that the Bulldog was one of
the first types of aircraft specifically and

deliberately equipped, and ground supported, with a communication system which ultimately became the Command/Group control system of Fighter Command for the Battle of Britain. Furthermore, although in complete ignorance of what we were actually doing, we made many flights over Suffolk and Norfolk, pinpointing ourselves with as much accuracy as possible, for the benefit of what later transpired to have been the machinations of a chap named Watson Watt.'

Sir Edouard Grundy continues with his impressions of Bulldog itself:

'It was a heavy, rugged, aircraft which, during its comparatively short life, became heavier and heavier as successive modifications were made and additional equipment fitted. It was therefore not nearly as joyful to fly as its generic predecessor the Grebe, but it was much more useful. It was stable in flight and although mechanically noisy, not too electrically noisy for the limited capabilities of the TR9.'

Graham Wallace in his well researched book *RAF Biggin Hill* records that the Air Ministry had, by 1934, established a committee with H. T. Tizard as its chairman, in order to explore every available avenue of aircraft detection. Within a few months R. Watson Watt had demonstrated the practicability of depicting the reflections of radio waves from a flying aircraft on a cathode ray tube. And so the beginnings of a British radar system started to take shape; initially with the building of Chain Home stations (known as Air Ministry Experimental Stations Type I) at Bawdsey, Canewdon and Dover in 1937, and subsequently with a network of similar stations around the country by 1940.

Pilot Officer W. 'Eddie' Carr (later to become Group Captain Glennie-Carr) arrived at 56(F) North Weald in 1935 and recalls his initial impressions of the aeroplane and of the men who flew it:

'I did my first night flying in a Bulldog and was much alarmed by the "cherry-red" exhaust collector ring which no one had warned me about.

'We did some trials of a carburettor icing-up warning device, whereby a red light came on to tell you that the air-intake was full of ice, but as, by this time, your engine had stopped it seemed rather superfluous.

'I well remember I. C. "Blondie" Bird who was later posted to Uxbridge, in January 1936, in order to attend a course in Russian at Kings College, London; also on the squadron at the same time was Arthur Donaldson, the youngest

of the three famous Donaldson brothers.* M. V. Gibbon was a great charmer who always had "the" most attractive girl-friends and a very pretty Riley 9 — perhaps there was some connection! A. W. Sandeman was a Flight Commander who resigned his commission in September 1935 to become a priest, whilst Sergeant Wilcox I remember with affection for looking after me when I arrived in the squadron as the "Junior Bog-rat" and saving me from being sent to fetch "long stands" and "oxometers", etc.

'Guy Menzies (see chapter 8) achieved some fame by falling out of the window of his upstairs room in the Mess and being found by a batman the next morning badly broken up, but he recovered and went on to Flying Boats and among other things took Haile Selassie back, after the Italians were chucked out of Abyssinia.

'I have left to the last A. E. ("Scruffy") Taylor, my Flight Commander, who was the nicest of men, a splendid leader and one from whom I learnt so much. Sadly he died young from ill-health otherwise I'm sure that he would have achieved Air Rank.'

Although 1936 was to be the final year for 56(F)'s Bulldogs, flying activity was no less hectic. February saw seven of the Squadron's aircraft, led by CO Squadron Leader C. L. Lea-Cox, fly to Hornchurch for a three-day period of Winter Air Exercises, whilst in April a week was spent in Affiliation Exercises with No 4 Army Co-Operation Squadron at Farnborough.

Squadron successes, both in the Sassoon Map Reading and Flight Attack competitions, were achieved when visiting Tangmere and Hornchurch in April and Northolt in May, and where second place was gained in each of the events. A two-night exercise, in co-operation with the 26th and 27th AA Battalions of the RE, was carried out in March with a total of seven hours flying being logged. By May, the first of the Gauntlet II replacements had begun to arrive at North Weald and these were to accompany the Bulldogs to Sutton Bridge on 16 May for the squadron's annual fortnight at No 3 ATC. It was whilst here, on the 23rd, that the Bulldogs of 56(F) were to be seen in public for the last time when they took part in the Empire Air Day Display.

* * *

* Teddy had served with 3(F) on Bulldogs and was, during the Battle of Britain, to command the Hurricanes of 151 Squadron. Jack was to be killed when the aircraft carrier HMS *Glorious* was sunk in June 1940 and whilst he was CO of 263 Squadron equipped with Gladiators.

No 54 Squadron was formed on 15 May 1916 and after a period of training exchanged its Farnborough BE2cs for Sopwith's new single-seat scout, the Pup, in December. Although they were the first RFC squadron to be equipped with the Kingston product, the first six had already been delivered earlier in the year to the RNAS and it was with this Service that the Pup was to achieve the distinction of being the first aircraft to land on a ship under way, when one touched down on the deck of HMS *Furious* on 2 August 1917.

The squadron arrived at St Omer on 24 December 1916, and within a few weeks flew to the Western Front, where the highly manoeuvrable Pups were soon in action, participating in balloon attacks and light bombing raids until replaced by the more powerful Camels, in December 1917. The final year of the war saw 54's Camels initially flying cover patrols for the 5th Brigade's Army Co-operation squadrons, and then during the summer in the final offensive of the war it was given the specific role of carrying out ground attacks on the retreating German army.

The squadron remained in France for a further three months after the Armistice, whereupon it returned to England and was disbanded at Yatesbury on 25 October 1919. Upon being re-formed at Hornchurch (previously known as Sutton's Farm but renamed on 1 June 1928) on 15 January 1930, under the command of Squadron Leader W. Bryant, MBE, 54(F) was allocated Bulldogs. There was, however, some delay in delivering the new fighters because of lubrication problems that were being experienced with the Jupiter VIIF engines, and as a temporary measure the squadron was equipped with Siskin IIIAs. The first of the Bulldog IIAs, complete with its yellow bar markings along the side of the fuselage and upper mainplane (this was changed to a red bar, broken by an oblique white stripe on the Gauntlet replacements in August 1936), arrived at Hornchurch on 8 April 1930 and by 18 October the squadron was completely re-equipped.

The first 54(F) Bulldog to be seen in public was *K1604* when it was flown by Pilot Officer Ken Knocker to Croydon Airport, on 25 October 1930, for exhibition to the Imperial Premiers during their visit to London for the Commonwealth Conference.

This pilot was to be promoted to the rank of Flying Officer by the end of the year and subsequently appointed Squadron Adjutant, before being posted to No 3 FTS as an instructor during 1931. Jeffrey Quill recalls that he was to have the privilege of being instructed by Knocker at Grantham during his senior term as a pupil

pilot, and that sadly he was to be killed in 1942 whilst serving with Bomber Command.

The squadron's ORB records that night flying exercises with Bulldogs commenced on 10 November 1930 and that by the following May eleven officer and NCO pilots, including the CO, had qualified. These exercises included, in the month of April, co-operation with the Anti-Aircraft and Searchlight batteries of Romford, Upminster, Brentwood, Ingatestone, Stanford-le-Hope, Gravesend and Chatham, during which the Bulldogs would fly a pre-arranged course over an area within the batteries' sector. Allen Wheeler recalls that when similarly engaged on such exercises in the North London area, pilots were instructed that if they were embarrassed by the concentration of searchlights, to fire a signal cartridge from their Very pistol whereupon the beams would move away. When the searchlight crews were satisfied that the evening's work had been worthwhile and that they were ready to conclude the exercise, they would wave their beams about and the pilot would then, with his navigation lamps switched on, put his aircraft into a loop to signal 'message understood'. During the time of these exercises, in the month of February, modifications were carried out on 54(F)'s Bulldogs

Flying Officer John Grandy of 54(F) Squadron, Hornchurch *(Sir John Grandy).*

which included the welcome addition of experimental cockpit heating to four of the fighters, as well as the fitting of a special type of 4.5-in ring sight to five other aircraft.

Air displays not only provided valuable training for the air crews of ADGB during the inter-war years, but they also raised money for RAF charities and at the same time enabled the taxpayer to see tangible evidence of exactly how some of his hard-earned income was being used. It meant that a considerable portion of the squadron's time was spent, during the early months of the year, practising for either the Hendon or Andover displays, and for 54(F) in 1931 it was to be the latter venue. On 23 April four of the Bulldogs, piloted by the CO and Flight Commanders Flight Lieutenant F. W. Moxham and Flying Officers C. M. D. Chambers and N. C. Singer, flew from Hornchurch to Upavon where they joined with their counterparts from Nos 3 and 17(F) in a preliminary practice for the June event. Five weeks later the whole of 54(F) Squadron moved to Upavon, to spend three weeks of intensive formation flying exercises with the two home squadrons. Such a move meant a busy time of preparation by the ground staff beforehand, with the loading of spare engines, airframe parts, fitters' toolkits and equipment on to the trailers, which would then eventually be towed by the Leyland three-tonners fully laden with the squadron members. On the day of departure the convoy of RAF vehicles would wend its way through the busy streets of East London, through the City and out on to the Great West Road — quite a journey in those days, especially in solid-tyred vehicles. The joint exercise culminated in the Andover Air Display, on Friday 19 June, when the 27 Bulldogs of the three squadrons combined for a formation flypast, whilst No 3(F) carried out Air Drill practice later in the day.

Formation flying, or more particularly formation aerobatics, requires a high degree of flying ability and, depending upon how tightly the formation is performing, has its own particular hazards. Apart from human error there is always the possibility of an unexpected encounter with turbulent air which can bring about a disastrous situation. One such incident did occur in 54(F) on 23 November 1933 — fortunately it did have a happy ending as well as its humorous aspects. Flying Officer John Grandy (later to become Marshal of the Royal Air Force Sir John, GCB, KBE, DSO) recalls the event clearly:

'Pilot Officers Hill Harkness, Ian Mackay and I agreed to meet up and do some formation loops, but because we were not all three in the same Flight this was "unauthorised" formation aerobatics and frowned upon. I was leading a normal formation of three in *K1660*, above ten/tenths cloud cover, and we had performed a few manoeuvres including loops during the last of which, just as we neared going over the top, Mackay (no 3 on my left) collided with me; Harkness pulled away clear. I remember a loud bang, lots of bits of fabric floating about, and then seeing the top wing of Mackay's Bulldog appearing to come off as he disappeared into the cloud cover.

'My port aileron looked a mess, the stick was very heavy fore and aft, almost solid, but it was hard to see what had gone wrong with my tail (just as well as it turned out!) so I tried a dummy landing on the cloud tops. This seemed OK with judicious use of the trimming wheel so, not at all relishing the idea of a bale out, I gingerly started my descent. On emerging through the cloud base somewhere over the Thames Docks' area, to the east of Hornchurch, my faithful and much loved *K1660* continued descending — I could not get her to hold level flight. This was disconcerting, but after some experimenting I discovered to my relief that with a little more throttle and trim juggling I was able to regain a reasonable amount of control and stop the descent. I set course for Hornchurch.

'I made a long straight "rumble" approach with minimum turns and managed to get *K1660* safely on to the ground first time and taxy in; I was pretty certain that it had to be first time "or else", so although I had never heard of the word in those days the adrenalin must have been working pretty hard!

'When I did see the tailplane, or what was left of it, I was horrified for it had suffered quite considerable damage and very little of its control surfaces remained. If I had been able to see this from the cockpit then I believe that any doubts I had about baling out would have rapidly disappeared.

'So that was it. Ian Mackay did bale, no alternative, and landed safely in, I think, a garden, his aircraft and mainplane crashing in open country.

'To round off the story, I had of course some explaining to do. After a quick word with my Flight Commander, Flight Lieutenant St. J. Arbuthnott, a delightful chap who was very relaxed, even amused about the whole thing except that we were a bit worried about Mackay, not by then having heard word from him, I duly presented myself to the CO, Squadron Leader Ivor M. Rodney, who was very busy in the squadron HQ office that morning.

' "Yes Grandy, you can see I'm very busy, what is it?"

' "I'm afraid P/O Mackay and I have had a bit of a collision Sir."

' "Really? — not too much damage to the cars I hope?"

' "No Sir, I mean — well, you see Sir, this was in the air."

' "Mmmmm *WHAT*? Where is Mackay?"

' "I, er, don't know Sir."

' "What do you mean, *you don't know?*"

' "Well, er, when I last saw him, Sir, he was going in to a cloud without his top wing."

'Squadron Leader Rodney was *very* angry.

'The Court of Inquiry, chaired by Squadron Leader "Bunty" Frew, OC 111(F) Squadron, an excellent and most understanding officer, established that we should not have been flying as we were [unauthorised] and we got a rocket for that, but they never did ascertain exactly why we collided. We were pretty proud of how close we flew in those days; not admitted at the time of course but now, over fifty years later, I rather suspect this *may* have had something to do with it.

'Lastly, Cyril Uwins, Chief Test Pilot of the Bristol Aeroplane Co, was delighted at this fortuitous demonstration of how strong the Bulldog was, how well it could stand up to damage; when the fuss had died down he gave me a super Board Room lunch with the Directors and a day out at the Filton works.'

It was the aim of every squadron within the Fighting Area of ADGB to have the honour of appearing during the summer time at Hendon, the most prestigious venue for air displays, and 54(F) as a newly re-formed squadron was no exception. Their turn came in 1933, and then in 1934 when they participated in the 'Set Piece', an event which formed the climax of the display and which normally involved the bombing of 'enemy warships', 'stations' or 'villages'. For the finale during the hot Saturday afternoon sunshine of the 1934 event, 54(F)'s Bulldogs were given a paint disguise of white tipped wings and wide white bands around their fuselages when, as the defending force, they were required to prevent the attack on the 'magazine'. Unfortunately, just prior to this part in the proceedings there was to be a fatal accident, marring what would otherwise have been a day of perfect enjoyment for all concerned. Sir John Grandy recalls his impressions of that afternoon:

'We flew in the "Set Piece" and my log book shows a number of rehearsals. Nothing else remembered other than just before we were about to climb into our cockpits for our show a Hawker Hart was making I think, a genuine forced landing when it crashed in the middle of the aerodrome and was a flamer.

'Squadron Leader G. D. Daly, our CO and formation leader, called us all together and said, very forcefully, something to the effect that . . . "if any of you have an engine failure DON'T put it down here, anywhere else OK but NOT Hendon — plenty of open fields around." We then started up and, all eyes glued to oil pressure gauges, had to taxy past the smoking wreck (grim) for a squadron take-off.'

Whilst Hendon was a prize event, lesser displays local to RAF Hornchurch were not neglected. On 24 September 1932, three Bulldogs from 54(F) together with five Westland Wapitis (also Jupiter-powered) of 600(B), acted as an escort to the Lord Mayor's Spartan Cruiser aircraft as it arrived at Maylands aerodrome, Romford, for the Essex Air Pageant. The event had been master-minded by E. H. Hillman in order to celebrate the expansion of his airline and its aerodrome. Hillman had entered the airline business after he had scored a remarkable success with his private coaches which had broken the monopoly of LPTB's red bus service by providing a faster, cheaper alternative for London's commuters.

Two final entries in the squadron's ORB record the 1935 Affiliation Exercises and the 1936 Hendon Air Display. The former took place during the period 6-21 May when the Bulldogs flew to Roborough, Devon, for joint exercises with 204 (FB) Squadron, and where Flight and Squadron attacks were carried out on the Southampton flying boats over the sea. One can only conjecture just how long a Bulldog would have floated before sinking if forced to make a sea ditching — presumably the risks involved were minimised by the 'enemy's' ability to effect an immediate sea rescue. Early in 1936 Acting/Pilot Officer R. C. Love (later Group Captain, DSO, DFC) joined 54(F) and recalls his first impressions of the Squadron and his part in the Hendon event:

'When I joined 54 Squadron from Flying Training School the squadron was commanded by Flight Lieutenant J. Rhys-Jones . . . Joining on the same day were Acting/Pilot Officers G. Feeny, R. Milward and Flying Officer D. O. Finlay. On arrival we were immediately involved in converting to the Bulldog before the squadron moved to Sutton Bridge, Lincs, for two weeks annual armament training at the Holbeach ranges.

Investigators examine the wreckage of a Bulldog Mark IIA, *K2487*, from No 3(F) Squadron, RAF Kenley 1934 *(RAF Museum)*.

'On return to Hornchurch we were then detailed to practice for the 1936 RAF Display at Hendon. Our item was formation flying by a "V" of five aircraft which ended in a formation loop trailing coloured smoke . . . I well remember we were all covered in rather nasty dyes and there was some difficulty in finding a solvent to clean ourselves.

'Soon after the Hendon display the squadron closed down for four weeks' leave and on return we were busy flying the Bulldogs to the storage unit at Waddington and collecting our new Gauntlets from Gloucester.'

*   *   *

No 111 Squadron, or 'Treble One' as it was (and still is) affectionately known, was formed on 1 August 1917 from a nucleus Flight of No 14 Squadron's personnel at Deir-el-Belah in Palestine. Initially the squadron was equipped with a variety of scout aircraft including Bristol's Scout,

Monoplane M1b, and Brisfit F2B; DH2, Vickers FB19 and Nieuport, but it was to eventually score its major successes with the SE5a which it used in low-level strafing and bombing attacks during the defeat of the Turkish 7th and 8th Armies in the summer of 1918. These victories were to be immortalised in the squadron's crest when it was devised in 1932, for not only does it depict the gold Cross of Jerusalem behind which lies the two red swords in Saltire of the City of London, but it also carries three black notched seaux; these three swords bear allusion to the defeat of the Turkish Armies as well as to the arms borne on the crest of the County of Essex. With the cessation of hostilities 111 withdrew to Kantara in Egypt, until recalled to Ramleh in February 1919 where, equipped with Bristol F2Bs, it carried out security patrol duties in Palestine until it was disbanded there on 1 February 1920.

'Treble One' was re-formed at Duxford on 1 October 1923, being successively equipped with Snipes, Grebes, Siskin IIIs and IIIAs, with which it moved to Sutton's Farm in April 1928 (subsequently to be renamed Hornchurch a few weeks later). It was an aerodrome which, owing to its close proximity to low-lying marshland around the Thames, was notorious for its fogs during the winter months — squadron ORB records that in December 1929 the airfield was fog-bound for 22 days during the month.

The first new black-striped Bulldog allocated to 111(F) flew into Hornchurch from Filton on 20 January 1931, and within a few weeks the squadron was completely equipped with the type, whilst its Siskin IIIAs were re-allocated to 19(F) at Duxford. A busy programme of familiarisation ensued straight away with R/T tests in February, whilst throughout March (during which time 407 flying hours were logged — a squadron record), all pilots completed a short course in the dropping of $8\frac{1}{2}$ lb practice bombs. Such practice was not restricted to the annual visits to the Sutton Bridge or Lydd ranges but was also carried out on the home station. Every aerodrome had its own 200-yd diameter landing circle which was used not only for simulated forced-landings but also for bombing exercises. Within the circle was painted a Bisley type target having the usual two concentric rings and a bullseye, with scoring of five for a bull, four for an inner, three for a magpie and two for an outer. The Bulldog would approach in a shallow dive from 1,000 ft and, without the use of any bombsight, the pilot would release his bombs singly or in a salvo. Meanwhile an armourer would be positioned at a respectable distance away, but sufficiently near enough to record the score, which meant an anxious eye upon the aircraft up until the point of release, whereupon he would mark the position of the hits upon a simulated target drawn upon his score pad. The type of bomb that could have been used in a real live situation — the 20 lb Cooper HE anti-personnel bomb — were rarely, or if ever, dropped, except on the permanent armament ranges.

On 26 May the squadron flew to Andover for Affiliation Exercises with the Sidestrand bomber crews of 101(B) Squadron and here, for one part of the exercises, 111(F)'s pilots flew as air gunners in order to gain experience in the defender's position. It no doubt helped to imbue the young pilots from 111(F) with a certain sympathy for the Sidestrand's rear gunners, as they were dived upon, at 200 mph plus, by a screaming Bulldog, piloted by a budding McCudden or Ball.

July saw the squadron participating in the ADGB Air Exercises where the Bulldogs were involved in sound location practice as well as co-operation with the ground defence's searchlights, in order to attack 9 and 10(B)'s bombers. Evaluation trials of various pieces of new equipment were conducted by 111(F) throughout

the year and included a new type of reflector sight successfully used at Sutton Bridge; three types of oxygen masks with integral R/T microphone; recently developed Very cartridges; use of portable identification beacons; special flying helmets; as well as the testing of downward recognition lamps during October and November.

'Treble One' was invited to participate in the 'Set Piece' of the 1932 Hendon Air Display and during practice for the event at Upavon in May, managed to have the nine Bulldogs into the air, from call to scramble, within fourteen seconds. These early beginnings in public air displays were to foreshadow the squadron's role on the international aerobatic scene, where as the crack squadron of RAF's Fighter Command and flying Hawker Hunters in the later 1950s and early '60s they were known as the 'Black Arrows'.

One notable pilot during 111(F)'s early Bulldog era at Hornchurch was Pilot Officer H. J. 'Willie' Wilson (later to become Group Captain, CBE, AFC and Bar), who had joined the squadron in 1930 after obtaining a Short Service Commission and learning to fly at No 5 FTS, Sealand. Upon termination of his commission he became a test pilot with the Blackburn Aircraft Co at Brough and subsequently filled a similar post at the RAE Farnborough, eventually becoming their CTP, in 1941, with the rank of Wing Commander. He is chiefly remembered today for the establishment of a world speed record in a Gloster Meteor, the first jet-propelled aircraft to do so, when on 7 November 1945 he, and his partner Eric Greenwood, were timed over a set course at 606.262 mph. For his services and contribution to aviation in general he was awarded the AFC and Bar, and then in 1946 the Britannia Trophy. There was, amongst RAF pilots, a well-known aphorism concerning the DFC and AFC awards, where it was said with some truth that the former was awarded for 'flying in the face of the enemy', whilst the red and white ribbon of the latter was worn as an award for 'flying in the face of providence'.

In all, three of 'Treble One's' pilots were to be killed during its Bulldog era, with two of the fatalities occurring in 1933. Flying Officer J. L. Armstrong was killed when the ill-fated R5 broke up in the air over Norton Heath on 4 January, whilst Pilot Officer J. J. Murphy was tragically lost in a flying accident over Shenfield on 29 December. The squadron was to move from Hornchurch on 12 July 1934 to join 41(F) Squadron at Northolt just as the latter was exchanging its Bulldogs for the two-seat Demons. It was from the Middlesex station that the squadron flew to Sutton Bridge in 1936 for what was to be its last fortnight's camp with Bulldogs on air firing practice. Poor visibility bothered Acting/Pilot Officer J. H. W. Radice of 'C' Flight in *K1683* on 5 May as he was returning to the ATC base from nearby Holbeach Air Firing Range, and tragically he descended through the mist, crashed and was drowned in the River Nene. Nine days later, during the period of the camp, another potentially dangerous accident, in the same area, almost claimed its fourth 111(F) victim. Acting/Pilot Officer M. S. Bosquet's Bulldog

K1672 experienced jamming of its controls and the young pilot was obliged to bale out from only 800 ft — fortunately he landed unharmed on the Holbeach ranges.

Almost as soon as the squadron returned to Northolt from the camp the Gloster Gauntlet Is were beginning to arrive, and by June the last of the Bulldogs departed, either to be re-allocated or to become instructional air frames.

Chapter 7
Foreign Bulldogs

The Directors of the Bristol Aeroplane Co were very wise in their policy of building the prototype Bulldog as a private venture, for not only did it enable them to avoid the delays inevitable with official decisions, but it also meant that they were free to sell abroad to foreign national air forces. No doubt the first prototype Bulldog's appearance in the 'New Types Park' enclosure at Hendon in 1927, as well as the second prototype's display at the Paris *Salon de l'Aéronautique* of 1928, did attract overseas customers. Two further factors were to help; firstly, the Jupiter engine was renowned for reliability and was being made under licence by the Gnôme-Rhône Co of France, as well as other licensees throughout the world, and secondly, the company was busy exhibiting its Bulldog demonstrators *G-AAHH, G-AATR* and *G-ABBB* around Europe.

Cyril Uwins made his first flight in *G-AAHH*, resplendent in its silver paint trim with dark green fuselage decking and side stripe, on 14 June 1929.

Two further short test-flights were made the next day, before he took it on its first demonstration tour to Belgium and France. He made the fifty-minute flight from Filton to Croydon airport, where he stayed overnight, before making a ninety-minute flight across the Channel to Brussels on the 16th. During the next eight days he made four demonstration flights in *G-AAHH* in Brussels and Ostende, interspersed with visits to Le Bourget and Villacoublay before returning to Filton. More demonstration flights were made at Upavon, Filton and Heston in July, before he flew the aircraft to Switzerland on 26 August. The flight to Thun was made in a total flying time of three hours ten minutes, landing at Lympne, Le Bourget and Zurich on the way. Demonstration flights were made at Thun before flying to Dubendorf for the same purpose on the 30th, whilst a final flight home, via Paris, was made on the next day.

The Belgians, or their near neighbours, must have been showing some keen interest in Bulldog

The first Japanese Bulldog, *701*, built by Nakajima, Tokyo in 1930 *(British Aerospace, Filton).*

for Uwins was to fly the second company demonstrator, the Mercury-engined *G-AATR* to Brussels on 14 January 1930, returning the next day and calling in at St Inglevert and Croydon on the way back. He was also to make five demonstration flights in Brussels on 8 and 10 February, again in the same aircraft, but without receiving any orders from that country.

A third company demonstrator, the Gnôme-Rhône Jupiter VI-engined *G-ABAC*, which was a conversion of the Mercury-engined *R1*, was destined for a European tour, but was abandoned in flight by T. W. Campbell on 4 June 1930. This aircraft only appears in Uwins' flying log on one occasion, when he flew it in the heats and final of the Bristol Derby Air Races held on 30 and 31 May.

A fourth and final demonstrator was built to replace *G-ABAC* and this was, apart from its GR-9ASB engine, the prototype of Bulldog Mark IIA; it was finished in silver, with a blue decking, and was registered on 12 June 1930 as *G-ABBB*. Only one brief demonstration tour is recorded for this aircraft, when Uwins flew it to Villacoublay on 24 April 1931 and where it remained until 7 May before returning to Filton.

The end result of all this flag waving was to be quite considerable, for Bulldog was to eventually be supplied to eight other national air forces as well as the RAF. Furthermore, apart from a strong interest shown by three further countries (Chile, Switzerland and Romania), it was to be built under licence in one country and evaluated by another.

* * *

Fedden, in a sense, paved the way for the interest that was to be shown by Japan, for a licence to build Bristol's Jupiter radial had been sold to the Nakajima Aircraft Co in Tokyo. As a consequence, an airframe, no 7341, from the first production batch of Bulldog Mark IIs, was despatched in 1929 to the company's agents, the Mitsui Co, for evaluation purposes and with the possibility of the aircraft being built under licence. Although the Japanese aircraft industry was in its infancy, a specification had been issued in 1927 by the Japanese military to their aircraft manufacturers for a fighter plane, and both Mitsubishi and Nakajima had responded.

The airframe was fitted with a Jupiter-Nakajima engine and successfully flown in Japan, which prompted their government to request assistance from Filton to build their own Bulldogs under licence. Obviously their aircraft industry was

The second Japanese Bulldog, *702*, fitted with wheel spats and which achieved a maximum speed of 196mph *(British Aerospace, Filton).*

anxious to catch up with western technology, and they welcomed Bristol's offer to send aircraft designer Leslie Frise and draughtsman H. W. 'Micky' Dunn, to their country in March 1930. The Filton men took a complete set of Bulldog production drawings with them to Japan, their main task being to assist in their conversion to metric dimensioning and tolerancing. The Japanese at that time were not particularly innovative, but they were absolutely meticulous and accurate in their production methods and quality control — early warning of things to come in their motor industry!

The prototypes, *701* and *702*, were built — designated Japanese Single Seat Fighter (JSSF) — and finished in silver, with red sun insignias on fuselage sides as well as upper and lower wings. Both incorporated 'N' type interplane struts; four, instead of six, centre mainplane support struts; larger fuel tanks; modified undercarriage, fin and rudder; and strut-bracing on the underside of the tailplane.

The first prototype, *701*, had the nine cylinders of its Jupiter-Nakajima VII engine individually cowled, and carried its serial number on port and starboard sides of its top wing, as well as fuselage sides. The second prototype, *702*, was fitted with a short cord Townend cowling ring and wheel spats which gave it a remarkable resemblance to the Mark IIIA Bulldog. In this its final form *702* achieved a maximum speed of 196 mph, some 18 mph faster than its British counterpart, the Bulldog Mark IIA.

The trials of *701* and *702* were very successful, but the Japanese government did not follow them up with any orders or even a request to manufacture under licence. However, shortly afterwards, in 1931, the first all-Japanese designed fighter, the Nakajima Army Type 91 — a parasol monoplane bearing a striking resemblance to the JSSF — was built and went into production in December of that year.

* * *

The once independent Baltic state of Latvia is today a satellite of the Soviet Union, but during the inter-war years at the time of Bulldog it was a nation in its own right. Prior to World War 1 it had been ruled intermittently by Germany, Poland, Sweden and Russia, but with the armistice in November 1918 it took the chance to seize its independence.

The Latvian Air Force placed an order, the first from a foreign nation, with the Bristol Aeroplane Co for five Bulldog Mark IIs from the second production batch to be made at Filton. The aircraft, nos 7353-7357, were fitted with Gnôme-Rhône Jupiter VI engines and Oerlikon machine-guns in place of the standard Vickers armament and were finished in silver paint, apart from plan view surfaces which were a drab olive green. The aircraft were despatched to Latvia via Hull in September 1929, complete with right-handed swastika insignias, four years before Hitler came to power as Chancellor of Nazi Germany. The swastika in its left-handed form was originally an ancient symbol connected with sun worship and used in early Indian and Buddhist religions. On the Latvian Bulldogs the symbol was, as in the case of the Nazi emblem, placed with its leading arm at 45 degrees, unlike the Finnish swastika which was placed vertically. It appeared in red, on a white disc background, on the fuselage sides as well as asymmetrically on the upper and lower mainplane wing surfaces.

The aircraft were allocated to No 1 Squadron of the Latvian Air Force based at Spilve, a grass airfield quite near Riga, the capital. It was rather an unfortunate site for an airfield because that flat low-lying area of the country is prone to flooding, particularly in the springtime. The five Bulldogs were joined by a second batch of seven Mark IIs, ordered by the LAF in July 1930 and allocated to Nos 2 and 3 Squadrons; the first five (nos 7439-7443) being fitted with the G.R. Jupiter VI engine, whilst the remaining two (nos 7444-7445) were powered by GR-9ASBs. Several of the Bulldogs

A Latvian Bulldog Mark II with officials from the Latvian government *(RAF Museum)*.

Latvian Bulldog Mark II in 1929 with swastika markings being used long before Hitler came to power
(British Aerospace, Filton).

were destroyed in the pre-war years when they were involved in aerobatic accidents whilst being flown by young, over-zealous and inexperienced Latvian pilots. A small number of the Bulldogs (the numbers are uncertain) survived right up until the time of the Soviet occupation, in October 1940, when they were then placed into storage. One or two went into store in the Provodnik rubber tyre factory on the outskirts of Riga, whilst the remainder were stored, along with the remainder of the 26 Gladiators which had been supplied in 1937, in wooden sheds in the eastern part of Latvia. All the aircraft were subsequently destroyed by fire when *Luftwaffe* bombers attacked Latvia on 1 July 1941, as the Germans invaded the Soviet Union.

Very little is known of Latvian Bulldog pilots, but No 3(F) Squadron's ORB does record the visit of Captain N. Balodis and Lieutenant A. Graudinš to RAF Kenley in June 1937, where they were attached for experience on Gladiator Is, having previously attended a blind-flying course at the CFS. Captain Balodis, who had taken part in the

Latvian uprising in 1918, in order to free the country from Russian domination, was murdered by the Soviets during their occupation of 1940/41. It is believed that his body, along with those of fellow-officers, was buried in the sandhills around Riga. Lieutenant Graudinš, who also served for some considerable time on Bulldogs, was due to visit England in 1939, in order to accept Hurricanes on behalf of Latvia, but the deal was cancelled at the last moment. He was to leave Latvia during the German retreat in 1944 and eventually retired to live in Munchen-Gladbach where he died in 1984. Warrant Officer Janis Abolinš, former Latvian Bulldog pilot of No 1 Squadron, who resigned from the LAF in 1936 in order to become a civilian airline pilot flying DH Dragon Rapides, now lives in Upsalla in Sweden.

★ ★ ★

The United States began to show an interest in Bulldog as a dive bomber, being impressed by its performance and maintainability; they were particularly intrigued by Pollard's method of high tensile steel construction. Their own equivalent aircraft, the Boeing P-12 (F4B-1 in USN nomenclature) which first appeared early in 1928, lagged behind Bulldog in performance and method of construction. It used bolted square aluminium tubing for its fuselage but retained the traditional wooden construction for its wings. It was not the normal policy of the US Forces to purchase foreign military aeroplanes and Bulldog was the only British aircraft to be supplied during the inter-war years.

The Bureau of Naval Aeronautics placed an order for a Mark II in order to evaluate and test it at their Anacostia Naval Air Station, Washington DC. The aircraft (no 7358), which was without armament, was flight-tested by Uwins at Filton on 14, 21 and 22 October 1929, before being shipped to the United States on the 25th. It arrived at Anacostia on 18 November and was given the registration *A8485* before undergoing its evaluation trials. On 25 November, whilst being flown by Lieutenant George T. Cuddihy, USN, it experienced aileron flutter in a terminal velocity dive and crashed, killing the pilot. At the time of the accident *A8485* had a total flying time of 3 hours 25 minutes whilst the details of the crash are recorded as follows:

'At 10,000 ft pilot started a nearly vertical dive. At 6,000 ft pilot appeared to start pull-out, and as he did so a part of the right wing and right aileron were seen to leave the plane. The plane continued the recovery from the dive, but as the nose came up the plane slowly rolled to the right into inverted flight. This was repeated once, and then from 1,500 ft the plane dived straight into the ground.'

Lieutenant Cuddihy was particularly well known as a Schneider Trophy pilot, having formed part of the strong American Service team entries in 1925 and 1926, when he flew the Curtiss biplane racers. At the time of his death he had some 2,000 hours flying time to his credit, and a wide experience of many different types of aircraft. The accident record card does not go into any detail of the examination of the wreckage, but merely gives the 'immediate cause of accident' as a 100 per cent structural failure. It should be borne in mind that wing flutter was not an uncommon occurrence in those days, and that a terminal velocity dive would impose increased dynamic loadings, and stresses, of as much as 70 per cent above normal.

This was the first fatal accident due to aileron flutter on a Bulldog and no doubt much heart-searching took place at Filton. Modifications to wing and aileron spars were quickly incorporated after static testing of the wing structure, and a replacement aircraft (no 7398), which had been ordered in February 1930, was test-flown by Uwins on 21 March before being shipped to the United States. The aircraft was, upon arrival, registered as *A8607* and used to continue the evaluation trials at Anacostia, logging a total flying time of 32 hours 35 minutes before being struck off the USN list on 27 August 1931. A careful stress-analysis was made of Bulldog's construction, and the airframe was tested statically to destruction, the results of which were shared with the manufacturers and the RAF. In addition, recommendations were made for a wider track undercarriage and wheel brakes, to improve its ground handling.

* * *

The Royal Siamese Air Force were supplied with two Mark II Bulldogs (nos 7387-7388) in January 1930, which appear to have been based at Don Muang airfield, near Bangkok. They were purchased, together with samples of the Heinkel He 43 and Boeing 100E biplanes, for evaluation trials so that future fighter aircraft needs could be determined (the American aircraft was finally selected). The eventual fate of the two Bulldogs is unknown. Markings for these aircraft included wing roundels which were the equivalent of those used by the RAF, except that they had two additional outer bands of white and red, whilst the rudder was horizontally striped in red, white, blue, white and red.

* * *

Eight Bulldog Mark IIs (nos 7389-7396) powered by the unsupercharged Jupiter VIF engine, and carrying identity markings *A12-1* to *A12-8* arrived in Australia on board the SS *Fordsdale* in February 1930. They were assembled and allocated to an unnumbered Fighter Squadron of the RAAF, under the command of Squadron Leader J. H. Summers, at the No 1 Flying Training School at Point Cook, near Melbourne. By 30 April the first of the batch to be flown, *A12-2*, was given a short acceptance test flight by Flight Lieutenant F. R. W.

Specification	Bristol Bulldog Mk II	Boeing F4B-1	Svenska J6A Jaktfalk
Date first flown	21 Jan 1928	25 Jun 1928	1931
Engine	440 hp Jupiter VII	450 hp Pratt & Whitney Wasp Junior	500 hp Jupiter VIIF
Span	33 ft 10 in	30 ft	28 ft 10 in
Length	25 ft 2 in	20 ft 1⅜ in	24 ft 7 in
Height	8 ft 9 in	9 ft 4½	11 ft 4 in
Crew	1	1	1
Empty weight	2,281 lb	1,916 lb	Not known
Gross weight	3,490 lb	2,536 lb	3,240 lb
Fuel capacity	70 gallons	57 gallons	Not known
Armament	2 Vickers .303in	2 Browning .30in	2 Oerlikon
Maximum speed	178 mph	166.3 mph*	193 mph
Service ceiling	29,300 ft	26,400 ft	26,200 ft
*176 mph with Pratt & Whitney R-1340-C.			

Scherger (later to become Air Marshal Sir Frederick).

The brand new Bulldogs, which represented the peak of fighter development at that time, were quickly tested to the limit by the enthusiastic young RAAF pilots. On 9 May Flying Officer C. Henry flew *A12-3* into first place in the Victorian Aerial Derby at 183 mph (Summers was to win the 1931 event), whilst Pilot Officer W. G. Rae's *A12-4* broke up in the air over Point Cook six days later when he attempted an outside loop.

Over the next eight years the Bulldogs and their pilots became firm favourites with the air-minded public as they performed aerobatic displays at Empire Air Days, and notably the 1937 Coronation Review Flypast and 1938 RAAF Displays at Laverton and Richmond. Group Captain E. Glennie-Carr, former Bulldog pilot with No 56(F) Squadron, North Weald, and now living in Portugal, went through the Cadet College at Point Cook and was commissioned in the RAF in January 1935, under a scheme then existing between the RAF and the RAAF. He remembers a 'Fighter Flight' of Bulldogs (three operational plus one reserve at that time) at Point Cook and recalls that 'as Cadets we were inclined to regard these pilots as "gods"'.

Scherger, who was considered to be one of the RAAF's best aerobatic pilots, gained public prominence when he participated in the Adelaide Aero Pageant on 17 October 1931. En route from Point Cook to Adelaide in *A12-1* he had nosed over upon landing to refuel at Nhill in the outback and damaged a wingtip, fortunately without injury. A photograph of the Bulldog, with Scherger standing on a step-ladder refuelling from two drums carried on the back of a horse-drawn cart, achieved worldwide publicity as it illustrated the primitive conditions under which he competed. A terse entry in his flying log two days later read, 'Adelaide Aerial Derby — won at 180.98 mph'. On another occasion, again flying *A12-1*, whilst visiting Tasmania for a display at Elwick racecourse he was seen to be flying inverted, almost below the building line of Hobart's main thoroughfare, when the Bulldog's Jupiter cut out. Fortunately for him, and others, he had sufficient speed to roll over in time for the engine to fire again.

Another well-known pilot, Air Commodore Paddy Heffernan, who logged more hours in Bulldog than any other Australian, recalls his impressions of the aeroplane and its use during that period:

'Apart from training in single-seat fighter

"Travelling down the Trans Line to Cook" *(P. G. Heffernan).*

RAAF Bulldogs, Mark II, serial numbers *A12-1* to *A12-8* in course of erection at Filton in 1929 *(British Aerospace, Filton).*

Heffernan's Bulldog being loaded onto a truck after a forced landing in the outback *(P. G. Heffernan)*.

Flying Officer Paddy Heffernan prepared for the "Met" Flight *(P. G. Heffernan)*.

tactics, a lot of time was spent in demonstrations at pageants around Australia, and in co-operation with the Army during their annual exercises. Another activity was introduced when the Meteorological Department asked for a daily flight to 16,000 ft to record wet and dry temperatures every two thousand feet, cloud formations, etc. This introduced some interesting aspects of the skills of the pilots. At that time the only blind flying instruments were a bubble and compass. Some time later a turn and bank indicator was installed but it proved to be so inaccurate as to be dangerous. About 1932 the Reid and Sigrist turn and bank instrument replaced it and, once the pilot got used to its peculiarities, it was used with confidence. No radio was carried, as the sets available at that time were quite useless, whilst oxygen was not considered necessary. It was amazing that in the nine years from 1930 to 1939, the flights were carried out on about 330 days of each year and during this time there was only one crash. The pilot, Flying Officer E. Read, got caught out in low cloud whilst flying *(A12-7)* down a valley on 14 December 1936, hit a tree and remained trapped in the wreck for 32 hours, with two broken legs and a badly cut face. He scraped raindrops off the fabric to quench his thirst and kept notes of his ordeal on a pad. Believe it or not, he was flying again

RAAF pilots (reading left to right) Squadron Leader Johnnie Summers and Flying Officers Paddy Heffernan and Dixie Chapman, 1934. Note the plaque on the engine cowling panel *(P. G. Heffernan).*

within a year and during the war was awarded the AFC.

'The Bulldogs were considered almost sacrosanct and a pilot had to be of a B1 instructor rating before being allowed to fly one, but towards the end of their time the novelty had worn off and any pilot who wanted to try could have a go. In spite of this there were only two fatal crashes. In the first one, the pilot dived into the water while doing gunnery practice and the second was caused by overconfidence when the pilot misjudged his height whilst doing low aerobatics. Another aircraft was lost when the pilot, Flying Officer W. Rae, attempted an outside loop. Instead of starting from a stalled position and becoming inverted as quickly as possible, he pushed the nose down and was almost at terminal velocity when he tried to push the nose up from the inverted position thus causing the wings to collapse. He managed to bale out safely, so becoming the first RAAF member of the Caterpillar Club.

'As part of the training, several long cross country flights took place annually. Point Cook

to Perth involved refuelling every two hours, and as petrol stocks in those days were held in four gallon tins and had to be poured through a chamois filter, it does not require much imagination to understand the problems of the pilot. All pilots were trained in minor maintenance, ie, cleaning plugs, oil filters, etc. Members of other Air Forces do not realise the problems we, of the RAAF, had in organising cross country flights. I recall on one flight, I rang the postmaster, the usual source of such information, at an intermediate refuelling stop to enquire the state of the weather and was told it was 'OK'. We ran into heavy rain and low cloud, but managed to locate the paddock and on registering a rather forceful complaint as to the inaccuracy of the forecast, we were told that as he knew where the paddock was and as we had used it before, he couldn't see what our problem was!

'Operating from country paddocks usually produced clouds of dust and the local fuel suppliers seemed to have no regard for the damage that dust could do to an engine. To quote an incident which happened to myself.

Three of us were going to Perth and on the way, we put on a show at Moonta, in South Australia, operating in a cloud of red dust. Next refuelling was at Whyalla in similar conditions and then on to Ceduna again in a red cloud. Next stop was Cook, a small siding on the Trans-Continental railway. About half way, I noticed that the oil pressure was slowly dropping, but considerable latitude was allowed in the Jupiter engine. However, the temperature did not rise, but when the pressure had dropped to 15 pounds, I began to worry, so I cut the corner and headed directly for the rail, which was only about 20 miles away, whereas Cook was some 60 miles. Just as I reached the line, I got a whiff of very hot metal and the engine seized solid. I was flying at 5,000 feet and saw an old dry salt pan close to the line. Here I should say that the Nullabor Plain is covered with limestone rocks and small clumps of salt bush, none of which are conducive to a smooth landing. So I made a very careful approach on to the salt pan and finished the landing on the very edge, which fortunately had a slight rising edge. I removed the cowl and took out the oil filter, which was so clogged with dust that it was almost sucked flat. Then it hit me as to why the temperature had not risen, as no oil was passing over the temperature bulb, it did not register until the last few seconds.

'An hour or so later, one of the Hawker Demons who were accompanying us came looking for me and landed on the strip which I had cleared for it. I tied the Bulldog down and returned to Cook in the Demon. I rang Point Cook that night, told them the story and another Bulldog was on the way the next day, also a new engine and fitter were on the next train. I left for Perth in the replacement aircraft and the Bulldog was pushed over to the line by a gang of enthusiastic railway fettlers and brought to Cook, where the new engine was installed.

'The serviceability of the Bulldogs was remarkable. I know of only two other forced landings, one caused by a broken connecting rod and the other by ice forming on the breather pipe for the fuel tanks.

'About this time the Army developed a craze for night displays, so naturally we got roped in to add to the excitement. Wingtip flares were installed and the Vickers guns adjusted to fire blank cartridges. At the appropriate time, the aircraft would be picked up by searchlights and we would dive into the arena, madly firing the guns. Naturally one of the Bulldogs would be shot down, so a flare would be ignited and the Bulldog would disappear in flames, saving the other flare for landing back at Point Cook.

'When HRH the Duke of Gloucester came to Australia in 1934 to greet the winner of the air race, England to Australia, three of us were detailed to provide an air escort and to participate in pageants in Melbourne, Sydney and Brisbane. It was a very busy time as every time HRH appeared we had to be in the air to escort his retinue.

'So much for the odd story of the Bulldog. It was a delight to fly, easy to land and in fact could be landed in a shorter run than a Gipsy Moth; a sideslipping turn into wind, a bit of a wag tail to wash off any surplus speed and it would sit down on three points. Cross winds of up to twenty miles per hour could be coped with easily. As a firing platform it was very stable. We did not have drogue targets at that time, but firing on to a ground target six feet square, an average of 75% hits was common. By the time World War 2 broke out, the four remaining Bulldogs *(A12-1/-3/-6/-8)* were relegated to the schools of technical training and used for teaching skills in metal rigging. I had my last flight in a Bulldog on 3 October 1938, making a total of 511 hours and felt as though I had lost an old friend and as a matter of interest, it was the same aircraft in which I had my first flight on 25 May 1931'.

By 1935 the remaining six Bulldogs, *A12-1, -2, -3, -6, -7* and *-8 (A12-5* was written off in a crash-landing on 3 July 1935), joined the two flights of Demons, at Laverton, as part of No 1 Squadron which was now designated a fighter-bomber unit. *A12-2* was involved in a major crash at Richmond, on 22 April 1938, during a practice upward roll from low level on the eve of display. The four remaining aircraft were taken out of service on 15 April 1940, but it was not until 1942 that they were replaced by Curtiss Kittyhawks. (Interest had been shown by the Australian government in the Bulldog Mark IVA when it appeared in 1934 and had sought to place an order for 45. However, the order was declined by Bristol because of their commitment to production of the Blenheim at that time.)

* * *

The Swedish government were in 1931 to show an early interest in Bulldog, for they wished to

Swedish Bulldog pilots (left to right standing) Lieutenants Olle Carlgren, Lars Gasta Hägglöf, Captain Nils Söderberg and Lieutenant Gustav Adolf Weskring. (Left to right seated) Engineer Claus Sparre and Lieutenant Erik Ekman *(British Aerospace, Filton)*.

compare its performance and construction, in evaluation trials, with their own Svenska J6A Jaktfalk biplane fighter. The prototype Jaktfalk was powered by a 465 hp Armstrong Siddeley Jaguar radial air-cooled engine, but the following two pre-production aircraft were to be equipped with Jupiter VIIF engines, so that comparisons in performance could be made. An added incentive to their interest was the granting of a licence by Bristol to one of their own manufacturers, Nydqvist & Holm (Nohab Flygmotor-fabriken), for them to build Jupiter engines. And so the Royal Swedish Air Force placed an initial order for three Mark II Bulldogs (nos 7400-7402) to be powered by G.R. Jupiter VI engines. Two members of the *Flygvapnet*, officer pilots Cloes Sparre and Erik Ekman, were sent to Filton to have oversight of testing prior to delivery of the aircraft to Sweden.

Cyril Uwins carried out test flights on the three aircraft, which were given the Swedish serial numbers *1201-1203*, on 26 July, 18 and 21 August 1930 respectively, before their delivery to *Västerås Flygkär* (F1). In Sweden the Bulldog was designated J7 and carried the three crowns in black, on a white disc background, on fuselage sides and top and bottom wings. In addition three black hooped rings were marked on the fuselage between the serial number and the tailplane. The rudder carried two vertical stripes, leading in yellow and then blue, whilst the fin carried the customary Bulldog insignia.

The result of the evaluation trial with the Jaktfalk fighter was that, although the home-produced competitor had a higher maximum speed of 193 mph at 14,700 ft when fitted with the Jupiter VIIF, the Bulldog was the better of the two. Only fifteen Jaktfalk J6As were made in all; eight being built by the Svenska Aero AB Co which went into liquidation, and the remainder being supplied by the ASJA Co which took over Svenska.

Early in 1931 the Royal Swedish Air Force placed a further order, this time for eight Bulldog Mark IIAs (nos 7582-7589) which were allocated Swedish serial numbers *5211* to *5218*. The aircraft were flight-tested in May and air-ferried to Malmslatt by Swedish service pilots Olle Carlgren, Lars G. Hägglöf, Nils Söderberg and Gustav A. Weskring, in two flights of four, on 13 and 16 May. The aircraft were allocated for squadron service with F1 where they served, sometimes with ski-landing equipment, until they were eventually relegated to the Central Flying School F5. Three of the second batch of Mark IIAs, *5214, 5215* and *5216*, were donated to the Finnish Air Force for use as trainers when that country was attacked by the Soviet Union in December 1939. The RSAF had quite close links with the RAF as a result of their purchases, and it was not uncommon for their

Service pilots to be attached for short periods to RAF Bulldog squadrons for training. Two such pilots were Captains E. M. Bang and L. Jungdahl, the former being with No 17(F) Squadron, Upavon, in February 1932, whilst the latter was with No 23(F) Squadron, Kenley, in December 1934.

★　★　★

Estonia, like its Baltic state neighbours Latvia and Lithuania, had suffered a turbulent and bloody history, having been occupied and ruled at various times by Danish crusaders, German Teutonic knights, Swedish kings, and tsars of Russia. At the time of World War 1 they were under a Czarist government which began to crumble under the weight of Lenin's revolution in October 1917. Not wishing to have any part in a communist utopia, and being fiercely nationalistic, they took up arms

Swedish Bulldogs in course of erection at Filton in May 1931. Note the hand-holds for the pilot on the cut-out of the top mainplane on *5217* (British Aerospace, Filton).

to gain their independence on 24 February 1918. Their new-found freedom was, however, to be shortlived, for the German army soon invaded and occupied the country, until they too surrendered to the Allies on 11 November 1918. Eleven days later the Red Army invaded and occupied Estonia, but were themselves, with help from Finland, France and Great Britain, driven out by February 1919. After much political turmoil in which the Baltic Germans attempted to control the country, a peace treaty was eventually signed between Estonia and the Soviet Union on 2 February 1920.

The birth of the Estonian Air Force began with the formation of a small military Aviation Co on 11 November 1918. Their pilots, about twenty in number, who had been trained in Russia, England and Germany, were based at Lasnamägi, near Tallinn, the capital, where they flew a variety of odd aircraft. These included aircraft obtained from Finland, Russia and England, amongst which were a Farman HF-30, a Shchetinin M-16 seaplane, a Sopwith 1 ½ strutter, two BE2es, two Norman Thompson NT2B flying boats, nine Avro 504Ks, eight DH9s, six Short 184s and a Sopwith Camel 2F.1 which arrived in July 1919. The Aviation Co was reorganised in 1925 as the Aviation Regiment, and expanded with bases now at Rakvere (No 1 Division), Tartu (No 2 Division), and Jägala, as well as Lasnamägi (No 3 Division). The Commanding Officer of No 3 Division, which was

responsible for air defence, was Lieutenant Eduard Reissar. He had attended a short course of instruction in 'Administration of a Fighter Squadron', as well as carrying out flying duties on Bulldogs, whilst with the RAF's No 3(F) Squadron at Upavon in August 1929. He was promoted to the rank of Lieutenant Colonel on 24 February 1940, having remained with the 3rd Division during the whole time of its existence until the country was invaded, along with Latvia and Lithuania, on 17 June 1940, by Soviet forces. Reissar fled to the West, along with other EAF personnel, and took up residence in the USA in 1945.

In an attempt to modernise its Air Force the Estonian government, no doubt encouraged by Reissar's enthusiasm for the Bulldog, placed an order with Filton for twelve Mark IIs (nos 7447-7458), which were taken from the third and final batch to be produced. The twelve aircraft, all of which were fitted with G.R. Jupiter VI engines, were flight-tested during the period 17 July to 1 August 1930 by Uwins; this entailed some 27 flights with a total flying time of eleven hours. They were shipped to Estonia and allocated to the 3rd Division with serial numbers *122* to *133*, where they replaced the ageing French Gourdou-Leseurre GL-22 fighters. All twelve aircraft were finished in silver doped fabric, with the Estonian national insignia of an inverted black triangle, surrounded by another triangle in blue, which were

Estonian Bulldog at Filton 1930 *(British Aerospace, Filton).*

carried on the upper and lower mainplane surfaces. The serial number was carried on each side of the fuselage, whilst the rudder carried three horizontal stripes of blue, black and white, in descending order. The Bulldogs were joined in 1932 by four Hawker Harts, serial numbers *145* to *148*, making the 3rd Division the biggest unit in the EAF until 1934, when the Harts were transferred to the 1st Division at Rakvere. By April 1936 it was reported that the twelve Bulldogs were all still serviceable, each having made more than a thousand landings. The aircraft were operating during the winter months from snow-bound airfields using ski landing gear, and no major components, having been replaced, apart from those parts needed to repair damage caused during two bad landings.

Little is known of Estonian pilots who flew Bulldog, apart from Lieutenant H. Kirsipuu who was at one time OC of the 2nd Salk (flight) of the 3rd Division, and Pilot Officer Alfred Kriisk. The former pilot crashed Bulldog serial no *123*, whilst landing at Jöhvi in the summer of 1933 (one of the two bad landings previously mentioned and which must have been repairable), breaking the back of the aircraft. Fortunately he was unhurt, and went on to be promoted to the rank of Captain in 1940, when he became head of operations of the staff at Ohukaitse. All that is known of Kriisk is that he regularly flew serial no *131* and was subsequently killed during World War 2.

By late 1936 the Bulldog was becoming obsolescent and the Estonian government were seeking to modernise the EAF. They took advantage of the Spanish Civil War, which broke out in July 1936, to sell eight of the twelve Bulldogs, as well as eight Potez 25A2s (purchased in 1925), to the Republican government. The Estonians did consider updating the performance of the four remaining Bulldogs to Mark IVa standard, by fitting the Mercury VIS2 engine, as they had already done with their four Letov S228Es. However, the conversion did not take place and they continued to serve with their Jupiter engines until 17 June 1940 when the Soviet forces invaded Estonia, Latvia and Lithuania. The aircraft were then stored in the open at Jägala, along with all other Estonian aircraft, until June 1941 when the Germans mounted Operation 'Barbarossa' which took them into the Soviet-held territories. The Russians ordered that the aircraft should be burned rather than let them fall into German hands. And so on 27 June, five days after the German invasion, the Bulldogs were fired and destroyed.

* * *

The Royal Danish Air Force were to order four Bulldogs (nos 7564-7567) in 1931 to their own specification requirements, and these were designated Type 105D at Filton. They were taken from the first production batch of Mark IIAs, but differed inasmuch as they were fitted with the Jupiter VIFH engines, the 'H' signifying that they were fitted with high compression ratio pistons. The Jupiter VI had gained an enviable reputation for reliability, having been used by Imperial Airways in their five DH Hercules aircraft on the Cairo to Basra air route during 1927. By January 1928 *The Times* had reported that during the first year of service, over 134,000 miles had been flown on that particular route without engine trouble of any kind. Viet gas-starters were also specified, in place of the standard RAE Mark 1 and 2 gas-starter installations. No doubt the Danes had little faith in the Vickers gun, for they specified the Madsen counterpart which used .30 calibre ammunition. They were positioned lower along the fuselage, directing their fire between cylinders 3 and 4, and 7 and 8.

The first of the four 105Ds was test-flown by Uwins on 15 March 1931; the remaining three are not recorded in Uwins' log, so they were most likely flown by test-pilot colleagues T. W. Campbell or C. T. Holmes, both of whom worked closely with, and under the supervision of, Uwins. The aircraft were given serial numbers *J151-J154*

Danish Bulldog, Type *105D*. Note the position of the Madsen 0.3 machine guns and cowling bulge
(British Aerospace, Filton).

and allocated to No 1 Squadron of the Army Aviation Troops (*Haerens Flyvertropper*), initially based at Kastrup, where they arrived on 31 March 1931. The aircraft were finished in the normal silver paint, with their serial numbers in small lettering on the rudder, whilst the national insignia roundels, which consisted of a white disc surrounded by a red circle, were carried on upper and lower mainplane surfaces and fuselage sides.

The Danish government had subsequently shown an interest in building Bulldogs under licence in their Naval Dockyard, and had in fact received such a licence in March 1932, but conditional upon the Bulldog Mark IIIA receiving firm production orders from the RAF. However, at that time the outcome of the trials with the IIIA, AW16 and SS19B had not been decided. The serial numbers of all four Danish Bulldogs were changed in 1932 to *J301-J304*, and on 2 May *J304* was loaned, for evaluation purposes, to the Naval Air Force, where it remained until 31 August before returning to squadron service. A further change was made in the serial numbers of the four aircraft when in 1933 they were re-numbered *J1* to *J4*. The serial number was now moved from its position on the rudder and appeared in large lettering on the fuselage sides, leading the national insignia.

The deal between the RDAF and Filton involved more than aircraft, for on 17 April 1932 three Danish officers, Captains Bjarkov, Braunstein and Pojarkorf, were posted to No 17(F) Squadron at Upavon, where they received familiarisation training on Bulldog. The latter two were given flying instruction on 25 April in the station's dual-Siskin *J7760*, by Flight Lieutenant J. Oliver, OC 'B' Flight of No 3(F) Squadron. Their visit was reinforced by one from their senior officer, Colonel Foerslev, who was Chief of the RDAF, when on 16 June he too visited Upavon. No doubt closer ties were envisaged when Bulldog Mark IIIA was manufactured in Denmark under licence. Unfortunately this was not to be, for the IIIA failed to obtain an Air Ministry production contract, when the SS19B (Gauntlet) was chosen from the trials.

Bulldog *J2* was being flown by Corporal V. C. Lauritsen at Vaerløse, where the aircraft were now stationed, when on 29 October 1936 he hit a fence with his undercarriage. Although the pilot was unhurt, apart from minor bruises, the aircraft was heavily damaged and was struck off charge on 29 July 1937, having logged 726 hours 25 minutes flying time. The remaining trio continued in service, without armament, in a training role, but were in storage at the time of the German invasion of Denmark on Tuesday, 9 April 1940. The military airfield at Vaerløse was bombed by the *Luftwaffe*, with token resistance bravely offered by a lone Danish aircraft which was immediately shot down. During this time the Danish Army, comprising only 7,000 men, was hopelessly outnumbered by an invading German force of 40,000 troops. Eventually *J1, J3* and *J4* were scrapped on 27 February 1942, having logged 845 hours 5 minutes, 868 hours and 974 hours 10 minutes respectively.

★   ★   ★

Finland, the last country to be directly supplied with Bulldog, had historically, like its Baltic neighbours Estonia, Latvia and Lithuania, been the constant victim of aggression by its larger and more powerful neighbours Sweden and Russia. The Swedes gradually took control of Finland during the 12th and 13th centuries, to the point where it merely became a province of that country. It remained a part of the Swedish kingdom until 1809 when it was ceded to Russia during the Napoleonic wars. The Finns are a determined and fiercely nationalistic people, and in 1905 they forced Russia, by means of strikes, to grant them a modicum of independence in which they formed their own parliament. They showed themselves to be progressive in political outlook and were the first European country to grant the franchise to women. The collapse of Russia in October 1917 encouraged them to complete the process of full self-government, and in 1919, after their War of Independence during which General Carl Gustav Mannerheim led them to victory, the Republic of Finland was established.

The natural consequence of their new found autonomy was to protect themselves from further aggression, by equipping their small but efficient armed forces with modern equipment. On 6 March 1918, what was to be the forerunner of the Finnish Air Force, the *Ilmailuvoimat*, was formed. The new force was divided initially into two Flying Divisions, one based at Kolho near Tampere, and the other at Antra near Viipuri, using a wide variety of aircraft acquired mainly from Russian, Swedish and French sources. A State Aircraft Factory was founded in 1920 which built foreign aircraft under licence, such as the French Caudron C60.

The first British aircraft to join the new force in 1923 were fifteen Martinsyde F4 fighters which had been sold off as war surplus, joining twenty

A line up of Bulldogs at Suur-Merijokı, near Viipuri on the Karelian Isthmus (today in the USSR) during an air display on 3 August 1935 *(Keski-Suomen Ilmailumuseo)*.

A line up of Bulldogs near Viipuri in the late 1930s. One of the few photographs depicting the peacetime service of the type with skis *(Keski-Suomen Ilmailumuseo)*

Gourdou-Leseurre GL21 fighters which had been purchased earlier from France. In 1924 the *Ilmailuvoimat* was reorganised into three Flying Divisions, with No 1 as a fighter squadron at Utti, No 2 a bomber squadron at Viipuri, and No 3 a floatplane squadron at Sortavala. Two Gloster Gamecock IIs were ordered in 1927, with fifteen more being manufactured under licence; together with 26 Blackburn Ripon IIF land and floatplanes a few years later. The Finnish government began to show an interest in the Bristol Bulldog in the early 1930s by which time the *Ilmailuvoimat,* now using the abridged title *Ilmavoimat,* comprised only a land-based squadron at Suur-Merijoki, and three maritime squadrons at Tervaniem, Sortavala and Turkinsaari. It should not be forgotten that Finland has more than 60,000 lakes, most of which make readily available landing places, and which occupy an area of some 13,000 square miles. However, it was recognised by the mid-1930s that the floatplane could not, as a military aircraft, achieve the performance of its land-based counterpart. This realisation, together with a growing awareness of the increasing military strength of the USSR, led to a further reorganisation and expansion, in which six Air Bases *(Lentoasema)*, each occupied by squadrons *(Lentolaivue)*, were placed at Utti (LLv10 and 24), Santahamina (LLv36), Sortavala (LLv38), Turkinsaari (LLv34), Suur-Merijoki and Viipuri (LLv44).

The Finnish government invited the Bristol Aeroplane Co, in December 1933, to supply a batch of seventeen Bulldog Mark IVA fighters (nos 7810-7826), for the FAF with a delivery deadline of 31 October 1934. However, owing to protests from the French Gnôme-Rhône Co, who objected to the export of Bristol manufactured Mercury engines, with the tenuous argument that under the Jupiter licence they were the rightful suppliers to Finland, the contract, which was placed on 28 March, was not signed until the following month. The French protests, although causing delays in delivery, were ignored by the Company who soon after terminated their licensing agreement with the Gnôme-Rhône Co. The aircraft were allocated FAF serial numbers *BU59-BU75,* and were finished in a drab olive green paintwork to all top surfaces, with silver doped undersides. The national insignia was a pale blue swastika set square (the Latvian swastika was set on the corner of its profile), on a white disc background, and appeared on upper and lower mainplane surfaces as well as fuselage sides.

The design specification was tailored to meet the vagaries of the severe Finnish climate, where temperatures as low as -40°C are not uncommon and where the sun never appears for 51 days in mid-winter. This meant modifications to the electrical system, to cater for heated clothing, gun-heating (two-gun armament was used, in spite of the Mark IVA being built to meet Air Ministry

Ex-Royal Swedish Air Force Bulldog, *BU-216*, being used as an FAF trainer at Vesivehmaa, near Lahti. This aircraft was written off on 20 December 1942 *(Keski-Suomen Ilmailumuseo).*

The last remaining Bulldog Mark IVA, *BU-59*, pictured at Filton in 1934 and now on static display in a Finnish Air Museum *(British Aerospace, Filton)*.

specification F7/30 as a four-gun fighter), and provision for engine heating. In addition, a landing-lamp, positioned in the leading edge of the lower starboard wing to assist in Arctic night landings, was used, instead of the usual Holt flare equipment, standard on the Mark IIA.

The first of the batch, *BU59*, was flight-tested by Uwins on 27 September 1934, whilst the remainder had been completed by 7 January 1935, over-running the agreed delivery date by some two months and incurring a penalty payment of £232. The aircraft were crated and shipped to Finland, the first arriving on 20 December and the last by 10 January 1935. All seventeen Bulldogs were allocated to LLv26 at Suur-Merijoki near Viipuri where the following Flights were formed: 1st Flight *BU61-65;* 2nd Flight *BU66-70* and 3rd Flight *BU71-75.* One of the remaining two aircraft, *BU59*, was allocated to the Squadron Commander, Major Einar E. Nuotio, and the other, *BU60,* to Lieutenant Eino A. Carlsson, the ADC. Warrant Officer T. J. Kleemola, an LLv26 Bulldog pilot at that time, has recorded that the aircraft were assembled by British mechanics. He also claims to be the first Finnish pilot to perform climbing and near vertical rolls with Bulldog.

State Aircraft Factory Inspector U. E. Makelä

was the first to fly the Bulldog on 20 February 1935, when he took *BU62* on a fifteen-minute test flight. Ski landing gear was fitted to the aircraft during the winter months, for snow starts to fall as early as October or November, and usually lasts until May before it clears. During the winter months it was soon found that the size of the foothold on the port side of the fuselage needed enlarging, for it was too small to accommodate the foot of a heavily-booted pilot.

Carl-Erik Bruun, now living in Turku, was a former FAF and LLv26 pilot, who flew Bulldog as part of his advanced training. He recalls his impressions of the aircraft:

'I saw the Bulldog for the first time in a flying display at Turku in 1938 (the newer Fokker DXXIs had already arrived and served alongside Bulldog in HLeLv24 at Utti). Because of the dihedral and shorter span lower wings, the Bulldogs, which were finished in standard green paint, swastikas in ultramarine blue and undersurfaces silver doped, looked as if they were taking off even when standing on the ground — a typical Bulldog-look.

'I myself flew the Bulldog for the first time on 1 March 1940, while serving with *Täydennyslentolaivue* [OTU Squadron] at

An FAF Bulldog used as a trainer at Pori in 1941.
Note the Luftwaffe Ju52 in the background
(Keski-Suomen Ilmailumuseo).

Tyrväntö, under the command of Captain Bo
von Willebrand. The aircraft was *BU72*. . . The
pilot's seat was located relatively forward under
the upper wing from which a section was
removed to improve visibility, but the upper
wing was still quite disturbing as in all biplanes.
A big man had a hard time trying to squeeze
into the cockpit, but once inside there was
enough room even when clothed in a fur-lined
flying suit. The height of the seat was
adjustable, which was a good thing, and the
control column had a spade-grip with the R/T
microphone switch on top, and machine-gun
triggers in the middle. The aircraft was
equipped with the basic instruments typical for
the period; engine and air speed indicators,
altimeter, turn-and-bank indicator, fore-and-
aft level indicator, and compass, all of which
enabled the aircraft to be flown solely on
instruments. The Bulldogs were originally
equipped with P-12-17 radio which were fairly
ineffective, although they did come in useful
during the war.

'On both sides of the cockpit, level with the
pilot's elbow, were the 7.62 mm Vickers
machine-guns with interrupter gear. Provision
for other armament included bomb racks of
type Tolfvan XII-A-II, which were installed on
the undersides of the lower wings. The engine
was turned over with the Eclipse inertia starter,
normally cranked by two men, whereupon it
usually started easily, although during the
winter months it needed the assistance of a pre-
heater.

'Taxying with wheel landing gear was no
problem, although care was needed because of
poor forward visibility, whilst with skis some
skill was needed, particularly if it was windy.
Take-off was quite straightforward, only slight
rudder pressure being needed to maintain the
correct heading — just like any other trainer in
this respect.

'Once in the air the cockpit provided
adequate protection against the slipstream,
whilst the aircraft was highly manoeuvrable,
responding without any unpleasant
characteristics to its well-harmonised controls.
Mock dog fights were very popular with the
flying pupils and considering that *BU72* had
already flown over 530 hours, and participated
in air battles with Soviet aircraft, it performed
well, although some pupils claimed that in a
slow roll the rear fuselage turned much later
than the nose and wings! All normal aerobatics
were possible, in spite of the fact that the engine
did not run inverted, and when new it was
possible to make one upward, near vertical,
roll. In a prolonged dive a flutter could develop,
particularly if the aircraft was badly trimmed.
However, since Bulldog presented no extra
"gadgets", like retractable landing gear, flaps
or variable-pitch propeller, it was considered an
ideal advanced trainer. In gunnery training
against ground targets it was very easy to get
over 50 per cent hits, although the Finnish
machine-guns, used later, proved to be more
reliable.

'Landing-speed was slightly above 100 km/h
[62 mph] when the aircraft could be made to
touch down in a beautiful three-pointer.
However, because of poor forward visibility the
aircraft was usually held in a side-slip up to the
last moment during its landing approach, in
order to avoid possible obstacles.

'The Bulldog presented no major problems
for our fitters either, for its Mercury VIS2
engine was quite easy to maintain, and spare
parts were fully interchangeable. Damage to its
fabric covering was normally repaired in the
field, whilst more severe structural damage was
repaired at the State Aircraft Factory.

'To summarise, I think the Bulldog was a nice
aircraft and particularly pleasant for the pupil
to fly — pilot skills were greatly improved and
"aviation was lovely".'

FAF fighter pilot Lieutenant Eino Luukkanen
was posted to *Lentoasema* No 5 on 21 March 1935
where he joined LLv26 at Suur-Merijoki, near
Viipuri. He was destined to fly Bulldogs during the
next four years and he recalls:

'We practised continually until we were

conversant with every mood, idiosyncrasy and foible of our little Bulldog, whose name belied its delightfully sprightly qualities . . .'

During the summer of 1937 the Bulldogs of LLv26 operated from Käkisalmi airfield, alongside Lake Ladoga, whilst during the following winter it took part in the 'War Games' held at Sortavala, at a time which was intensely cold. By 1938 both Hitler and Stalin were beginning to flex their military muscles, with the latter casting an envious eye over certain Finnish bases that he felt Russia should possess in order to assure the security of Leningrad. War clouds were gathering over Finland, as well as the rest of Europe, and these acted as a catalyst for a further reorganisation of the FAF. The previous six Air Bases *(Lentoasema)*, with their attached squadrons *(Lentolaivue)*, were ended and became Air Regiments *(Lentorymentti)*. No 2 LeR, with headquarters at Utti, embraced two fighter squadrons, HLeLv24 *(Havittajalentolaivue)* with its newly acquired Fokker DXXI single-seat monoplanes, and HLeLv26, equipped with Bulldogs, all under the command of Colonel Yrjö Oppas. Lieutenant Eino Luukkanen was appointed as Adjutant to Regimental Commander Oppas, whom he found to be highly efficient although autocratic in manner and not particularly easy to please.

The Finns were determined not to yield to Stalin's demands for bases such as the Aaland

A Bulldog trainer at Kauhava "Air War School" during the Continuation War. Note the yellow band around the rear fuselage and yellow wingtips on undersurfaces *(Keski-Suomen Ilmailumuseo).*

Islands, and air bases in Finland, and so in August 1939 the FAF put on defiant air-exercises over Karelia to show the Soviets their resolve. The ten Bulldogs of HLeLv26, now based at Raulampi, were near obsolescent amongst a total defence force of some 150 aircraft, not all of which were serviceable. Their pilots were ready waiting for the Red invader and they were not to be disappointed for long.

Chapter 8
Bulldogs at war

Every young peacetime fighter pilot must consider, at one time or another, being called upon to put into practice all that he has been taught in a war situation — Bulldog pilots were no exception. No doubt it was a topic of conversation that occupied some of their off-duty hours, in the Mess, or during preparation for ADGB air exercises in 1935. Would their opponents be the Heinkel 51s of Göring's newly formed *Luftwaffe*, or the Fiat CR32s of Mussolini's *Regia Aeronautica*, for they seemed to be the most likely candidates as Britain began to take rearmament seriously. For RAF Bulldog and Demon squadron pilots the moment became a near reality when in October 1935 Mussolini's forces invaded Abyssinia.

Abyssinia, or to give it its present day name Ethiopia, had historically experienced bad relationships with Italy since 1885, when the Italians had occupied the port of Massawa on the Red Sea. The Abyssinians ordered their withdrawal, and after some sporadic fighting, a war broke out in 1895 leading to the defeat of the Italians at Adowa a year later. The country was eventually guaranteed its independence in 1906, when a treaty was signed with Britain, France and Italy as the signatories. An uneasy peace ensued, until a border incident at Wal-Wal on 5 December 1934 gave the Italian leader, Benito Mussolini, all the excuse that he needed in order to fulfil his military aspirations in East Africa. Although the Italians were pledged by a treaty they had signed in 1928, to go to arbitration through the League of Nations, they invaded the country in October 1935. Meeting little opposition from the Abyssinian troops led by Emperor Haile Selassie, and using poison gas and aerial bombing of defenceless villages, they had completely occupied the country by 30 April 1936 when they entered the capital, Addis Ababa. Mussolini is on record as saying that he was fascinated by the patterns made by the exploding bombs as they fell from his Savoia Marchetti bombers, and no doubt encouraged by this 'victory', he began to cast envious eyes on other prizes, particularly in the Mediterranean area.

The British government had obviously been closely watching events in East Africa since the border incident occurred late in 1934, and had made contingency plans. On 20 September 1935, a Secret Document (Operational Order No 1) was issued to various RAF fighter and bomber squadrons. Squadron Leader G. Martyn, OC No 3(F) at Kenley, was instructed to fly with his squadron of eighteen Bulldogs (this number included six reserve aircraft) to RAF Sealand near Chester on the next day. The squadron pilots comprised seven officers, all from No 3(F), and eleven NCOs, two of whom (Sergeants Brunner and Rogers) were from No 17(F) and three (Sergeants Cooper, Gommshall and Price) from No 32(F) based at Biggin Hill. Six flights of Bulldogs took off on 21 September and landed without mishap at Sealand, whereupon they awaited the arrival of the squadron's ground staff who would dismantle the aircraft and hand them over to OC of the Packing Depot. The ground staff included fitters, riggers, armourers, electricians, MT personnel, medical and administrative groups who were kitted out with tropical gear whilst they awaited embarkation. Little speculation was needed amongst pilots and ground staff to deduce the proposed destination, for it was almost self-evident that the only places of British interest, and within striking distance of Abyssinia, were the Sudan and Aden.

At 10:00 on the morning of 4 October, the squadron boarded TSS *Cameronia* at Liverpool docks, destination East Africa — somewhere! Eight days later the ship docked at Alexandria in Egypt, in order to take on provisions before sailing through the Suez Canal and down the Red Sea, arriving at Port Sudan in the early hours of the morning on the 18th. The squadrons were ordered to disembark — it was to be the Sudan after all — whereupon Pilot Officer N. M. Hall (who was to be killed some five years later when his Hurricane was shot down off St Catherine's Point by Bf 109s of 111/JG27) and 62 members of the ground staff left by train at 08:30 for Khartoum, arriving there at 08:00 on 22 October 1935. The crated Bulldogs, stored in the hold of SS *Antilochus*, arrived at Port Sudan on the 20th, and were speedily unpacked

No 3(F) Squadron Bulldogs Mark IIA, *K2140*, *K2494* and *K2232* over the Sudan during the Abyssinian crisis 1935/1936 *(MoD)*.

and assembled by the thirteen members of ground staff who had arrived two days earlier. After assembly and flight-testing of the eighteen Bulldogs it was soon found that the heat of the Sudan was to cause problems. Vaporisation of fuel lines, combined with leaking gas-starter bottles, made for difficult starting of the Jupiter engines, particularly when already hot. However, the aircraft were, within a few days, flown across country to the capital of Khartoum where they were based until January 1936.

Sudan had been ruled under the joint sovereignty of Britain and Egypt since 1898, when Lord Kitchener had recovered the province from the Mahdi uprising in which General Charles Gordon had been killed. The British government were demonstrating to the Italian leader that they were determined to defend their interests in that part of the world. Hawker Demons of No 29(F) Squadron from North Weald were despatched to Amriya, arriving there on 31 October, whilst Vickers Vildebeest bombers from the Coastal Defence Development Flight were also sent. Demons of No 41(F) went from Northolt to Aden on 4 October arriving at Khormaksar on the 20th to join with a flight of Demons from No 8(F) Squadron.

As the prospect of a 'showdown' with the *Regia Aeronautica* receded in the early days of 1936, the pilots of No 3 kept themselves busy with exercises and displays. On 16 January at Khartoum, along with bombers from No 47(B) Squadron, they put on an air display much to the delight of the local sheikhs and their tribesmen. No doubt the pilots enjoyed the warm air over the cockpit when flying, which was a welcome relief from the cold damp air of England's southern counties in January! The problem of icing carburettors was exchanged for that of desert sand and flies, particularly the insidiousness of the former. Sand was not only reported as being troublesome for the Kestrel engines of the Demons, but it was also a problem for the Bendix brakes on Bulldogs.

On 20 January 1936 No 3's Bulldogs flew back to Port Sudan where they continued to keep themselves in a state of readiness. One of the aircraft, *K1628*, crashed whilst coming in to land after night-flying practice and was written off; fortunately the pilot, Pilot Officer J. W. McGuire, was only slightly injured. Whilst the one-sided war was dragging on across the Sudanese border, Britain, France and the USA sought to restrain Italy by imposing sanctions. The attempt was a fiasco, with the French and the Americans failing to agree on oil sanctions, and Britain failing to close the Suez Canal or put on a naval blockade of the Italian-held coastal ports. By May the war had ended with Haile Selassie seeking asylum initially in Sudan, and later in England, whilst his country became a part of the Italian Empire of East Africa. The British forces were to linger for a further three months before they were ordered home.

On 3 August 1936 fifteen of the original eighteen Bulldogs took off like disillusioned migratory birds from Port Sudan, climbing into the warm and bumpy air of the coastal mountains on the first leg of the way home. As they came in to land at Gebeit, Pilot Officer Eyres' aircraft, *K1671,* turned over on to its back as the brake drums filled with sand and clogged. The remaining Bulldogs refuelled and took off for Atbara, where they remained overnight. On the morning of the 4th the fourteen aircraft headed north across the Nubian desert to Wadi Halfa, breaking their journey at Landing Ground No 10 to refuel on the way. After an overnight stay they left the Sudan and crossed into Egypt, following the Nile until they landed at Assuan. Here they were met by quite high winds, which caused one of the aircraft to turn over, damaging a wing whilst taxying — and then there were thirteen! The diminished squadron flew on to Luxor on the Nile where they stayed overnight before flying on to Aboukir, with landings at Asyut and Helwan on route. Thirteen weary pilots proceeded to No 4 FTS at Abu Sueir where they were accommodated prior to embarking for the UK. In the meantime all ground staff had embarked on the *Somersetshire* at Port Sudan on

14 August, arriving at Port Said three days later, where they were joined by the rest of the squadron. On 28 August the *Somersetshire* sailed up the Solent into Southampton water where the squadron disembarked and proceeded by rail to RAF Kenley.

No 3(F) Squadron had been away for almost eleven months and its members were ready for a well-deserved and long-awaited leave. The whole affair had been an abortive one as far as the pilots were concerned, for their RAF Bulldogs had never fired a shot in anger. Little did they, or anyone else, realise that within a few weeks the little biplane fighter would be in action over other foreign skies, in Spain, against the very enemy aircraft that they had so nearly engaged.

There was yet to be a final link between Bulldog and Abyssinia — some four years later. Former No 23(F) and No 56(F) Squadron Bulldog pilot, Flying Officer Guy L. Menzies, was to be the pilot of the Short Sunderland flying boat which secretly flew the Emperor Haile Selassie — 'The Lion of Judah' — back to his homeland. In July 1940 the Sunderland crossed Nazi-occupied France and

Republican Bulldog exhibited as a "spoil of war" at San Sebastian circa 1937 *(Patrick Laureau/Editions Lariviere).*

Republican Bulldog exhibited as a "spoil of war" at San Sebastian circa 1937 *(Patrick Laureau/Editions Lariviere).*

made its way across the Mediterranean to Alexandria in Egypt, from where the Abyssinian leader was to make his way home; first to the Sudan, and then finally on 15 January 1941, into his own country. As a token of his appreciation, Selassie had presented Menzies with a gold watch engraved with a crown, remarking at the time that he would soon be back in Addis Ababa wearing one. Flying Officer Menzies was subsequently to be lost, somewhere in the eastern Mediterranean later during the war, whilst flying Sunderlands.

* * *

On 18 July 1936 Spain was plunged into a bitter and bloody civil war that was to last for almost three years, and which was to be responsible for the deaths of at least some 700,000 of its people. Elections held in February 1936 led, by a small majority, to the establishment of a Republican government which was supported by the trade unions, socialists, communists, anarchists and separatist regional groups. Opposition to this government came from the Nationalists, who were supported by the Army and the church, and who believed that the Republicans had become merely a pawn of the Soviet Union. They did not consider their uprising to be an insurrection or *coup d'état* of a democratically elected government, but rather as a move to restore law and order and to prevent Spain from becoming a Soviet satellite state.

The Nationalists held support in the south of the mainland, at Cadiz, Seville, Cordoba and Granada; the western side of the country neighbouring Portugal; as well as the provinces of Galicia, Leon and Navarre in the north; together with Morocco and the islands of Majorca and Ibiza. The uprising failed in Madrid, Valencia, Barcelona and Bilbao, which together with the island of Minorca remained loyal to the Republican government. Unfortunately, the civil war did not remain a domestic issue for long, but attracted foreign powers who were motivated not only by ideological belief, but were also anxious to use the war as a training ground for new weapons. The Soviet Union and France began to ship aircraft and other war equipment to the Republican forces, whilst the Italians and the Germans rallied to the aid of Franco who had become the natural leader of the Nationalist uprising.

At the commencement of the war the Republican air force comprised some 170 aircraft, which included three unarmed Hawker Furys, 26 Vickers Vildebeests, Breguet XIXs, Nieuport NiD 52s, Savoia and Dornier Wal flying boats, DC2s and Fokker FVIIs. They were opposed by a Nationalist air force of approximately fifty aircraft which included a de Havilland Dragon, Nieuport NiD 52s, Breguet XIXs, Dornier Wals, Fokker FVIIs and various trainers.

The first aircraft from foreign powers began to arrive in support of the Nationalists in August, these being Junkers Ju52 transports and Heinkel He 51 biplane fighters from Germany, as well as Savoia SM81 bombers and Fiat CR32 biplane fighters from Italy. Nationalist markings were a black St Andrew's cross on white rudder; white cross inboard of upper wingtips and three black stripes running chordwise on upper and lower surfaces of wingtips. In addition, plain black discs were added to the undersurfaces of wings and fuselage sides.

The French were to supply Potez 540 twin-engined bombers to the Republicans on 8 August, which were soon pressed into action. Meanwhile Russian freighters began to unload Tupolev SB2 (Katiuska) bombers at Cartegena in September, after the Republicans had taken over the naval base there. In the north the Basque nationalists who had been given a degree of autonomy, had been desperately searching the arms dealers of Europe in order to buy whatever second-hand aircraft they could. Estonia, who saw the Spanish *débâcle* as an opportunity to sell their obsolescent Bulldogs and Potez aircraft, offered them for sale to the Basques. A deal was concluded through an import/export agency in Prague and the aircraft were secretly transported to their purchaser. The eight Bulldogs and eight Potez 25As arrived in northern Spain in October 1936, whereupon the Bulldogs were allocated to the base at Lamiaco, near Bilbao, under the command of Lieutenant Jose Gonzalez Feo. They bore the Republican markings in which a red hooped-band encircled the fuselage from cockpit to tailplane, whilst the rudder carried the Republican tricolour which comprised horizontal stripes descending in red, yellow and mauve. Red bands were carried on upper wing surfaces inboard from the wingtips, and on lower wing surfaces the wingtips were painted red. The general camouflage colour scheme of the aircraft was a yellow ochre with smudged olive green patches on all upper surfaces, whilst undersurfaces were in a pale blue. Spinners and fabric wheel disc covers had been removed from the Bulldogs, and although they did not carry identification letters, as on the majority of Republican aircraft, they were marked with a small white numeral on the lower part of the fin.

The Bulldogs at Zone Nord, Lamiaco, were soon joined by fifteen more modern Russian Polikarpov I-15 biplane fighters, nicknamed 'Chatos' (the Cat) which arrived on board the Russian freighter *A Andreu* at Bilbao on 1 November. Despite its distinctive upper wing arrangement the I-15 was sometimes confused with the Bulldog by Nationalist fighter pilots. The Chatos were formed into two squadrons at Lamiaco, one with Russian pilots under the command of Boris Maranchov and the other with Spanish pilots, including Felipe del Rio, Leopoldo Morquillas and Baquedano (the latter was to be killed in a flying accident at Santander in June 1937).

The Nationalist forces were anxious to gain control of the north of the country for it contained rich industrial areas as well as the Asturian mines which were vital to the economy of Spain. The Republicans, although contained along a line from the Cantabrian mountains to the Bay of Biscay, from Aviles to Guernica, were determined not only to hold on to the major cities of Santander and Bilbao but to break out and capture Nationalist held Vitoria. The Bulldogs from Lamiaco had so far been used, along with the Potez 25As based at Sondica, to attack enemy shipping along the coastline; but on 30 November when the Villareal offensive began, they were allocated to a ground-strafing role in support of Basque troops. The offensive, which was supported by government bomber aircraft such as the three-engined Farmans and Douglas DC2s failed to achieve its target and the Republicans were forced to withdraw.

Very little is known of the combat pilots who flew Bulldog, apart from Carlos Lazaro Casajust, one time head of the Basque air force, who is recorded as having flown the type on two occasions. The Bulldogs flew missions daily and were quite literally flown to a standstill, being grounded for want of spares, particularly for their Jupiter engines. Although none were ever reported to have been destroyed in aerial combat, two were quite severely damaged by AA fire, whilst operating from La Vega airfield, during a small offensive against the town of Oviedo. Reinforcements, including eight Koolhoven FK-51s, a Beech 17, a Lockheed Vega and an Orion for the Republican forces, began to arrive in January 1937, and at that time seven Bulldogs were reported to be still in flying condition. On 4 April 1937 the airfields of Lamiaco and Santander came under attack from Nationalist aircraft who were at that time being supported by the German 'Condor Legion'. German Me 109Bs were in action and it was towards the end of April that Felipe del Rio was shot down in combat and killed. It is not known exactly which type of aircraft he was flying at the time, but it is unlikely to have been a

Bulldog.

The last Bulldogs were relegated to what was to become known as the *Circo Krone* (Krone Circus), which, as its name suggests, included a group of obsolescent aircraft such as Nieuports, Letovs, Breguets and Dewoitines. According to a late pilot of the *Circo Krone,* there were still one or two serviceable Bulldogs with the unit in the period July to August 1937, when they were based at Torrelavega. On the ground, General Davila's forces went on to break through the so-called 'Iron Ring' fortifications around Bilbao, which, after a period of sustained shelling from artillery and aerial bombing, was overrun on 19 July 1937.

Santander was the next major objective for Nationalist troops, and the Government forces, who were determined to defend it to the last, put all their aircraft into its defence. Heavy air fighting took place during which the Nationalists reported that, in the period 21 to 23 August, they had destroyed forty enemy aircraft for the loss of four of their own. The 'Condor Legion' took part in these air battles and the Republican fighter pilot Tarazona records that the 'Krone Circus' were involved, as were the Chatos, commenting that they were flown with the courage of brave men. The last of the Bulldogs — the precise number is not known — were captured at Carreno-Santander when on 26 August General Davila's troops entered Santander. Souvenir hunters tore the fabric from the Bulldogs, after which at least one of the aircraft was exhibited by the victors in the 'Gran Kursal' at San Sebastian amongst its spoils of war.

* * *

On the pretext of a border incident, in which the Soviet forces accused the Finns of having fired seven shots — killing one of their NCOs and several of their soldiers — Red Army troops invaded Finland at 06:15 on the morning of 30 November 1939, in what was to become known as the Winter War. The attack had long been expected by the Finns, and therefore came as no surprise, for ever since Hitler and Stalin had signed their German-Soviet pact of Non-Aggression, some two months earlier, their fate had been sealed. Events moved swiftly, for the pact was to pave the way for the *Wehrmacht's* attack on Poland on Friday 1 September. Stalin administered the *coup de grâce* when on the 17th Red Army tanks attacked from the rear in order to 'liberate' the Poles, bringing about a surrender of that country by the end of the month. Within days, the ministers

of Estonia, Latvia and Lithuania were summoned to the Kremlin, with a 24-hour notice of attendance, where they were offered and signed, pacts of 'mutual assistance' which became a euphemism for their surrender. Stalin, who now controlled the Gulf of Finland along its coastline from Kronstadt down to Libau on the Baltic Sea, turned his eyes towards Finland — but the Finns were to prove tougher opponents than their Baltic neighbours!

The demands on the Finns included cession of several islands at the entrance to Kronstadt Bay, gateway to Leningrad; a withdrawal of her forces from the frontier at the Karelian Isthmus of up to sixteen miles, as well as a promise not to fortify the Aaland Islands. The latter demand would ensure that the Soviets could control the Gulf of Bothnia, thereby giving them the power to stop vital Swedish ore from reaching Germany's war factories if need be. The Finns would yield to none of these territorial demands and so the Soviets, confident that they could sweep aside any opposition, invaded.

At the time of the Russian invasion the Finnish Air Force could only muster two Fighter Squadrons *(Hävittäjalentolaivue)*, HLeLv24 and 26, comprising 46 aircraft — 36 Fokker DXXIs and ten Bulldogs — under the command of Colonel Riku Lorentz; the remainder of the FAF totalling 83 aircraft, and comprising trainers, floatplanes and reconnaissance types. In opposition were some 900 aircraft of the Red Air Force which were soon in action on the first day, bombing the Finnish capital of Helsinki, as well as other towns and airfields. On land the Russians attacked on five fronts, from Petsamo in the far north to the Karelian Isthmus in the south, vastly outnumbering the Finnish forces who fought back fiercely. Ironically, the Bulldogs of HLeLv26 which were based at Raulampi airfield near Heinjoki, on the Karelian Isthmus, were fighting against the very aircraft — Tupolev SB-2 bombers and Polikarpov I-15 and I-16 fighters — that they had fought alongside in the Spanish Civil War three years earlier! The squadron, which was commanded by Captain E. Heinilä, was scrambled, along with the Fokker DXXIs of HLeLv24 based at Immola, on the morning of 30 November, to meet the Russian bombers that were attacking Viipuri. Fokker fighter pilot Lieutenant Eino Luukkanen has recorded that the cloud base was down to 2,000 ft over Viipuri on that day as he patrolled in the area. He saw fires burning at the railway yards of Maaskola but apart from sighting some of the Bulldogs of HLeLv26 no other aircraft were seen.

The most famous Bulldog of all, FAF Mark IVA, *BU-68*. It accounted for two Soviet SB-2s and a I-16 before it was relegated to a training role *(Keski-Suomen Ilmailumuseo)*.

Warrant Officer Lasse Lautamäki (b. 28.10.1909)
(Keski-Suomen Ilmailumuseo).

The Russian aircraft were not to elude the Finnish fighters much longer, for on 1 December the first FAF aerial victory of the war was to be gained by Bulldog pilot Sergeant Toivo Uuttu whilst flying *BU-64*. He was attacked by five Polikarpov I-16 (Rata) fighters — the first low-wing monoplane incorporating a retractable undercarriage to enter service anywhere in the world — to the south-east of Muolaanjärvi. Although outnumbered by aircraft with superior armament and performance, he engaged one of them in an air battle which resulted in both of them making a forced landing — but in Finnish-held territory. The distinction of being the first pilot to down a Russian bomber went to Fokker pilot Lieutenant Luukkanen who, on the same day, intercepted two SB-2s over Koljola and destroyed one. Luukkanen went on to participate in a further 161 aerial battles in which he was credited with a total of 54 enemy aircraft destroyed. A further SB-2 fell, later in the day, to the guns of Sergeant Valio Porvari's Bulldog *BU-68* when he intercepted the bomber over Taspernaja and destroyed it. The Finnish Bulldog pilots may have been flying obsolescent biplane fighters against more modern aircraft, but their skill and determination in defending over their own soil, more than made up for such deficiencies.

On 6 December the Bulldogs moved from Raulampi to Mensuvaara, but were only there for three days before moving to Käkisalmi alongside Lake Ladoga. The weather deteriorated and little flying took place for the next two weeks. On the 18th the temperature began to drop and snow fell, by which time the ground crews had removed the wheel landing gear on the fighters and replaced them with skis. On land the Russian 13th Army, comprising five divisions backed up by 280 tanks, was making the main thrust of its attack on the Karelian Isthmus where the Soviet troops were meeting fierce opposition. If the French and Germans had their Maginot and Siegfried Lines then the Finns had their equivalent defence system, but unlike the French system it was not to be easily outflanked. Named after their military leader, Field Marshal Carl Gustav Mannerheim, it stretched from Taipale on the shores of Lake Ladoga, to Koivisto on the Gulf of Finland, a distance of some 75 miles. It was not a single fortified line, but rather a zone of defence some twenty miles deep, comprising a matrix of linked tank traps, short lengths of trench, gun-emplacements and mined lakes. The eyes of the world were upon the heroic Finns as they brought the might of the Red Army to a standstill, inspiring many foreign nationals such as Swedes, Danes and Italians to volunteer as pilots with the FAF. Not only men but equipment too was volunteered — this included two of the original Swedish Bulldogs, *5214* and *5216*, which were handed over on 15 December. The two aircraft received FAF serials

BU-214 and *BU-216*, and being Mark IIAs were relegated solely to a training role.

The temperature was down to -20°C on 21 December when the Bulldog pilots were scrambled to their open-cockpit fighters to intercept eight SB-2s near Taipale. The Fokker DXXIs of HLeLv24 had been alerted to the same mission, and although it was Stalin's birthday the Soviet bomber crews were obviously not anxious to sacrifice themselves for 'mother Russia', for they turned tail when they saw the Fokker fighters and headed home. Luukkanen was flying one of the Fokkers at the time and he recalls his anxious feelings of sympathy for the Bulldog pilots, flying those outdated biplanes against a better equipped enemy.

On 23 December a patrol of Bulldogs, led by Lieutenant Pentti Teva in *BU-68,* was directed to search for Russian bombers in an area near the shores of Lake Ladoga. They intercepted and engaged a formation of thirteen SB-2s, two of which they destroyed without loss to themselves. The first was shot down by Warrant Officer Lennart Mildh in *BU-74* over Käkisalmi, whilst Tevä accounted for another which fell over

Finnish fighter pilots (left to right) Aarne Alitalo, Tapani Harmaja, Erkki Heinilä, Valio Porvari, Pate Berg and Jussi Tolkki with Bulldog in 1939 *(Keski-Suomen Ilmailumuseo).*

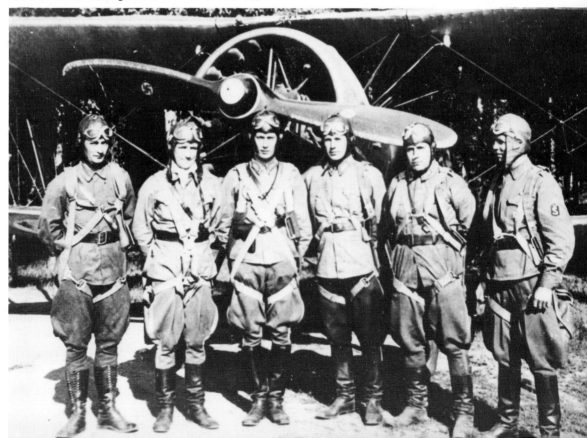

Sergeant Pilot Valio Porvari (b. 13.11.1913)
(Keski-Suomen Ilmailumuseo).

Laatokka. It says quite a lot for the skill and training of those Finnish pilots for the SB-2 was no slouch, being powered by two 880 hp Klimov twelve-cylinder liquid-cooled in-line engines, giving it a maximum speed of 282 mph. The Bulldogs would initially need to have the height advantage, so that they could gain speed in the dive and engage the SB-2 before it dropped its bombs, if they were to have any success at all.

Andrei N. Tupolev had conceived the fast, modern, mid-wing monoplane in 1935 as the ANT 40, which went into production a year later as the SB-2 *(SkorostnyiBombardirovshchik*, meaning Fast Bomber). One of its distinctive design features was the semi-retracting undercarriage, which left the wheels protruding below the engine nacelle for use during a crash landing. Another feature was the positioning of the radiators in front of the in-line engines, which gave the appearance of a radial-powered aircraft. The SB-2 carried a crew of three, and was armed with four 7.62 mm machine-guns, two in the nose turret and two in the rear dorsal and ventral positions.

After almost four weeks of air fighting the Soviet air chiefs had come to treat the FAF fighters, obsolescent or not, with a healthy respect, for no longer were the SB-2s alone, but were escorted by more numerous Russian fighters. Heinilä's BUs were scrambled on 25 December to intercept a large formation of Red aircraft approaching Käkisalmi, comprising forty SB-2 bombers escorted by twenty Polikarpov I-16 fighters. An air battle developed in which the SB-2s escaped, but not before Sergeant Porvari's *BU-68* had a squat Polikarpov I-16 irretrievably in its sights, sending it down over Ostamonjärvi. It was Porvari's second victory (he went on to claim two more enemy aircraft whilst flying a Gloster Gladiator) and *BU-68's* third victim. Porvari must have been jubilant when he returned to base, for the I-16, or 'Rata' as it was nicknamed had a speed advantage of almost 60 mph over the Bristol-built biplane. In addition, it was a highly manoeuvrable fighter, which, in the right hands, could deliver a lethal punch from its four 7.62 mm ShKAS machine-guns. The type had been successfully used by the Republican government in the Spanish Civil War, as well as by the Chinese in the Sino-Japanese War during 1937-1939. It did, however, finally go out of service in 1942, when it proved to be no match, on the Russian front, for the *Luftwaffe's* Bf 109s.

The Bulldogs continued to fly missions daily on the Karelian front, often in a ground-strafing role where their lack of speed was not the handicap that it was in air fighting. As the early weeks of the war passed the Russians began to step up their attacks both on the land and in the air, where their aircraft now numbered some 1,500. Reinforcements of aircraft for the FAF, particularly fighters, began to arrive in late December, with Fiat G-50s from Italy, Morane 406s from France, and unwanted Gauntlets and Gladiator IIs from Great Britain, as well as Blenheim I/IVs. Foreign volunteer pilots, Danes, Swedes, Hungarians, Poles and Italians (the latter mostly to bomber squadrons) were also arriving to fly these aircraft.

On 28 December five of Heinilä's Bulldogs were moved back from the front to Immola, and then to Parola near Hämeenlinna, finally operating from the frozen Lake of Littoinen, near Turku. Finnish cities were particular targets for the Red Air Force bombers, with Helsinki, the capital, Viipuri and Turku bearing the brunt of the attacks. New Year's Day 1940 arrived with temperatures down to - 42°C, the severe and bitter cold acting as an ally to the Finns, for the Soviet troops were ill-equipped for such weather. Stalin had been misled by his easy 'victories' in Poland and the Baltic States, into believing that the Finnish war would be a brief one.

Russian blood reddened the white snow as his troops fell by the thousand in their attack on the unyielding Mannerheim Line, their dead frozen bodies totalling 40,000 by 14 February. In addition the Finns claimed the destruction or capture of 327 aircraft, 594 tanks and 552 military vehicles up to the same period.

As the air raid warning sirens sounded in Turku on 14 January 1940, the recalcitrant Mercury radials of HLeLv26's Bulldogs were cranked into life, whilst their heavily clothed pilots squeezed into open cheerless cockpits. With a flurry of propeller swept snow their skis began to slide across the frozen lake, gathering speed until the six little fighters began to lift into the cold crisp air. Warrant Officer *(Lentomestari)* Lasse Lautamäki was to claim his first kill, a Soviet SB-2, which fell to his guns over Perniö. It is not recorded in which Bulldog he was flying at the time but he was to claim two more Russian aircraft, as well as a shared victory, later in the Winter War whilst flying a Gladiator.

On 2 February the Bulldogs of HLeLv26 were withdrawn from front line service, being replaced by fourteen Gloster Gladiator IIs. They were then allocated to No 2 OTU *(Täydennyslentorykmentti)*, where they joined *BU-214* and *BU-216* as advanced trainers at Tyrväntö under the command of Captain Bo von Willebrand. Finnish fighter pilot Carl-Erik Bruun, who was to see combat service flying Fiat G-50s and Brewster B-239s in the Continuation War, remembers flying *BU-75* during his early training in March 1940. He flew various other fighter trainers during his time in the FAF, including the Gamecock II, Jaktfalk and Gauntlet II. He records his impressions of these types in comparison to Bulldog.

'The Gamecock had the shortest take-off run of any of the four aircraft, being airborne well before the throttle was even fully open. It was a very manoeuvrable aeroplane with better visibility than Bulldog, making it very popular with pupil pilots.

'Jaktfalk was a pleasant fighter to fly and although slower than Bulldog it was its equal in manoeuvrability, and marginally better for visibility. The outcome of practice "dog fights" was very much dependent upon whoever was the better pilot.'

Surprisingly, Bruun adds, 'The other Gloster product — the Gauntlets — were much newer than the other trainers, giving them a slightly more "solid" feel. Manoeuvrability was about the same as Bulldog, but the Bristol fighter was faster and would probably have won in a battle.'

Other British biplane fighters were to participate in the Winter War when four Pegasus-engined Hawker Harts, together with twelve Gloster Gladiator Is, all ex-Swedish Air Force and manned by Swedish volunteer pilots, joined the fray. They operated from a base on frozen Lake Kemi on the northern front under Flight Regiment LeR19, and on 11 January were responsible for shooting down six Soviet fighters and six bombers, sustaining the loss of three of their Harts and three Gladiators. HLeLv26's Gladiators took heavy punishment during the closing weeks of the war, losing thirteen of their number in combat before being withdrawn. During this period Porvari, who had exchanged his faithful *BU-68* for Gladiator *GL-264*, was to increase his score to four, when he destroyed a Ilyushin DB-3 on 15 February and a I-16 on the next day. The Gladiator was to be criticised for its lack of pilot protection, both with respect to omission of armour and fire-wall. The latter aspect meant that should the fuel tank catch fire during an attack, the pilot was immediately engulfed in flames, causing severe burn injuries. This criticism was to be verified later in 1940 during the RAF's defence of Malta.

Towards the end of February the overwhelming weight of the USSR was beginning to tell, with fierce fighting on all fronts from Petsamo in the far north to Karelia in the south. On 26 February the Finns evacuated Koivisto at the western end of the Mannerheim Line, whilst Taipale at the other end held. By 9 March Russian troops had gained a foothold on the outskirts of Viipuri — the brave Finns were beginning to buckle — and on the 10th, Finnish representatives were in Moscow seeking a cessation of hostilities. At 11:00 on Wednesday, 13 March 1940, an official cease-fire was announced and the Winter War was over.

Flags were flying at half mast throughout Finland, as the peace terms that would save the country from complete Soviet occupation were announced. They included the ceding of the whole of the Karelian Isthmus; territory around the shores of Lake Ladoga and islands in the Gulf of Finland, while Hango was to be leased to the USSR for a period of thirty years; finally, there was to be a corridor of access across Petsamo territory as well as a pledge of non-aggression.

On 2 March 1940, *BU-214* was destroyed and struck off charge, and later in April all the remaining Bulldogs were transferred to tactical reconnaissance squadrons *(Täydennyslentolaivue)* TLLv35 and LLv34. Peace was not to reign for long, for on 22 June 1941 Germany attacked the Soviet Union, whereupon Finland allied itself to the Axis powers and the Finnish Continuation

War, as it came to be known, began. At the outbreak of this war the Bulldogs, now numbering eight serviceable aircraft, were to play a minor role with TLLv17 and 29, before being allocated to the Air Fighting School *(LentosotaKoulu)* at Kauhava, in 1942. Here they were seven in number, and were intensively used as advanced trainers, some eighteen years after their manufacture at Filton. They were gradually written off in service, until the last *BU-59*, was withdrawn, after overturning whilst landing, on 22 February 1944.

Just as Gladiator has its place in the history books of the defence of Malta, and Spitfire and Hurricane in the Battle of Britain, so too has Bulldog in the defence, albeit an unsuccessful one, of Finland. The Finns hold the little biplane fighter from Bristol in high esteem, for it became a symbol at a time when they stood alone against the might of the Soviet Union.

★   ★   ★

Chapter 9
Last in the pack

With the completion of production of the Finnish Bulldog Mark IVAs in January 1935, the airfield at Filton was to reverberate to a new sound of heavier, larger aircraft, as the Bristol Aeroplane Co became involved in the production of the twin-engined Blenheim Mark I bombers. The last of the company's Bulldogs, demonstrator IIA *G-ABBB* (no 7446), had, by September 1935, completed its part in the Aquila I's engine test programme and was placed into storage at Filton. As war clouds loomed over Britain in 1938 (by which time production of Blenheim Mark IV had began to supersede the Mark I), factory space was at a premium and but for the timely intervention of company Director Herbert J. Thomas, *G-ABBB* might well have been sold for scrap. An offer was made to, and accepted by, the South Kensington Science Museum, London, for the aircraft to be handed over and exhibited to the public. Arthur G. Gregory, who retired from the company in 1981, was a member of the Inspection Department at the time and remembers accompanying the aircraft (now with one side of its fabric removed for exhibition purposes) to London for the presentation in February 1938. He further recalls that *G-ABBB* was moved from the museum for safety reasons during the war and was stored for the duration at a warehouse in Wapping alongside the Thames, before being returned.

By the end of World War 2, in 1945, Douglas Bader's exploits, both in the air and as a PoW at Colditz, had made him a household name. Bader was patently a man of action, rather than a man of letters, and if his story was to be recorded then it needed a biographer. It was therefore no surprise when the Australian author, Paul Brickhill, agreed to write Bader's biography *Reach for the Sky* in 1954. The legless war veteran was advised to accept a 'once and for all' payment of £10,000, rather than a percentage share in royalties, for the supply of material for both book and film. There is no doubt that in retrospect he was ill-advised, but it does commend his modesty inasmuch as he did not envisage what a great success both book and film were to be. The actor, Kenneth More, was chosen in 1955 to play the part of Bader in the film but he

was not to be the only star, for *G-ABBB* also appeared, having been loaned to Pinewood Studios by the museum. The film not only made Bader even more popular as a post-war hero, but it also prompted the restoration of Bulldog *G-ABBB* to flying condition. And so it was decided, in 1957, that the biplane fighter should be returned to the Filton factory for all the necessary work, whereupon the aircraft would be presented to the Shuttleworth Collection — a unique gathering of historic aeroplanes displayed and flown at Old Warden aerodrome, Biggleswade, Bedfordshire.

Restoration work commenced in 1958, on a low priority basis, in the company's Experimental Department, under the supervision of H. F. 'Bert' Clatworthy who had, during the days of its production, been a fitter on Bulldogs. Apprentices were used to carry out much of the work on the airframe under the guidance of the senior foreman George Kington, aided by R. G. Brown from 188 Department. The airframe was, apart from its fabric and aluminium panelling, basically sound, bearing ample testimony to the protective powers of its original stove-enamelled paint finish. The major part of the restorative work on the airframe concerned gas starter, braking, control and electrical systems, as well as instruments, which meant calling upon archive drawings, or hand drawn sketches, for the machining of replacement parts.

A search was made by the company for a suitable Jupiter VIIF engine to install in *G-ABBB*, with the result that a 1931-built VIIFP (no J7508), which had been in the possession of No 391 Squadron of the ATC at Wilmslow, Cheshire, was purchased from the Air Ministry. The engine, which was kept in the Nissen hut building used by the ATC squadron, had to be partially dismantled by the company's representative before it would pass through the doorway and on to the lorry that was waiting to transport it back to Bristol. In addition, three more Jupiter engines were discovered in their packing cases in a barn at Tockington, near Fedden's old home, allegedly put there in Barnwell's day. The ex-ATC engine J7508 was stripped and examined, revealing certain

Bristol Chief Test Pilot Godfrey Auty with the restored Bulldog, *G-ABBB*, at Filton 1961 *(British Aerospace, Filton).*

shortages, whilst the other three engines were similarly stripped in order to provide spares. Any missing parts that they were required were made in the Apprentices' School of Bristol Siddeley Engines Ltd.

The engine was finally rebuilt and installed on a dynamometer in the Piston Engine Development and Test Department of BSE, on 26 January 1961, for testing prior to flight in the Bulldog. The tests, which were conducted during the next two weeks, included thirty minutes' light running at 600 rpm, followed by thirty minutes' progressive opening up to 90 per cent power at 1,775 rpm, with fuel consumption checks being made throughout the test-programme. A further one hour's running at 90 per cent power, at 1,775 rpm, in order to check oil consumption was made, followed by two spells of five minutes each at 1,775 and 1,950 rpm with zero boost. This was followed by slow running checks and adjustment to give 530 rpm, as well as three accelerations from slow running to 1,775 rpm with the dynamometer set to 405 bhp. Apart from oil leakage caused by paint under the ball seatings

of the priming nipples lubricating the blower gears, which was quickly remedied, all the tests were completed satisfactorily. The final report dated 21 February 1961 showed that the engine came up to the required standards and commented that the Jupiter was 'truly ship-shape and Bristol fashion'.

The company was able to draw upon the experience of older craftsmen for such things as the renovation of the wooden Watts propeller, made in February 1929 by the Airscrew Co of Weybridge. One former employee, 84-year-old Ralph Harris of the Woodwork Shop, was still able to impart some of the 'tricks of the trade' when called upon for advice on the propeller! Problems in manufacturing a new spinner for *G-ABBB* were also resolved when an archive drawing of the component revealed that it had been drawn by former draughtsman, Freddie W. Stokes. He was still with the company at that time, now as the manager of Technical Publications, and was therefore able to advise on its precise construction.

When the aircraft had last been in use, as a test-bed for the Aquila I sleeve valve engine, it had been installed with an electric starter, and not the standard RAE Mark II gas starter system normally used with the Jupiter engine. To recreate the complete original system meant the manufacture of some items from old drawings, replacement of certain parts with more readily available alternatives and lastly, with components obtained as a result of enquiries to the original suppliers of ancillary equipment. Further work resulted in apprentices machining a new press cock, vaporiser and master cock, under the supervision of C. Walker of Manufacturing Development, whilst a 750-litre aircraft type nitrogen bottle replaced the original air bottle which was of riveted construction.

One particularly helpful contribution was made by the joint Managing Director of Ki-Glass Ltd, Leamington Spa, Group Captain R. B. Wardman, in the form of a replica of the original primer pump. He presented the vital component to the company with his compliments, adding that it gave him great pleasure as he was himself 'an old Bulldog pilot'. All the parts were finally assembled

on the bench for proof pressure (to 300 psi) and functional tests of the separate components and the complete system. In the interests of safety kerosene instead of petrol was used in the functional tests in order to verify complete atomisation of the fuel at 200 psi. Satisfactory results were obtained during twelve operations of the system, which was witnessed by test pilot J. Ian Williamson and members of the Inspection Department, before it was all installed into *G-ABBB*. On 8 June 1961 the rebuilt and overhauled Jupiter VIIFP engine was installed, complete with its 8 ft 10.5 in diameter propeller (8 ft 3.5 in pitch), prior to its endurance and check test before flight. During the engine run, checks were made at maximum rpm for zero boost, oil pressure, slow running, and on the Watford SP9/2 magnetos which each gave an acceptable drop in engine speed of 30 rpm. Furthermore, airframe rigging checks for incidence, dihedral, stagger and symmetry of mainplanes, as well as verification of aileron, elevator and rudder ranges were made, before the aircraft was deemed fit for flight.

Two members of the company's inspection staff with the restored *G-ABBB* at Filton, 1961 *(A. Gregory)*.

Bristol Test Pilot Ian Williamson *(British Aerospace, Filton).*

Company sales demonstrator, Bulldog *G-ABBB,* made its 'first flight' over Filton at 08:04 on 23 June 1961 with Godfrey L. Auty, the company's chief test pilot, at the controls. It was to be the beginning of a series of test flights to satisfy airworthiness standards for the purposes of demonstration at public displays, and for general flying under Class B registration. What nostalgia for all those old-timers who had remembered the aircraft flying over the factory almost 26 years ago — this was the last flying example of a Bulldog anywhere in the world! The initial flight lasted for 36 minutes and its pilot was to recall some time later:

'The aircraft was a joy to fly, plenty of power, manoeuvrable, and a lovely aerobatic aircraft which was very stable in the climb and cruise, being able to be flown 'hands off' without trouble. The elevator was a little lacking in power making it less easy to do a true three-point landing. Ground manoeuvring was not helped by the awkwardly positioned footbrake pedals, although this may not have been so noticeable on the old grass airfields and when a tailskid was fitted. However, I regard myself as having been most fortunate to have flown the aircraft and I thoroughly enjoyed the experience.'

Test pilot Ian Williamson, who took the aircraft up for his own first flight later that same morning, was to perform low-level rolls and loops at Filton in July, much to the delight of those watching. In view of the age of the aircraft and its historic value, certain restrictions were placed upon aerobatics involving high 'g' forces such as flick rolls, spinning and manoeuvres in the bunting plane.

Godfrey Auty's flight-test report dated 21 August 1961 makes the following comments:

'Take-off

'The take-off was made on the grass and into wind. The elevator was trimmed one complete turn nose-up. Mixture setting was "Rich" and the air intake "Warm".

'The throttle was opened with brakes off and the aircraft rolled forward with little torque effect, directional control being easily maintained with the rudder. The stick was eased forward slightly and the tail raised. At 65 mph the stick was gently eased back, approximately 2 in, and the aircraft rotated easily, reaching the 50 ft point approximately 600-700 ft from the commencement of roll, the engine at T.O. producing 1,520 rpm.

'Climb

'From the 50 ft point the aircraft accelerated quickly to the climbing speed of 82 mph. The aircraft trimmed nicely at this speed and could be flown hands-off with only a small amount of rudder. Max continuous 1,775 rpm were not achieved until 9,000 ft.

'Level flight

'The aircraft can be trimmed to fly hands-off in level flight, the amount of rudder required to maintain directional trim varying with speed and power. Quite a pronounced rolling moment is produced with rudder application and rudder is necessary for a balanced turn.

'Stalls

'The aircraft was trimmed power-off 800 rpm at 80 mph at 10,000 ft, and two stalls carried out. As the speed was reduced, mild buffet commenced at 55 mph increasing slightly in intensity just before the right wing started to drop at 51 mph, this being held by aileron, followed by a straight nose drop at 50 mph.

'By accelerating the stall, aileron snatch can be produced.

'Aerobatics

'The following manoeuvres were carried out at the speeds quoted, the aircraft responding to the controls in the normal manner and the control forces remaining positive:

Power on dive 220 mph

Loop 180 mph
Roll 140 mph
Stall turn 140 mph
Roll off the top 210 mph

'Approach and Landing

'The approach for landing was made with mixture "Rich" and air intake "Warm" at a speed of 1.4 Vs 70 mph. This speed was easy to maintain and the rate of descent was controlled by use of the throttle. The aircraft touched down at 60 mph on the mainwheels, elevator power being inadequate for a three-point landing. During the landing run there was tendency for the right wing to drop, but this was corrected by immediate use of aileron and rudder.

'Conclusions

'After the first flight of the aircraft there were only two snags. The first was the inability of the throttle friction damper to hold the throttle setting constant in the wider-open range. The second fault was the fast, slow-running setting of the engine.

'The aircraft was a delight to fly and the persons associated with its rebuild are to be highly commended for doing a really first-class job.'

★   ★   ★

Saturday 24 June 1961 saw the Bulldog make its first public appearance at nearby Lulsgate aerodrome where, after an early morning sea mist, the weather gave way to a hot, sunny afternoon. The main event of the day was the Bristol Air Race which had last been held in 1951. It was a handicap race over three laps of a sixteen-mile course and was won by A. J. Spinner in a Percival Proctor. However, the highlight of the day for many was to be a flypast of three military biplanes, which included Shuttleworth's Bristol F2B Fighter and Gloster Gladiator, together with the Bulldog in its pristine silver paintwork. No doubt the camera shutters were clicking furiously as these three famous fighters brought pleasure to young and old alike. The Shuttleworth Collection felt that *G-ABBB* would be more in keeping with its 'Brisfit' and 'Gladiator' exhibits, as well as more truly reflecting the large RAF usage of the type with the ten pre-war squadrons, if it too were finished in military livery. A decision was therefore made to finish the Bulldog in No 56(F) Squadron's red and white chequerboard markings, and to allocate it with one of their old Bulldog serial numbers — *K2227*. It was in this form that, on 12 September 1961, a handing over ceremony took place at Filton, with representatives of the Shuttleworth Trust receiving their new addition to the collection.

G-ABBB coming in to land at Filton 1961 *(British Aerospace, Filton)*.

Shuttleworth wasted no time in displaying their new acquisition, for only four days later *K2227* was flown by Ian Williamson accompanied by Godfrey Auty in the Bristol Fighter, *D8096*, to RAF Coltishall. Here *K2227*, now with Godfrey Auty at the controls was to join with No 56(F) Squadron's Hawker Hurricane, Gloster Meteor, Hawker Hunter and English-Electric Lightning in order to participate in a Battle of Britain flypast. The next day a photographic sortie was arranged in which four of the aircraft would attempt a formation pose, with the photographs being taken from the Meteor. Squadron Leader J. R. Rogers (later to become Air Chief Marshal Sir John Rogers, KCB, CBE) was piloting the Lightning on that day and he recalls:

'Due to runway resurfacing at Wattisham the sortie was flown from Coltishall on 17 September 1961. We could not actually fly formation, even in a turn, as the minimum safe speed of the Lightning was some fifty knots above the maximum of the Bulldog. The

Meteor was also some ten knots "too fast", thus we had to do a double fly-by, one on either side of *K2227*, and hope that the photographer could get a reasonable shot . . .

'The other difficulty was that it was a misty day with no horizon, not great for low level, low speed manoeuvring in a Lightning. In fact we almost got a close-up of Norwich Cathedral in one pass!'

The outcome of that historic sortie was to be at least two memorable photographs, both of which are, to this day, proudly displayed at RAF Wattisham, the home of No 56(F) Squadron, now equipped with Phantoms. One man who would dearly loved to have witnessed the event on the day, but had to be satisfied with the photographer's efforts, was Wing Commander Leslie S. Holman, AFC, now living in quiet retirement with his wife in their beautiful Avon home. He joined the RAF in January 1924 as a 15½ year old to become, on ten shillings a week, what was customarily known as one of 'Trenchard's

K2227 coming in to land at Filton 1961 *(British Aerospace, Filton).*

The original 56(F) Squadron *K2227* fitted with polygonal plate type cowling *(MoD).*

brats' — a boy apprentice — at Halton's No 1 School of Technical Training in their fourth entry. After a three-year apprenticeship with rigging and engine instruction on DH9As, Bristol Fighters, Avro 504Ks and Sopwith Snipes, he was posted, as a lowly Aircraftman, to Calshot. This station was at the time the home of the RAF's 'High Speed Flight', which was engaged in the technical development of the Supermarine S4 and S5 Schneider Trophy floatplanes. He was, in May 1928, posted to an FAA Spotter Reconnaissance Flight using Fairey IIIDs, and it was during his two-year spell with HMS *Vindictive* that he volunteered and was accepted for pilot training. On 1 April 1930 he arrived at No 5 FTS Sealand as a pupil pilot where he was to receive dual-instruction in the ubiquitous 504K, from First World War veteran pilot and tutor, Flight Lieutenant Alan Jerrard, VC. He remembers his time there with some humour, particularly when recalling a solo cross-country flight that he and others were required to do as part of their flying training. The route included a landing at No 3 FTS at Grantham before returning to Sealand, which, owing to poor weather conditions with low cloud, took more than a little difficulty in locating. Realising that he was hopelessly lost he decided to 'fly by Bradshaw', which meant finding a suitable

railway line leading to a station and taking the Siskin down low enough to read the name on the platform-board. He saw a railway line running north to south and passed between a station's platforms, past the signal-box, low enough to read 'Godmanchester' and with his bearing now established he soon landed at Grantham. A few moments later an agitated fitter was examining the Siskin's undercarriage, around which was wrapped a trailing length of telephone wire, exclaiming to the red-faced pilot, 'Eh, Sarge, where have you been with this aeroplane?'

Sergeant Pilot Holman gained an 'above average' pilot's assessment at Sealand, and on 13 March 1931 was posted to No 56(F) Squadron, North Weald, which at that time was equipped with Siskin IIIAs. He made rather an inauspicious start with the squadron for within a few days he had crashed a Siskin on landing. Being unaccustomed to the increased weight of the fully equipped fighter carrying armament, he had not taken this into account when making his landing approach and had held off too early. In October 1932 the squadron was re-equipped with Bulldog Mark IIAs and on the 21st of that month he made his first flight in a mint, oil-stain free specimen — *K2227*!

Leslie Holman was to remain in 'B' Flight with

Godfrey Auty in *K2227* alongside Squadron Leader John Rogers in Lightning *XM174* over Coltishall on 17 September 1961 *(British Aerospace, Filton)*.

the squadron for five years logging over 600 hours in Bulldogs and, although his regular aircraft was *K2224,* many of these hours were in *K2227*. At one time later during its operational usage *K2227,* along with *K2206,* was fitted with the thin polygonal plate type experimental Townend cowling ring. The aircraft remained with the squadron throughout the whole of its operational life until declared obsolete in July 1937, whereupon it was allocated to a School of Technical Training, as instructional airframe No 978M.

The Shuttleworth Bulldog, *K2227,* left Coltishall on the day of its aerial meeting with its younger brethren and was flown to RAF Henlow, where it was stored throughout the winter. Its Jupiter was given occasional runs on a regular basis whilst it was in storage, and on 6 June 1962 it made the short flight from Henlow to Old Warden for an RAFA display. Five days later Godfrey Auty flew it to a Whit-Monday flying display at North Weald, where it vied in competition with the F-100s and F-101s of the USAF before an estimated crowd of some 30,000 spectators. Bristol's chief test pilot put on a spectacular aerobatic performance under leaden skies, much to the enjoyment of the crowd. Unfortunately, he applied the aircraft's brakes a little too vigorously upon landing, and *K2227* did a nose-over, finishing up on its back. Luckily the pilot was little more than shaken, but considerable damage had been sustained by the Bulldog which was, a few days later, returned by road to Filton for check and repair.

Back at the factory the engine was removed to enable repairs to be carried out to its engine bearers, whilst repairs were also made to the mainplanes and tailplane structure. The original propeller was damaged beyond repair by the mishap and a search was made for a replacement. Enquiries were soon rewarded when a brand new, unused, specimen was found behind the bar of the Officers' Mess at RAF Leeming in Yorkshire. After some negotiation it was procured and fitted to the aircraft ready for its first test flight, since repair, on 7 August 1963.

K2227 was in great demand around the country from the organisers of the traditional September Battle of Britain Air Displays, and on the 14th it was flown from Filton to the Midlands for events at Tern Hill and Gaydon. Unfortunately, upon landing at Tern Hill the aircraft ground looped, due to the grass landing area being out of wind, and the port lower wingtip was slightly damaged. Temporary repairs were hastily carried out, in order not to disappoint the crowd, and *K2227* was put through its paces before being flown on to Gaydon for the final display of the day. Its performance here did not include the intended landing, due again to unfavourable cross-winds, and rather than chance more damage it was flown on to Bagington, near Coventry. After examination, it was decided that the damage did not warrant the delay of the aircraft's return, and so, on the next day, it was flown to RAF Henlow, where repairs were carried out by staff of the RAF Technical College before its winter storage.

Apart from a showing at Filton for an RAFA event on 19 June 1964, the restored Bulldog was to make only one further, and final, public appearance. This was to be for the SBAC Air Show at Farnborough on 13 September where Bristol's test pilot Ian Williamson was, just prior to the event, performing a low-level loop when the engine failed. He was not quite able to reach the touch-down area on the airfield, and as a consequence crashed heavily, completely wrecking the aircraft and injuring himself. An investigation into the cause of the crash was made later by the Accident Branch of the RAE, where suspicion was thrown upon the Bulldog's magnetos. Both of the Rotax 'Watford' units were sent to the Accident Investigation Unit of HMS *Daedalus*, Lee-on-Solent, where close examination in their Magneto Bay revealed that one magneto was 'dead' and the other, whilst still functioning, was well below specification. All of the wreckage worth retaining was removed from the RAE by the Shuttleworth Collection and transported back to Henlow and Cardington, where to this day it remains, along with a pair of Bulldog mainplanes largely complete but unconnected with *K2227*.

And so the final Bulldog — the last in the pack — made its ignominious departure from the skies, *K2227* being the last flying example of the type. Arguments will continue between the two schools of thought; to restore and fly, or merely to put on static display? Maybe one day another replica will be built and bring delight to a new generation of veteran aircraft enthusiasts. Until that day one must live with the memories!

Chapter 10
Epilogue

Barnwell and Frise's partnership was not to be harmed by the latter's success with Bulldog and the pair continued to work closely together until 1936, when Barnwell was appointed Chief Engineer and relinquished his post as Chief Aircraft Designer to the younger man. They were to achieve some remarkable successes, notably with the Bristol Bombay, a bomber/troop transport high wing monoplane with fixed faired undercarriage that went into production in 1937; Type 133, the first modern single-seat fighter to be built in the UK; Type 138A, a large single-seat high altitude monoplane that twice broke the world's altitude record, reaching 49,967 ft on 28 September 1936 when it broke the existing French record, and again on 30 June 1937 when it reached 53,937 ft to exceed an Italian record; Type 142, 'Britain First', a privately sponsored twin-engined low wing monoplane — the fastest civil aircraft of its day and forerunner of the famous wartime Blenheim.

The Type 133 is particularly worthy of note, for it was an aircraft ahead of its time and one designed specifically to meet the Air Ministry specification F7/30 for a four-gun single-seat fighter, after the company had failed to gain a foothold with the Bulldog IV or the Type 123 (the last biplane to come from Bristol). It was a low wing cantilever monoplane of all-metal, stressed-skin construction, with wing-flaps, hydraulically-operated semi-retracting undercarriage, a fully-cowled Mercury VIS4 air-cooled engine, enclosed cockpit with sliding hood and headrest, and a four-gun armament consisting of twin Vickers mounted in the fuselage and wing-mounted Lewis guns firing outside the airscrew disc. Test flights had shown a maximum speed of 260 mph, a rate of climb of 2,200 ft/min and excellent flying qualities. So confident was the Bristol Aeroplane Co that it would win the F7/30 competition against its rivals that preparations were, even before its entry, being made for its production. Although it made its maiden flight on 8 July 1934 (Hurricane and Spitfire prototypes first flew on 6 November 1935 and 5 March 1936 respectively), it was not ready for evaluation trials at Martlesham until the spring of 1935. Cyril Uwins had been putting the prototype through its paces just prior to its despatch to the 'Heath when he decided to allow test pilot colleague T. W. 'Jock' Campbell to make a thirty-minute test flight. Campbell took off and proceeded to carry out various manoeuvres before deciding to lower the undercarriage in preparation for his first landing. Just as he was making his approach he remembered that he had not spun the aircraft, so climbing to 15,000 ft he then put the prototype *R10* into a spin, completely forgetting that he had not raised the undercarriage. In the ensuing spin, the fin area of the wheels destabilised the aircraft and he found that he could not make a recovery. He was forced to abandon the aircraft over Longwell Green, south-east of Bristol, landing by parachute safely nearby. A. E. Russell was Chief Technician at the time and to this day has no doubt that had this unfortunate mishap not occurred, then the Bristol Aeroplane Co would have been producing single-seat fighters in the 1939-1945 period.

Barnwell's death in 1938 came as a shock to his colleagues and to the company, but it was not entirely unexpected for he insisted on flying, even though he had suffered some pretty close shaves in flying accidents over the years, beginning with his time in the RFC. Ever since he crashed the company's 'Brownie' — a two-seat light monoplane — at Farnborough in 1928, in almost the same spot that he had crashed the MR1 nine years earlier, there were grave doubts about his flying ability. By 1937 the Directors had forbidden him to fly any of the company's aircraft, deeming him to be uninsurable, but he persisted in flying privately. A great believer in the light aeroplane he had, with the help of his eldest son Tony and staff at Bristol Airport, Whitchurch, constructed an aircraft to his own design which he first flew in July 1938. It was a small wooden monoplane, designated BSW1, and powered by a 34 bhp Scott-Squirrel two-stroke twin-cylinder engine. Russell had offered to vet the design and Uwins had offered to fly it and give his opinion, but such was Barnwell's modesty that he would not even show drawings of it, and proffered the reply 'I wouldn't insult you . . .' Frank Owner had warned

Barnwell of the unreliability of the Scott engine for use in an aeroplane, having had experience with its motor cycle antecedents, but the 'Old Man' was undeterred and after making some modifications, made the second and final flight that was to end in tragedy.

Barnwell was truly a pioneer of aviation, a man of courage, modest to the point of being self-effacing and with endearing personal qualities that left him without enemies. Including those aircraft which did not reach the prototype stage, he was responsible for some 150 design types during his 27 years with the company — truly a remarkable achievement. His three young sons were to perish whilst on active service as pilots with the RAF within three years of their father's death. Ironically, two of them, Tony and John, were lost in Bristol Blenheims, whilst David, a Hurricane pilot, was killed in combat during the defence of Malta. The Barnwells were a brave and courageous family and one to whom people in Britain owe a great debt.

After Barnwell's death Frise was left to lead the Filton design team into the Second World War with some very useful, if not brilliant, aircraft including Blenheim I, IV and V and Beaufort. The Beaufighter which, with its large powerful Hercules radials and short snub nose, vied in appearance with its pugnacious predecessor Bulldog, was probably Frise's most successful wartime aeroplane. It was to be used in many theatres of war and in many different roles; from that of a radar-equipped night fighter, anti-shipping strike fighter, to that of a long-range day fighter where its ability to carry rockets, bombs, torpedo and cannon, combined with its high performance, made it a very formidable enemy indeed. The Brigand, a derivative of the Buckingham bomber, was originally designed by Frise in 1942 as a replacement for the Beaufighter in its torpedo carrying role and first flew late in 1944. It was, however, never as successful as the 'Beau' and was relegated to a ground-attack strike role against terrorist forces in the Malayan jungle in the early 1950s.

Frise was to leave Bristol in 1948, thereby ending a 32-year-long relationship with the company, but not before he had pioneered the use of nose-loading doors in the capacious Bristol Freighter — an aircraft which he had developed from the Bombay transport — as well as designing the giant Brabazon, probably his biggest undertaking. Fresh designs emerged from his fertile and talented brain when he moved to Percival, later Hunting Percival, first as their Technical Director, and finally as Chief Engineer. He came up with a string of successful aircraft over an eight-year period, producing Prince, and its highly versatile naval version Sea Prince which, apart from its uses in aerial survey and navigation training, was also a much sought-after small airliner and executive aircraft; Pembroke, piston-Provost and finally Jet Provost (from which BAC developed an export version, the light tactical strike aircraft, Strikemaster) followed. It says something for the genius of the man that Jet Provost, the RAF's present day basic trainer, has been in use for over thirty years both at home and abroad — and that from a man who worked on 'Brisfit' in World War I!

He left Hunting Percival in 1956 to become Director of Special Projects with the Blackburn Aircraft Co where he remained until his 'retirement' in 1962 but, being the visionary that he was, he became restless for new ideas, not necessarily confined to aircraft, and formed his own companies, Frise Patents Ltd and Frise Enterprises Ltd. He died, almost in obscurity, on 26 September 1979 at his home in Clifton, after suffering a series of strokes. His innovative flair as a pioneer aircraft designer had never made him a rich man, or rewarded him with the recognition that was his due, but as his charming wife Sidonie remarked, 'it never made him bitter either'. As I descended the staircase of his apartment, earlier in the year, my eye was greeted by an evocative painting of the Bristol Bulldog in full flight banking over the green English countryside. It spoke of a bygone age and seemed to be dipping its wings in salute to its creator, Leslie George Frise — one could almost hear the roar of Fedden's Jupiter and sense the sound of the wind singing in the wires!

Cyril F. Uwins, OBE, AFC, FRAeS, was to relinquish his post as Chief Test Pilot in 1947 having been responsible for the testing of 54 prototypes — all with the one company — and retired in 1964 as Deputy Chairman of the Bristol Aeroplane Co. He died in 1972, but will forever hold a place in the history of the Filton design office, for not only did he span the period from 'stick and string' biplane to modern all-metal monoplane, but he must take no small part of the credit for the flying qualities of Barnwell and Frise's designs.

Sir Archibald Russell and Frank Owner are both survivors from a very tough period indeed and one which has taken its toll of their contemporaries. They have both been highly honoured for their great contribution to British aviation and now live quietly in well-deserved retirement in the south-west of England.

Aerial warfare, particularly in the role of a fighter pilot, is a young man's task and by the time the skies of southern England were echoing to the roar of Merlin and Daimler-Benz, machine-gun and cannon fire, in the summer of 1940, the majority of the men who had flown Bulldog were already in their late twenties. Some such as John Rye had, in the pre-war years, become flying instructors where they fulfilled the valuable duty of training the very same young men who were then locked in combat with their German counterparts; others, more than thirty in number, were to become the leaders of the 68 squadrons, flights and units which took part in the Battle of Britain. In addition, some had previously seen action from the airfields of northern France, prior to the collapse and retreat from that country earlier in the year. Some were to fly and fight in Hurricane, Spitfire, Defiant, Blenheim, Beaufighter, Whirlwind, Havoc and Mosquito over other skies, in other battles.

Sadly, very few are still alive today. Many were to be killed in the air battles of World War 2, others have died with the passing years. Lack of space in this volume forbids more than a brief pen-picture of but a few.

Let us cast our minds back to that memorable summer of 1940.

Pilot Officer R. L. Wilkinson was posted to 'A' Flight of 3(F) at Upavon on 18 January 1931, and as a Squadron Leader commanding Spitfire Squadron 266 from Hornchurch, fell in flames over Eastry Court, Kent, on Friday 13 August 1940.

Acting/Pilot Officer J. T. Webster of 17(F) Kenley in 1936, a Flight Lieutenant with 41(F) in 1940, had an Me Bf 109E tantalisingly in the gunsight of his Spitfire I over the Channel on Sunday, 28 July. Several bursts from Webster's Brownings sent Major Werner Mölders of *Jagdgeschwader 51* seeking the safety of a French beach, upon which the German ace belly landed unceremoniously to a halt — alive to fight another day. Little respite was afforded Webster for the very next morning he was scrambled early and at 08:00 he crashlanded back at his Manston base having been damaged in action over Dover. Six weeks later, over the Thames estuary, he was heavily engaged with the Me 109 escorts of a flock of Dornier 17s when he collided with another Spitfire and sadly was killed as he attempted to bale out.

Sergeant Pilot George Lott of 'C' Flight 19(F) Duxford in 1932 was a Squadron Leader and CO of 43 Squadron in 1940. On patrol in his faithful Hurricane 'I was fool enough to joust head-on with an Me 110 over the Channel on 9 July (the Battle of Britain officially began on the 10th) — he had 20 mm cannon against my .303s — as a result of which I lost my right eye and my pilot's category'.

Pilot Officer Terence Gunion Lovell-Gregg, the young mustachioed New Zealander of 41(F)'s Northolt Bulldogs, was leading the last five serviceable Hurricanes of 87 Squadron, on 15th August 1940, to intercept a swarm of Bf 109s, and '110s escorting their Stukas over the Lyme Bay area. He had practised many 'Battle Climbs' but this one was for real and it was to be his last. Whilst going for the dive bombers the Hurricanes were bounced by the higher flying escort fighters, and within a short while the five were badly damaged and forced to break the engagement. The leader's lone Hurricane, trailing fire and smoke, crossed the coast at the western edge of Chesil Bank making for an emergency landing at Warmwell, but only to crash in a copse near Abbottsbury. At Exeter, 87 Squadron received the message from Warmwell during the late afternoon — 'Shovel' Gregg their commanding officer was dead.

To those who lost their lives; to those who lost their health; to those who lost their freedom — we salute you all — brave men of the Bulldog squadrons. Long may your people remember you!

Appendix 1
Technical data

Dimensions	*Bulldog I*	*Bulldog II*	*Bulldog IIA*	*Bulldog IIIA*
Span, upper	34 ft 0 in	33 ft 10 in	33 ft 10 in	33 ft 8 in
Span, lower	27 ft 6 in	27 ft 6 in	27 ft 6 in	27 ft 6 in
Chord, upper	6 ft 4 in	6 ft 4 in	6 ft 4 in	6 ft 4 in
Chord, lower	4 ft 9 in	4 ft 9 in	4 ft 9 in	4 ft 2 in
Gap	5 ft 0 in	5 ft 0 in	5 ft 0in	4 ft 10.5 in
Stagger	2 ft 0.5 in	2 ft 0.5 in	2 ft 0.5 in	2 ft 1.25 in
Dihedral	5°	5°	5°	5°
Sweepback	—	—	—	—
Wing area	307 sq ft	307 sq ft	307 sq ft	294 sq ft
Height	8 ft 9 in	8 ft 9 in	8 ft 9 in	9 ft 1 in
Length	23 ft 0 in	25 ft 2 in	25 ft 2 in	25 ft 4 in
Wheel track	5 ft 5 in	5 ft 5 in	6 ft 2.5 in	6 ft 2.5 in

Weights				
Empty	1,987 lb	2,200 lb	2,222 lb	2,800 lb
All-up weight	3,250 lb	3,490 lb	3,530 lb -3,660 lb	4,000 lb

Engine				
Type	440 hp Jupiter VII	440 hp Jupiter VII	440 hp Jupiter VIIF or 440 hp Jupiter VIIFP	Mercury IVA

Performance				
Maximum speed	173 mph	178 mph	178 mph	208 mph
Service ceiling	27,000 ft	29,300 ft	29,300 ft	31,000 ft
Climb	Not known	Not known	14.5 min to 20,000 ft	Not known
Range	350 m at 15,000 ft	350 m at 15,000 ft	350 m at 15,000 ft	Not known
Fuel capacity	70 gal	70 gal	70 gal	70 gal

Production				
Quantity	2	92	268	2

Dimensions	Bulldog IV	Bulldog IVA	Bulldog TM	Bullpup
Span, upper	33 ft 8 in	33 ft 8 in	34 ft 2 in	30 ft 0 in
Span, lower	27 ft 6 in	27 ft 6 in	27 ft 6 in	24 ft 0 in
Chord, upper	6 ft 4 in	6 ft 4 in	6 ft 4 in	5 ft 6 in
Chord, lower	4 ft 2 in	4 ft 2 in	4 ft 9 in	4 ft 0 in
Gap	4 ft 10.5 in	4 ft 10.5 in	5 ft 0 in	Not known
Stagger	2 ft 1.25 in	2 ft 1.25 in	2 ft 0.75 in	Not known
Dihedral	5°	5°	5°	5°
Sweepback	—	—	3.5°	—
Wing area	294 sq ft	294 sq ft	309 sq ft	230 sq ft
Height	9 ft 1 in	9 ft 1 in	8 ft 9 in	10 ft 0 in
Length	25 ft 4 in	25 ft 4 in	25 ft 3 in	23 ft 2.125 in
Wheel track	6 ft 2.5 in	6 ft 3.5 in	6 ft 0 in	5 ft 0 in
Weights				
Empty	2,810 lb	2,690 lb	2,200 lb	1,910 lb
All-up weight	4,100 lb	4,010 lb	3,300 lb	2,850 lb
Engine				
Type	560 hp Mercury IVS2	640 hp Mercury VIS2 or 600 hp Perseus IA	450 hp Jupiter VIFH, 350 hp Napier Rapier, 345 hp AS Cheetah IX or 480 hp Alvis Leonides	450 hp Jupiter VI, 450 hp Mercury IIA, 440 hp Jupiter VII, 400 hp Mercury Short stroke or 500 hp Aquila I
Performance				
Maximum speed	218 mph	224 mph	168 mph	190 mph (Mercury IIA)
Service ceiling	31,700 ft	33,400 ft	28,000 ft	Not known
Fuel capacity	70 gal	70 gal	70 gal	70 gal
Production				
Quantity	(1)	18	59	1

Armament

Twin Vickers .303 in machine-guns synchronised by Constantinesco gear; provision for carrying four 20 lb Cooper HE bombs under port wing.

Appendix 2
Bristol Type numbers referred to in the text

Type numbers were not allocated to any of the Bristol constructed or proposed aircraft until January 1924 whereupon they were introduced retrospectively (Types 1 to 89) and in a strict chronological order. Dates shown are the year in which the first flight was made.

Type No	Name	Engine	Year
1	Scout C	80 hp Gnôme	1914
2	Scout D	80 hp Gnôme	1915
3	Scout D	80 hp Le Rhône	1915
4	Scout D	100 hp Mono-Gnôme	1916
5	Scout D	130 hp Clerget	1916
10	M1A	110 hp Clerget	1916
11	M1B	110 hp Clerget or Le Rhône	1916
12	F2A	190 hp Rolls-Royce	1916
13	MR1	140 hp Hispano-Suiza	1916
14	F2B-1&11	190/275 hp Rolls-Royce Falcon	1917
15	F2B	200 hp Sunbeam Arab	1917
16	F2B	200 hp Hispano-Suiza	1917
17	F2B	300 hp Hispano-Suiza	1918
18	Scout E	200 hp RH Cruciform	1917
20	M1C	110 hp Le Rhône	1917
21	Scout F	200 hp Sunbeam Arab	1917
23	Badger	320 hp ABC Dragonfly 1A	1918
27	F2B Coupé	275 hp Rolls-Royce Falcon III	1919
28	Tourer (3-seat Coupé)	230 hp Siddeley Puma	1919
30	Babe Mk I	40 hp Viale	1919
32	Bullet	450 hp Jupiter II	1919
37	Tramp	Four 230 hp Siddeley Puma	1919
52	Bullfinch (SS Monoplane)	450 hp Jupiter	1920
53	Bullfinch (TS Biplane)	450 hp Jupiter	1920
83	PTM (L2S)	140 hp Lucifer	1923
84	Bloodhound	450 hp Jupiter VI	1923
89	Jupiter School	320 hp Jupiter	1923
90	Berkeley Mk I	650 hp Rolls-Royce Condor	1925
91	Brownie Mk I	35 hp Cherub	1924
93	Boarhound Mk I	425 hp Jupiter	1925
93A	Beaver	450 hp Jupiter	1927
99	Badminton I	510 hp Jupiter VI	1926

99A	Badminton II	525 hp Jupiter VI(SS)	1927
101	Fighter	450 hp Jupiter VI or VIA	1927
102A	Badminton F	510 hp Jupiter VI	1926
105A	Bulldog IIA	440 hp Jupiter VIIF	1927
105D	Bulldog (Danish)	450 hp Jupiter VIFH	1931
107	Bullpup	480 hp Mercury IIA	1928
123	F7/30 Biplane		
	Fighter	695 hp Rolls-Royce Goshawk III	1934
124	Bulldog TM	450 hp Jupiter VIFH	1932
130	Bombay	Two 1,010 hp Pegasus	1935
133	SS Monoplane		
	Fighter	640 hp Mercury	1934
138A	HA Monoplane	500 hp Pegasus PE6S	1936
142	'Britain First'	Two 650 hp Mercury VIS	1935
142M	Blenheim Mk I	Two 840 hp Mercury VIII	1936
149	Blenheim IV	Two 995 hp Mercury XV	1938
152	Beaufort	Two 1,130 hp Taurus II	1938
156	Beaufighter	Two 1,425 hp Hercules III	1939
160	Blenheim V	Two 950 hp Mercury	1941
163	Buckingham	Two 2,400 hp Centaurus	1943
164	Brigand	Two 2,400 hp Centaurus	1944
167	Brabazon I	Eight 2,500 hp Centaurus/Proteus	1949
170	Freighter/		
	Wayfarer	Two 1675 hp Hercules 131	1945

Appendix 3
RAF squadrons, bases and pilots

No 3(F) Squadron —
Tertius primus erit ('The third shall be first')

Bulldog II	(6/32 — 12/32)
Bulldog IIA	(2/31 — 1/32 and 12/32 — 7/37)
Upavon, Wiltshire	(4/24 — 5/34)
Kenley, Surrey	(5/34 — 10/35)
Khartoum	(10/35 — 1/36)
Port Sudan	(1/36 — 8/36)
Kenley	(8/36 — 5/39)

COs

Squadron Leader E. Digby Johnson, AFC	(9/27 — 8/30)
Squadron Leader C. A. Stevens, MC	(8/30 — 3/34)
Squadron Leader G. Martyn	(3/34 — 3/36)
Squadron Leader H. L. P. Lester	(3/36 — 7/38)

Rank	Name	Rank	Name
FL	J. L. Airey	PO	E. P. Mackay
FL	Bartlett	FO	P. L. Marett
FL	D. W. Bayne	FL	H. M. Mellor
FO	D. P. A. Boitel-Gill	SgtP	V. M. Montanini
FL	D. S. Brookes	PO	G. K. Moreby
PO	M. F. Calder	PO	J. S. O'Brien
PO	J. K. L. Carstairs	FL	J. Oliver
FO	W. I. Clarke	PO	J. J. Owen
FO	C. K. J. Coggle	PO	R. C. Parker
SgtP	D. I. Coote	PO	M. C. Pearson
PO	W. D. Disbrey	SgtP	W. Phillips
PO	E. M. Donaldson	PO	J. C. Pope
PO	M. A. Douglas-Hamilton	FO	H. D. Primrose
SgtP	J. K. Down	FO	H. J. Pringle
PO	E. S. D. Drury	PO	H. M. Prowse
PO	Eyres	SgtP	A. E. Rundle
FO	A. D. Gillmore	PO	T. C. Sanders
SgtP	P. C. Ginn	SgtP	R. S. Scrase
FO	E. S. Greenwood	FL	A. T. K. Shipwright
FL	C. Guppy	F/SgtP	F. H. P. Simpson
PO	N. M. Hall	PO	C. N. Smith

FO	M. B. Hamilton		PO	W. V. L. Spendlove
PO	P. J. W. Hawkins		SgtP	Strauss
A/PO	H. Henry-May		PO	V. C. F. Streatfield
FO	P. H. Heygate		FL	H. W. Taylor
A/PO	D. B. Hobson		PO	J. H. M. Teacher
PO	Hoskin		PO	H. R. Tidd
PO	J. W. A. Hunnard		FL	J. W. Turton-Jones
SgtP	L. G. James		A/SgtP	J. Watson
FO	H. Kerr		FO	S. H. White
FL	B. W. Knox		A/SgtP	J. P. Whitehead
PO	W. E. L. Lewis		PO	R. L. Wilkinson
A/PO	D. A. P. Lister		SgtP	Williams
PO	R. H. McDonald		SgtP	J. D. W. Willis
PO	J. W. McGuire			

*   *   *

No 17(F) Squadron —

Excellere contende ('Strive to excel')

Bulldog II	(10/29 —)
Bulldog IIA	(— 8/36)
Upavon, Wiltshire	(10/26 — 5/34)
Kenley, Surrey	(5/34 — 5/39)

COs

Squadron Leader A. R. Arnold, DSO, DFC	(4/28 — 5/30)
Squadron Leader R. Harrison, DFC	(5/30 — 11/31)
Squadron Leader A. L. Fiddament	(11/31 — 4/32)
Squadron Leader L. M. Elworthy	(5/32 — 6/32)
Squadron Leader F. J. Vincent	(11/32 — 8/34)
Squadron Leader H. S. Broughall, MC, DFC	(8/34 — 8/35)
Flight Lieutenant G. P. Chamberlain	(8/35 — 10/35)
Squadron Leader D. d'H. Humphreys	(10/35 — 1/37)

Rank	Name		Rank	Name
PO	C. F. G. Adye		PO	W. H. Kyle
SgtP	R. L. Amor		SgtP	R. H. Little
FL	G. C. A. Armstrong		PO	N. B. Littlejohn
PO	M. A. Aylmer		PO	G. O. Llewellyn
A/PO	M. R. Baillon		SgtP	G. McPherson
FL	I. A. Bertram		SgtP	W. C. Maher
SgtP	W. Birkinshaw		PO	P. H. Maxwell
PO	J. B. Black		A/PO	M. R. Milward
FL	E. S. Borthwick-Clarke		FO	E. J. H. F. Moreton
SgtP	G. C. Brunner		PO	W. F. Pharazym

FO	G. Burdick	PO	A. M. K. Phillips
FL	M. F. Calder	A/PO	P. C. Pinkham
FL	B. B. Caswell	PO	R. H. Preller
FL	G. P. Chamberlain	PO	R. Pyne
PO	G. F. Clarke	PO	J. Quill
PO	F. C. Cole	SgtP	F. C. W. Rogers
SgtP	H. F. Croft	FO	Q. W. A. Ross
PO	P. Y. Davoud	PO	J. K. Rotherham
PO	H. R. A. Edwards	PO	P. S. Salter
SgtP	W. J. Etherington	PO	A. C. Shearn
SgtP	C. E. Fooks	A/PO	J. Shepherd-Smith
PO	F. S. Gardner	SgtP	S. Spencer
PO.	M. V. Gibbon	PO	E. A. Springall
FO	P. S. Gomez	FO	W. L. Stedman
PO	A. D. Grace	SgtP	A. Steel
SgtP	E. G. Greenwood	PO	Stodart
PO	A. L. Holland	SgtP	Taylor
SgtP	J. C. Hopkins	SgtP	L. H. Thompson
PO	L. M. Hooper	PO	K. R. Warton
A/PO	L. C. Jones-Bateman	PO	C. A. Watt
A/PO	R. G. Ker-Ramsay	A/PO	J. T. Webster
		FO	E. W. Whitley

*   *   *

No 19(F) Squadron —

Possuit quia posse videntur ('They can because they think they can')

Bulldog IIA	(9/31 — 1/35)
Duxford, Cambridgeshire	(4/23 — 4/40)

COs
Squadron Leader A. C. Sanderson, DFC	(7/31 — 2/34)
Squadron Leader J. R. Cassidy	(2/34 — 1/36)

Rank	Name	Rank	Name
FL	J. S. L. Adams	FO	R. H. Hobbs
FO	S. H. A. Barrow	PO	G. T. Jarman
PO	L. G. Belchem	SgtP	J. C. Kay
SgtP	J. S. W. Bignall	FL	V. E. C. de Lart
PO	B. W. E. R. Bonsey	FO	J. H. Lock
FL	H. Broadhurst	SgtP	C. G. Lott
FO	J. A. S. Brown	FO	W. M. L. MacDonald
SgtP	R. B. Bryn	FO	A. W. S. Matheson
FO	T. H. Burleigh	FO	B. N. Matson
FL	V. Croome	SgtP	R. Parr

Rank	Name		Rank	Name
PO	E. B. C. Davies		FL	H. W. Pearson-Rogers
SgtP	R. E. Drake		PO	J. R. A. Peel
FL	C. S. Ellison		FL	C. B. R. Pelly
SgtP	A. E. Feather		SgtP	W. J. Rye
PO	E. Foster		PO	D. Scorgie
FO	S. F. Godden		FO	G. N. Snarey *
SgtP	J. S. Graham		FO	A. W. Vincent
SgtP	L. Gregory			

* Met Flight only

*   *   *

No 23(F) Squadron —
Semper Agressus ('Always on the attack')

Bulldog IIA	(7/31 — 4/33)
Kenley, Surrey	(2/27 — 9/32)
Biggin Hill, Kent	(9/32 — 12/36)

COs
Squadron Leader H. H. Woollett, DSO, MC	(1/30 — 12/31)
Squadron Leader A. L. Paxton, DFC	(12/31 — 2/33)
Squadron Leader H. G. Crowe, MC	(2/33 — 9/35)

Rank	Name		Rank	Name
PO	D. R. S. Bader		FO	J. F. McKenna
FL	W. L. Bateman		FO	G. L. Menzies
PO	N. Daunt		PO	G. E. B. Nixon
PO	H. M. A. Day		PO	C. M. H. Outram
PO	J. A. Dixon		FO	G. W. Phillips
PO	A. E. Dobell		PO	W. A. Richardson
FO	D. G. P. Fitzpatrick		FO	P. Ross
PO	A. P. Glenny		PO	F. W. Shute
FL	S. H. V. Harris		PO	D. G. Singleton
FO	F. B. H. Hayward		PO	G. D. Stephenson
FO	H. R. L. Hood		PO	F. E. Stokes
SgtP	E. D. Jack		FO	A. T. Tunnard
PO	A. C. Johnstone		FO	M. Watson
FL	P. W. Lowe-Holmes			

*   *   *

No 29(F) Squadron —
Impiger et acer ('Energetic and keen')

Bulldog IIA	(6/32 — 4/35)
North Weald, Essex	(4/28 — 10/35)
COs	
Squadron Leader H. D. O'Neill, AFC	(4/31 — 8/33)
Squadron Leader J. H. Butler	(8/33 — 8/34)
Squadron Leader C. Chapman, DSC	(8/34 — 12/35)

Rank	Name	Rank	Name
PO	D. Addenbrooke	FO	S. Keane
FO	J. R. S. Agar	FL	J. V. Kelly
FL	R. L. M. Barbour	FO	R. B. Lee
PO	D. C. T. Bennett	SgtP	G. E. Lillywhite
SgtP	F. G. Berry	FL	J. B. Lynch
FO	J. G. Bigelow	FL	R. L. McBarbour
FO	H. G. Blair	FL	J. W. F. Merer
FL	S. L. Blunt	SgtP	R. S. Mills
SgtP	W. Bradshaw	SgtP	W. Mormon
FL	H. H. Brookes	A/SgtP	M. Papworth
PO	G. Burdick	SgtP	J. J. Robertson
FL	C. Chapman	FO	M. V. Ridgeway
SgtP	W. A. Cheeseman	FO	W. R. Sadler
FO	R. N. Clarke	FL	C. F. Sealy
PO	R. Cleland	FO	J. C. W. Staveley
PO	W. G. Devas	SgtP	W. R. Suter
FL	A. L. Duke	FO	E. A. H. Tanner
PO	R. R. Fairweather	SgtP	B. R. Tribe
SgtP	H. Z. Foreman	PO	F. H. Tyson
PO	K. Gray	SgtP	L. J. West
SgtP	J. T. Holt	PO	S. C. Widdows
FL	S. L. Hunt	SgtP	E. E. Williams
SgtP	E. J. Johnson	FL	J. L. Wingate

*   *   *

No 32(F) Squadron —
Adeste comites ('Rally round comrades')

Bulldog IIA	(1/31 — 7/36)
Kenley, Surrey	(4/23 — 9/32)
Biggin Hill, Kent	(9/32 — 1/40)

COs
Squadron Leader B. E. Baker, DSO, MC   (11/29 — 12/32)
Squadron Leader D. L. Blackford   (12/32 — 4/34)
Squadron Leader G. T. Richardson   (4/34 — 4/37)

Rank	Name	Rank	Name
SgtP	G. Adams	PO	E. C. Ingham
FL	E. E. Arnold	SgtP	L. Jobbins
FL	C. E. J. Baines	SgtP	W. W. Loxton
FO	J. D. Baker-Carr	FL	E. J. H. Moreton
PO	E. F. E. Barnard	PO	L. J. Neale
SgtP	J. O. Barnes	SgtP	F. M. Nicholson
FL	H. A. J. Barrow	SgtP	Price
PO	R. T. P. Clarkson	SgtP	J. G. Priest
SgtP	Cooper	FO	N. C. Ross-Roberts
FO	L. J. Crosbie	SgtP	A. E. Rumble
FO	R. David	PO	G. F. A. Skelton
FO	E. W. Downing	PO	G. N. Snarey
FL	C. C. Edwards	PO	G. K. Tulloch
PO	H. Georgeson	SgtP	H. M. Walker
SgtP	F. Gommshall	PO	C. W. Williams
FL	D. J. Harrison	SgtP	R. G. Williams
PO	P. H. Heygate	PO	A. T. Wilson
FO	G. C. Holland	FO	H. P. Wilson
SgtP	M. H. Hooper	FL	F. W. Wiseman-Clarke
FL	J. H. Hutchinson		

*   *   *

No 41(F) Squadron —
'Seek and destroy'

Bulldog IIA   (10/31 — 8/34)

Northolt, Middlesex   (4/23 — 10/35)

COs
Squadron Leader S. F. Vincent, AFC   (9/31 — 5/33)
Squadron Leader J. A. Boret, MC, AFC   (5/33 — 2/37)

Rank	Name	Rank	Name
SgtP	F. Baker	SgtP	B. D. Larner
SgtP	Betty	PO	C. G. Lott

F/SgtP	Boucher	PO	T. G. Lovell-Gregg
FL	E. S. C. Davie	FO	J. N. McAirley
PO	M. Downey	PO	J. E. C. McClure
PO	P. W. Dustin	FL	J. A. McDonald
SgtP	Edwards	SgtP	B. J. Marsden
PO	H. Eeles	SgtP	Pearce
PO	D. O. Finlay	PO	J. B. Sims
FL	M. M. Freehill	PO	F. G. L. Smith
FO	W. H. Husbands	FL	R. T. Taaffe
FO	P. W. Johnson	SgtP	F. W. Upshall

*   *   *

No 54(F) Squadron —
Audax omnia perpeti ('Boldness endures everything')

Bulldog IIA	(4/30 — 9/36)
Hornchurch, Essex	(1/30 — 11/39)

COs
Squadron Leader W. E. G. Bryant, MBE	(1/30 — 2/32)
Squadron Leader S. L. G. Pope, DFC, AFC	(3/32 — 1/33)
Squadron Leader I. M. Rodney	(1/33 — 1/34)
Squadron Leader G. D. Daly, DFC	(1/34 — 10/35)
Flying Officer C. R. G. Lewis	(10/35 — 2/36)
Flight Lieutenant J. Rhys-Jones	(2/36 — 8/36)
Squadron Leader C. A. Bouchier, OBE, DFC	(8/36 — 4/38)

Rank	Name	Rank	Name
PO	A. A. Adams	A/PO	J. D. C. Joslin
FL	J. St Arburthnott	FO	K. D. Knocker
PO	R. E. Barnett	FO	C. G. R. Lewis
FO	R. J. Bennet	A/PO	R. C. Love
A/PO	E. R. Bitmead	PO	I. G. Mackay
FO	W. K. Brett	PO	L. E. P. Mahon
FL	E. S. Burns	A/PO	R. A. Milward
FO	T. B. Byrne	PO	J. W. C. More
FO	C. M. D. Chambers	FL	F. W. Moxham
FL	C. Chapman, DSC	FO	G. E. W. Parish
PO	A. L. Christian	SgtP	V. W. R. Penford
A/PO	R. Cluer	SgtP	N. T. Phillips
PO	A. J. Draper	FL	J. Rhys-Jones
FL	R. Duncanson	A/SgtP	S. A. Richens
SgtP	H. C. Evans	A/PO	W. Riley
A/PO	G. H. F. Feeny	FO	D. R. C. B. de Sarigny
FO	D. O. Finlay	FO	W. A. J. Satchell

FO	E. J. Finnegan	A/PO	W. R. Selkirk
SgtP	A. A. Forbes	FO	N. C. Singer
FO	J. Grandy	PO	E. W. Thornewill
FO	G. W. P. Grant	SgtP	S. Trout
PO	H. Harkness	PO	P. E. Warcup
PO	W. H. Harvey	SgtP	E. G. Watson
PO	H. Heyworth	FL	G. F. Wistondale
PO	W. F. C. Hobson	SgtP	E. Womphrey
PO	H. A. V. Hogan		

*   *   *

No 56(F) Squadron —

Quid siu coelum ruat ('What if heaven falls')

Bulldog IIA	(10/32 — 5/36)
North Weald, Essex	(10/27 — 10/39)

COs
Squadron Leader G. E. Wilson	(1/32 — 3/35)
Flight Lieutenant J. W. Colquhoun	(3/35 — 8/35)
Squadron Leader C. L. Lea-Cox	(8/35 — 8/38)

Rank	Name	Rank	Name
FL	G. C. Banting	FL	C. L. Lea-Cox
SgtP	W. Bastin	PO	D. H. Lee
PO	E. D. A. Bigg	PO	L. G. Levis
FO	I. C. Bird	PO	R. M. Longmore
PO	W. E. Carr	PO	J. C. MacDonald
FO	T. R. T. Carr-Ellison	FO	H. E. Mayes
FL	N. Carter	FO	G. L. Menzies
FL	J. W. Colquhoun	SgtP	D. Miles
PO	D. M. H. Craven	FO	L. R. Mouatt
FO	C. R. Davies	FL	L. G. Nixon
PO	A. H. Donaldson	A/PO	G. H. F. Plinston
PO	A. Foord-Kelcey	FO	W. S. Reed
FO	M. V. Gibbon	SgtP	R. Rudd
FO	H. R. Graham	FL	A. W. Sandeman
SgtP	W. Hardeman	FO	S. E. R. Shepard
SgtP	J. Harvey	PO	N. F. Simpson
SgtP	L. S. Holman	FO	L. C. Slee
PO	G. E. Horne	FO	R. Smith
FO	W. L. Houlbrook	PO	W. W. Stainthorpe
SgtP	A. Howell	FL	A. E. Taylor
FL	R. Ivelaw-Chapman	PO	J. M. Thompson
PO	W. A. W. Jameson	A/PO	A. J. Trumble

PO	D. V. Johnson	A/PO	E. L. A. Walter
FO	M. V. Johnstone	SgtP	P. C. Webb
SgtP	A. Jones	SgtP	A. Wheeler
PO	E. A. Kayser	SgtP	L. Wilcox
SgtP	T. Keill	FL	G. E. Wilson
SgtP	J. Lane		

*   *   *

No 111(F) Squadron —
Adstantes ('Standing to')

Bulldog IIA	(1/31 — 6/36)
Hornchurch, Essex	(4/28 — 7/34)
Northolt, Middlesex	(7/34 — 10/39)

COs
Squadron Leader E. R. Openshaw	(11/30 — 5/33)
Squadron Leader M. B. Frew, DSO, MC, AFC	(5/33 — 8/34)
Squadron Leader E. P. Mackay	(8/34 — 10/35)
Squadron Leader C. W. Weedon	(10/35 — 12/35)
Squadron Leader I. E. Brodie	(12/35 — 3/36)
Squadron Leader G. V. Howard, DFC	(3/36 — 10/37)

Rank	Name	Rank	Name
FO	J. L. Armstrong	PO	D. J. North-Bamford
PO	J. N. Baxter	FO	M. P. O. O'Reilly
PO	C. F. Birk	FL	J. T. Paine
FO	H. R. Black	PO	E. R. Pearce
FL	I. E. Brodie	PO	D. Prowse
PO	C. Broughton	PO	D. S. Radford
FO	J. Cherrill	PO	J. H. W. Radice
PO	F. Crump	PO	F. W. Richards
FO	G. H. Denholm	PO	M. W. S. Robinson
PO	D. Y. Feeney	FL	I. M. Rodney
FL	W. D. Gairdner	PO	J. S. Sabine
PO	G. W. P. Grant	FO	H. A. Simmons
PO	P. H. Hamley	FL	C. B. S. Spackman
PO	G. F. W. Heycock	FL	C. H. A. Stevens
FO	Johnson	FL	D. L. Thomson
FO	C. G. R. Lewis	PO	G. C. Tomlinson
FO	H. D. McGregor	PO	H. J. Wilson
PO	G. A. L. Manton	PO	R. I. B. Winn
PO	A. W. D. Miller	FL	A. B. Woodhall
PO	R. R. Murphy		

Appendix 4
RAF Squadron Bulldog serial numbers

Note: Time-expired, obsolete and damaged aircraft were often transferred to Schools of Technical Training for ground instruction. These were, with a few exceptions, given serial numbers in a numerical sequence with the suffix 'M'. In the tables the dates shown are those when the aircraft left active service, not necessarily the date on which the M-number was allotted.

25 Bulldog Mark IIs (24 delivered between May and October 1929)

Serial No	Sqdn	
J9567	3/A&AEE	Ground collision 27.8.36
J9568	3/41	SOC date NK
J9569	3/41	Ground collision with Horsley, J8604, 23.7.29; SOC date NK
J9570	3/41	Undercarriage damaged landing 22.1.31; Taxied into hedge and damaged wing, Biggin Hill, 13.7.31; SOC date NK.
J9571	3/41	SOC date NK
J9572	3/41	SOC date NK
J9573	3	SOC date NK
J9574	3	Collided in air with Horsley, J8005, on 12.6.30 — parachute descent
J9575	3	Ground collision with Horsley, J8604, 20.7.29; SOC date NK
J9576	3	Crashed and overturned Chipping Norton, 7.11.30; SOC date NK
J9577	3	Crashed at Eastchurch, 27.11.30; SOC date NK
J9578	3	Broke axle in dusk landing, 12.12.30; SOC date NK
J9579	3	Overturned and badly damaged, 27.11.30; SOC date NK
J9580	3	SOC date NK
J9581	3	SOC date NK
J9582	3	SOC date NK
J9583	3	Damaged wingtip landing at Northolt, 17.4.31; SOC date NK
J9584	3	Taxying accident, 19.5.30; damaged prop in forced landing at Dorking, 3.2.31; collided in air with K1605 on 19.4.33, both aircraft landed safely. SOC date NK
J9585	17	SOC date NK
J9586	17	Collided in air with J9588 on 6.3.30 aircraft landed safely; crashed at Sutton Bridge, 29.5.30; SOC date NK
J9587	17/29/32	Crashed at Arundel Park, Sussex, 30.9.30; SOC date NK
J9588	17	Collided in air with J9586 on 6.3.30 aircraft landed safely
J9589	17	Collided on ground with K1086 on 14.11.30 at Upavon
J9590	17	Collided at 14,000 ft with K1081 (parachute descent) and crashed at Wardington, nr Banbury, 6.5.31
J9591	MNFRS/17	SOC date NK

23 Bulldog Mark IIs delivered between March and June 1930

K1079	3	Spun into ground 9.3.31	K1087		SOC 2.2.32
			K1088	17	SOC 15.2.33
K1080	17/Eastchurch	SOC 19.12.32	K1089		SOC 27.2.33
K1081	17/29	Collided with J9590 and crashed 6.5.31 — parachute descent	K1090	3/54	SOC 15.2.33
			K1091		SOC 13.6.30
			K1092	54	SOC 5.3.31
			K1093	54	SOC 9.10.30
K1082	17	SOC date NK	K1094	54/17	SOC 9.9.31
K1083		SOC 20.10.30	K1095	54	SOC 6.8.31
K1084		SOC 4.2.32	K1096	17	SOC 9.5.32
K1085	17/29	SOC 20.10.30	K1097		SOC 6.5.32
K1086	17	Collided with J9589 on ground, Upavon, 14.11.30 and DBR	K1098		SOC 17.8.32
			K1099		SOC 1.9.31
			K1100		SOC 8.2.32
			K1101		SOC 6.5.33

92 Bulldog Mark IIAs delivered between October 1930 and May 1931

K1603	A&AEE	To 597M 9.3?	K1631	32	SOC 4.7.38
K1604	54	SOC 23.7.32	K1632	17/3	SOC 22.3.38
K1605	54/3	SOC 7.6.34	K1633	23/111/3	111 Squadron struck stationary Gamecock, J8084, of 23 Squadron at Hornchurch 31.3.31; to 700M 8.35
K1606	32	To 905M 11.36			
K1607	54/17/3	SOC 22.3.38			
K1608	54	SOC 1.4.31			
K1609		SOC 3.3.31			
K1610		SOC 8.6.38			
K1611	54	SOC 9.7.38			
K1612		SOC 1.9.31	K1634	111/3	Overturned at Assuan, 5.8.36; SOC 10.9.36
K1613	111	SOC 9.7.38			
K1614		SOC 2.8.38			
K1615	32	Crashed after collision, 24.11.31	K1635		SOC 1.9.31
			K1636	CFS	SOC 16.6.36
K1616	32	To 906M 11.36	K1637		SOC 22.8.34
K1617	32	To 907M 11.36	K1638	AAS	SOC 10.12.37
K1618		SOC 5.2.32	K1639		SOC 4.8.33
K1619	32	Overturned on landing, Biggin Hill, 22.5.36	K1640	3/54	Struck Sidestrand J9768 of 101 Squadron in practice combat, Upavon, 1.6.31; SOC 17.6.36
K1620	32	SOC 22.6.33			
K1621		SOC 8.7.32			
K1622	32	SOC 27.2.32			
K1623	32/17/54	Crashed on landing, Hornchurch, 9.7.36	K1641	54	SOC 17.7.36
			K1642		SOC 2.5.35
K1624	111/54/N. Coates	SOC 2.37	K1643		SOC 25.10.34
			K1644		SOC 10.1.33
K1625	111	SOC 5.7.35	K1645	17/54	SOC 13.7.32
K1626	111/17/3	Crashed on landing, Kenley, 31.3.37	K1646	54	Landing accident, Hornchurch, 10.1.36; SOC 23.1.36
K1627	111	To 701M 8.35			
K1628	111/3	Crashed on landing, Port Sudan, 18.2.36	K1647		SOC 3.10.33
K1629	111	SOC 2.2.32	K1648	AAS	To 1112M 8.38
K1630	111	SOC 27.10.32			

K1649	17/3	SOC 22.3.38	K1674		SOC 21.12.31
K1650		SOC 7.6.34	K1675	23	Collided with
K1651	54/3	Collided with			K1673 and
		K2486 and			crashed at
		crashed, 16.5.34			Hartfield, Sussex,
K1652	54	SOC 21.9.32			26.4.32
K1653	54	SOC 16.6.36	K1676	23	Crashed during
K1654	17	Collided with			aerobatics at
		K1659 and			Woodley, 14.12.31
		crashed at Milton	K1677	23	Collided with
		Lilbourne, 4.12.33			Moth K1210 over
K1655	54	SOC 10.12.37			Kenley, 24.11.31
K1656		SOC 14.4.32	K1678	23	SOC 2.8.38
K1657	32	SOC 10.12.37	K1679	23	SOC 4.7.32
K1658		SOC 8.8.32	K1680	32	Crashed in forced
K1659	A&AEE/17	Collided with			landing near
		K1654 and			Biggin Hill,
		crashed at Milton			2.5.35
		Lilbourne, 4.12.33	K1681	111	SOC 18.8.32
K1660	54/Met	Crashed at	K1682	3	Crashed in forced
	Flt Aldergrove	Parkgate, Ulster,			landing, 20.3.37
		14.4.37	K1683	111	Crashed in river
K1661	17/54	SOC 9.7.38			and sank, 5.5.36
K1662	56/54	Crashed in	K1684	111	To 920M 12.36
		forced landing,	K1685	111	SOC 10.1.34
		24.4.34	K1686	Met Flt	Crashed in
K1663	54	SOC 15.8.32		Aldergrove	snowstorm at
K1664	54	Crashed on landing,			Portadown,
		Waddington,			Ulster, 9.3.37
		3.9.36	K1687	23/Met Flt	To 951M 1.37
K1665	32/56/54	To 1129M 9.38		Aldergrove	
K1666	54	SOC 6.9.34	K1688		SOC 6.4.34
K1667	54/RAE/RAFC	To 655M 6.35	K1689		SOC 2.5.35
K1668	CFS	Overshot landing	K1690	32	To 908M/SOC
		at Wittering			20.5.40
		and overturned,	K1691	RAE/	Crashed in forced
		8.10.34			landing,
K1669	AAS	SOC 10.12.37		A&AEE	12.11.37
K1670	3/AAS	SOC 3.37	K1692		To 972M 9.37
K1671	17/23/3	Crashed on	K1693	RAFC	Spun into ground
		landing, Gebeit,			near Brauncewell,
		3.8.36			Lincs, 17.10.35
K1672	23/111	Abandoned when	K1694		SOC 9.5.32
		controls jammed			
		over Holbeach			
		ranges, 14.5.36			
K1673	23	Collided with			
		K1675 and			
		crashed at			
		Hartfield, Sussex,			
		26.4.32			

100 Bulldog Mark IIAs delivered between July 1931 and April 1932

K2135	54	To 954M 4.37	K2141	54	SOC 4.7.38
K2136	Mkrs	SOC 31.10.38	K2142	17	SOC 7.6.34
K2137	17/3	To 1075M 5.38	K2143		SOC 6.4.34
K2138	19	SOC 3.10.33	K2144	Met Flt	To 952M 4.37
K2139	111	To 986M 9.37		Aldergrove	
K2140	3	SOC 6.37	K2145	54	To 909M 11.36

K2146	54	Mid-air collision, 23.11.33 — parachute descent
K2147	32	SOC 10.12.37
K2148		SOC 2.37
K2149	23/54/111	SOC 10.12.37
K2150	3/54	Crashed on landing, Hendon, 6.1.36; SOC 11.4.36
K2151	23	SOC 27.2.33
K2152	23/56	To 921M 12.36
K2153	17	To 1010M 11.37
K2154		SOC 16.1.34
K2155	19/32	Crashed on landing, North Weald, 23.4.36
K2156	19/17/3	Hit by Gauntlet K5343 at Kenley, 9.3.37
K2157	19	SOC 2.5.33
K2158	19	SOC 6.9.34
K2159	19/17/3	SOC 4.7.38
K2160	19	SOC 17.11.33
K2161	19	SOC NK
K2162	19	SOC 6.37
K2163	19	SOC 10.8.33
K2164	19	SOC 6.37
K2165	19/54	To 955M 4.37
K2166	19/RAE/ RAFC	Abandoned in uncontrollable spin, Cranwell, 21.10.35
K2167	19/CFS	SOC 16.7.34
K2168	19/AAS	Overturned at Eastchurch, 28.10.36; to 941M
K2169	19	SOC 25.9.35
K2170	32/Met Flt Duxford/3	To 1076M 5.38
K2171	32	Broke up in dive and crashed in sea, 7.10.35
K2172	3	To 1077M 5.38
K2173	17	SOC 6.37
K2174		SOC 2.8.38
K2175		To 1150M 10.38
K2176	41	SOC 9.7.38
K2177	41	SOC 9.7.38
K2178	41	SOC 31.7.35
K2179	41	To 1012M 11.37
K2180	41	SOC 9.7.38
K2181	41	SOC NK
K2182	41	SOC 9.7.38
K2183	41	SOC 9.7.38
K2184	41	SOC 4.7.38
K2185	41/3	SOC 14.12.31
K2186	41	To 1078M 5.38
K2187	41	SOC 14.4.32
K2188	CFS/Mkrs & RAE	Two-seat trainer prototype; Cheetah test-bed; to 1923M 5.40
K2189	41	SOC 8.5.34
K2190		Crashed at Boxmore, 6.4.32
K2191	A&AEE	Collided with K2201 and crashed at Martlesham, 19.5.33
K2192	32	SOC 10.12.37
K2193	A&AEE	SOC 18.11.38
K2194	41	SOC 21.6.34
K2195	RAFC	To 778M 3.36
K2196	RAFC	SOC 20.11.35
K2197	111/54	To 956M 4.37
K2198		To 1011M 11.37
K2199	17/41	SOC 4.7.38
K2200		SOC 20.4.33
K2201	A&AEE	Collided in air with K2191 and crashed at Martlesham, 19.5.33
K2202	RAE	SOC 21.12.39
K2203	54	SOC 10.12.37
K2204	54	SOC 25.7.39
K2205	56/A Flt Lee	To 1079M 5.38
K2206	56	To 640M 4.35
K2207	54	To 899M 10.36
K2208	111	Crashed on take-off, 6.5.36
K2209	41/111/24	To 1159M 11.38
K2210	29/56/A Flt Lee	SOC 30.8.37
K2211	29/56/RAE	SOC 6.9.38
K2212	RAFC	Abandoned in spin, 12.4.35
K2213	RAFC/Met Flt Duxford/ Met Flt Aldergrove	To 953M 4.37
K2214	3	Crashed on landing, Kenley, 11.6.35
K2215	29/56/A&AEE & RAE	SOC 6.9.38
K2216	3/56/ RAE/17	Crashed on take-off, Kenley, 7.5.36
K2217		SOC 22.3.35
K2218		SOC 25.7.33
K2219	3/56	Ground collision, Boscombe Down, 18.9.35
K2220	29/3	SOC 6.37
K2221	A&AEE/ME	SOC 6.37
K2222	RAE	SOC 16.11.34
K2223	56	To 1151M 10.38
K2224	56	To 977M 7.37
K2225	56/3	SOC 4.7.38
K2226	56/3	SOC 22.3.38
K2227	56	To 978M 7.37
K2228	56	SOC 2.5.35
K2229	56	To 1152M 10.38
K2230		SOC 3.10.33

K2231	56	SOC 18.11.38	*K2233*	3	SOC 18.7.33
K2232	3	SOC 7.8.36	*K2234*	3	SOC 21.7.36

20 Bulldog Mark IIAs delivered between April and July 1932

K2476	RAE	To *714M* 10.35	*K2487*	3	SOC 21.6.34
K2477	ME	SOC 6.37	*K2488*	54	SOC 10.12.37
K2478		SOC 3.7.35	*K2489*	ME	SOC 6.37
K2479	3	SOC 4.2.36	*K2490*	32	SOC 10.12.37
K2480	32	SOC 6.37	*K2491*	17/3	SOC 4.7.38
K2481	32	To *900M* 10.36	*K2492*	56	Crashed near
K2482	17	SOC 6.9.34			Yelding, 12.5.36
K2483	17	SOC 6.37	*K2493*	32/Met Flt	SOC 4.7.38
K2484	ME	SOC 6.37		Aldergrove	
K2485	ME	SOC 19.5.37	*K2494*	3	SOC 6.37
K2486	3	Collided with	*K2495*	56/3	SOC 4.7.38
		K1650 and crashed			
		16.5.34 —			
		parachute descent			

14 Bulldog Mark IIAs delivered between July and December 1932

K2859		SOC 4.2.35	*K2865*	17/3	SOC 4.7.38
K2860	54/3	Crashed on	*K2866*	29	Crashed near
		landing, Kenley,			Shorncliffe, Kent,
		20.7.37			3.9.34
K2861	54/Met Flt	SOC 4.7.38	*K2867*	54	SOC 6.37
	Aldergrove		*K2868*	54	SOC 6.37
K2862	RAFC	Crashed in	*K2869*	3	Crashed on
		forced landing,			landing, Helwan,
		12.2.36			6.8.36
K2863	17/3	Crashed on	*K2870*	3	Crashed landing
		landing, 20.7.37			at night, Kenley,
K2864	17	Crashed on			25.7.35
		Kenley Common,	*K2871*	56	SOC 6.37
		Surrey, 23.5.36	*K2872*	17/3	SOC 4.7.38

18 Bulldog Mark IIAs delivered in March and April 1933

K2946		SOC 4.7.38;	*K2955*		To *1163M* 11.38
		believed to *884M*	*K2956*		SOC 30.4.35
K2947	17/3	SOC 4.7.38	*K2957*		To *1149M* 10.38
K2948	RAFC	To *1161M* 11.38	*K2958*		To *1164M* 11.38
K2949		SOC 6.37	*K2959*		SOC 15.6.37
K2950	17	SOC 8.10.37	*K2960*	54	Crashed on
K2951	54/Met Flt	SOC 4.7.38			landing,
	Aldergrove				Hornchurch, 3.3.36
K2952		To *1162M* 11.38	*K2961*		SOC 1.1.35
K2953	3 FTS	Crashed near	*K2962*	3 FTS	Overshot and
		Sandbach,			struck wall,
		Cheshire, whilst			13.1.36;
		on flight to N.			SOC 18.9.36
		Ireland, 22.1.35	*K2963*	32/Met Flt	Overshot in fog
K2954	3 FTS	Lost starboard		Duxford	and crashed,
		elevator and			Duxford, 22.9.36
		abandoned over			
		Culverthorpe,			
		Lincs, 16.8.35			

17 Bulldog Trainers delivered between December 1932 and February 1933

K3170	CFS	SOC 31.3.37	K3180		SOC 31.3.37
K3171		SOC 25.11.37	K3181	56/19	SOC 31.3.37
K3172	RAFC	To 910M 11.36	K3182	56	SOC 25.11.37
K3173		To 791M 3.36	K3183	Mkrs	Testbed for Napier
K3174	CFS	SOC 31.3.37			Rapier, Leonides
K3175	RAFC/1 FTS	To 911M 11.36			and Pelides;
K3176		SOC 22.5.36			SOC 7.5.40
K3177	17/3	SOC 25.11.37	K3184		SOC 22.5.36
K3178	54	SOC 25.11.37	K3185		To 829M 5.36
K3179	32	SOC 18.8.37	K3186		SOC 25.11.37

10 Bulldog Mark IIAs delivered by November 1933

K3504		To 885M 7.36	K3509		To 1015M 11.37
K3505	CFS	Pilot lost control	K3510		To 1016M 11.37
		and abandoned	K3511		To 1013M 11.37
		aircraft, 2.7.35	K3512	RAE	SOC 2.37
K3506		SOC 19.2.37	K3513	56	Crashed near
K3507		SOC 4.7.38			Bran End, Essex
K3508		To 1014M 11.37			30.1.36

31 Bulldog Trainers delivered between October 1933 and May 1934

K3923	RAFC	To 912M 11.36	K3937	3 FTS	SOC 22.5.36
K3924	RAFC	SOC 25.11.37	K3938	3 FTS	SOC 22.5.36
K3925	RAFC	SOC 9.9.37	K3939	3 FTS	SOC 22.5.36
K3926	RAFC	Undershot landing,	K3940	3 FTS	SOC 31.3.37
		10.5.35	K3941	AAS	SOC 25.11.37
K3927	RAFC	SOC 25.11.37	K3942	RAFC	SOC 25.4.37
K3928	RAFC	Collided with	K3943		SOC 22.5.36
		Hart Trainer	K3944		SOC 23.5.36
		K3152 and	K3945		SOC 23.5.36
		crashed, 1.5.34	K3946		SOC 23.5.36
K3929	5 FTS	SOC 3.37	K3947		SOC 25.11.37
K3930	5 FTS	SOC 31.3.37	K3948		SOC 25.11.37
K3931	5 FTS	SOC 3.37	K3949		SOC 23.5.36
K3932	5 FTS	To 1186M 11.38	K3950		SOC 23.5.36
K3933	5 FTS	Sold 25.11.37	K3951		SOC 23.5.36
K3934		To 1167M 11.38	K3952		SOC 23.5.36
K3935	5 FTS	SOC 8.2.35	K3953		SOC 23.5.36
K3936	5 FTS/3 FTS	Engine failure,			
		crashed in forced			
		landing, 4.1.36			

1 Bulldog Mark IIA to Specification 11/31

K4189	Mkrs & RAE	For static testing
		of stainless
		steel construction

1 Bulldog Mark IVA (ex-G-ABZW/R7) delivered in March 1935

K4292	Mkrs & A&AEE	To 1180M 11.38

11 Bulldog Trainers delivered between March and May 1935

K4566 to	All sold 25.11.37
K4576	

Appendix 5
Squadrons, bases and pilots of other national air forces

Royal Australian Air Force

Bulldog II — Jupiter VIF (A12-1 to A12-8) — April 1930
 Special Flight with No 1 Flying Training School, Point Cook (1930-1935)
 Fighter Flight, No 1 Squadron, Laverton (1935-1940)

Audax et Cautus

Pilots:

FO	D. R. Chapman (later Group Captain)		FO	W. G. Rae
SgtP	G. A. Cooper		FO	E. V. Read
SgtP	L. M. Diprose		FL	F. R. W. Scherger (later Air Marshal Sir Frederick)
PO	P. E. Heffernan (later Air Commodore)		FO	R. Simms
FO	C. M. Henry		Sqdn Ldr	J. H. Summers
FO	G. Jones (later Air Marshal Sir George)		FL	White
FO	J. McCauley (later Air Marshal Sir John)			

*　　*　　*

Royal Danish Air Force

Bulldog IIA — Jupiter VIFH *(J151-154/J301-304/J1-4)* — March 1931.
No 1 Squadron *(Haerens Flyvertropper)*; Kastrup and Vaerløse.

Pilots:

2nd Lieutenant O. S. V. Bernskov
2nd Lieutenant E. K. Birkhede
Captain H. L. V. Bjarkov
Captain I. A. W. Braunstein
2nd Lieutenant N. W. Buchave
Colonel Foerslev
Sergeant J. A. Hegner
2nd Lieutenant S. Høy
2nd Lieutenant P. Jensen

2nd Lieutenant H. Kierkegaard
Corporal V. C. Lauritsen
1st Lieutenant K. Pedersen
Captain Pojarkorf
2nd Lieutenant V. E. Prins
Lieutenant C. O. P. Schnack
Sergeant K. E. Simonsen
Sergeant H. Wolff

*　　*　　*

Estonian Air Force

Bulldog II — GR Jupiter VI *(122-133)* — August 1930.
No 3 Division: Lasnamägi and Jöhvi.

Pilots:
Lieutenant H. Kirsipuu
Pilot Officer A. Kriisk
Lieutenant E. Reissar

*   *   *

Finnish Air Force

Bulldog IVA — Mercury VIS2 *(BU-59* to *BU-75)* December 1934-January 1935.
Flights 1, 2 and 3; LLv26, *Lentoasema* No 5 TLLv35 and LLv34: Suur-Merijoki (near Viipuri), 1935;
Käkisalmi (near Lake Ladoga), 1937; Sortavala, 1938; Raulampi (near Heinjoki), 1939; Mensuvaara, 1939;
Immola (near Imatra), 1939; Parola (near Hämeenlinna), 1940; Lake Littoinen (near Turku), 1940.

Bulldog IIA — Jupiter *(BU-214* to *BU-216)* — December 1939.
No 2 OTU: Tyrväntö, 1940; Kauhava, 1942.

Pilots:
Warrant Officer C. E. Bruun
Lieutenant E. A. Carlsson
Captain E. Heinilä
Warrant Officer T. J. Kleemola
Warrant Officer L. Lautamäki
Lieutenant Colonel E. A. Luukkanen

Warrant Officer L. Mildh
Major E. E. Nuotio
Sergeant V. Porvari
Lieutenant P. Tĕvä
Sergeant T. Uuttu
Captain B. V. Willebrand

*   *   *

Latvian Air Force

Bulldog II — GR Jupiter VI (five in September 1929; seven in July 1930).
No 1 Squadron: Spilve (near Riga).
No 3 Squadron: Krustpils.

Pilots:
Warrant Office J. Aboliňš
Captain N. Balodis
Sergeant A. Danders
Sergeant A. Dulle
Captain H. Freimanis
Captain A. Graudiňš

Lieutenant A. Hvastkovs
Warrant Officer K. Iesalnieks
Lieutenant A. Lasmanis
Sergeant P. Lodziňš
Lieutenant K. Nagainis
Lieutenant E. Ruditis

*   *   *

Royal Siamese Air Force

Bulldog II Jupiter VII (two in January 1930)
Don Muang (near Bangkok)
Pilots:
Not Known

*   *   *

Royal Swedish Air Force

Bulldog II — GR Jupiter VI *(1201-1203)* — August 1930.
Bulldog IIA — GR Jupiter VI *(5211-5218)* — May 1931.
Västerås Flygkär (F1); Central Flying School (F5): Malmslatt

Pilots:
Captain E. M. Bang
Lieutenant O. Carlgren
Lieutenant E. Ekman
Lieutenant L. G. Hägglöf

Captain L. Jungdahl
Captain N. Söderberg
Engineer C. Sparre
Lieutenant A. Weskring

*   *   *

Bibliography

F. J. Adkin; *From the Ground Up* (A History of RAF Ground Crew); Airlife Publishing, 1983

C. F. Andrews; *The Bristol Bulldog Aircraft in Profile No 1;* Profile Publications, 1971

E. Angelucci & P. Matricardi; *World Aircraft 1918-1935;* Samson Low, 1975

C. Ashworth; *Action Stations* Vol 5; Patrick Stephens, 1982

Ralph Barker; *The Schneider Trophy Races;* Chatto & Windus, 1971

C. H. Barnes; *Bristol Aircraft since 1910;* Putnam, 1970

Charles Bowyer; *Pathfinders at War;* Ian Allan, 1977

Keith Braybrooke; *Wingspan: A History of Debden;* W. Hart & Son (Saffron Walden), 1957

Len Deighton; *Fighter* — The True Story of the Battle of Britain; Jonathan Cape, 1977

P. Flint; *RAF Kenley;* Terence Dalton, 1985

A. Granger; *The Bristol Bulldog* — Data plan No 2; Taurus Press, 1973

C. G. Grey; *The History of the Air Ministry;* Allen & Unwin, 1940

B. Gunston; *By Jupiter - The Life of Sir Roy Fedden;* Royal Aeronautical Society, 1978

B. Gunston; *World Encyclopaedia of Aero Engines;* Guild Publishing, 1986

B. Gunston; *The Encyclopaedia of the World's Combat Aircraft;* Hamlyn, 1976

B. B. Halfpenny; *Action Stations* Vol 8; Patrick Stephens, 1984

J. Halley; *RAF Unit Histories;* 2 Vols, Air Britain Ltd, 1969/73

J. Halley; *RAF Aircraft K1000-K9999;* Air Britain Ltd, 1976

A. J. Jackson; *British Civil Aircraft since 1919* (Vol 1); Putnam, 1973

Robert Jackson; *Douglas Bader;* Arthur Barker Ltd, 1983

D. N. James; *Schneider Trophy Aircraft, 1913-31;* Putnam, 1981

'Johnnie' Johnson; *Wing Leader;* Chatto & Windus, 1956

K. Keskinen, K. Stenman & K. Niska; *Suomen Ilmavoimien Lentokoneet 1918/38;* Tietoteos, 1976

K. Keskinen, K. Stenman & K. Niska; *The British Fighters in the Finnish Air Force;* Tietoteos, 1986

K. Keskinen, K. Stenman & K. Niska; *Finnish Fighter Aces;* Tietoteos, 1978

H. F. King; *The World's Fighters;* the Bodley Head, 1971

H. F. King; *Armament of British Aircraft, 1909/39;* Putnam, 1971

G. Kinsey; *Martlesham Heath;* Terence Dalton, 1983

Captain Jose Larios (Duke of Lerma); *Combat Over Spain;* Neville Spearman, 1967

J. S. Larrazabal; *Air War Over Spain;* Ian Allan, 1969

P. Laureau; *L'Aviation Republicaine Espagnole, 1936/39;* Lariviere, 1978

P. Lewis; *The British Fighter since 1912;* Putnam, 1979

P. Lewis; *Squadron Histories. RFC/RNAS/RAF since 1912;* Putnam

Bryan Little; *The City & Council of Bristol;* S.R. Publishers, 1967

P. B. 'Laddie' Lucas; *Flying Colours;* Hutchinson & Co, 1981

A. H. Lukins; *The Book of Bristol Aircraft;* Harborough Publishing, 1946

E. Luukkanen; *Fighter over Finland;* Macdonald, 1963

S. K. Mason; *Battle over Britain;* McWhirter Twins, 1969

P. R. Matt; *United States Navy & Marine Corps Fighters, 1918-1962;* Aero Publishers, 1962

Alan Morris; *Bloody April;* Arrow Books Ltd, 1968

K. Munson; *Fighters Between the Wars 1919-39;* Blandford Press, 1970

Brian Nolan; *Hero - the Falcon of Malta;* William Blackwood, 1982

J. D. Oughton; *Bristol - an Aircraft Album;* Ian Allan, 1973

A. J. Pegg; *Sent Flying;* Macdonald, 1959

John Pudney; *Bristol Fashion;* Putnam, 1960

Jeffrey Quill; *Spitfire;* John Murray, 1983

Winston G. Ramsey; *The Battle of Britain - Then and Now;* After the Battle, 1985

J. Rawlings; *Fighter Squadrons of the RAF;* Macdonald, 1969

H. Rayner; *Scherger;* Australian War Memorial, 1984

Bruce Robertson; *The RAF – A Pictorial History;* Robert Hale Ltd, 1978

A. Robinson; *In the Cockpit;* Orbis Publishers, 1984

D. A. Russell; *The Book of Bristol Aircraft;* Harborough Publishing Co, 1946

C. F. Shores; *Finnish Air Force, 1918-1968;* Osprey, 1969

C. F. Shores; *Spanish Civil War Air Forces;* Osprey, 1977

P. H. Sumner; *Aeroplanes, Seaplanes and Aero Engines;* Crosby Lockwood & Son, 1929

G. Swanborough & P. M. Bowers; *United States Navy Aircraft since 1911;* Putnam, 1979

O. Thetford; *Aircraft of the Royal Air Force since 1918;* Putnam, 1979

A. B. Tinsley; *One Rissole on my Plate;* Merlin Books Ltd, 1984

Frank Tredrey; *Pilots Summer;* Duckworth, 1939

C. C. Turner; *My Flying Scrapbook;* Samson Low, 1940

Graham Wallace; *RAF Biggin Hill;* Putnam, c 1960

Allen Wheeler; *Flying Between the Wars;* G. T. Foulis & Co, 1972

Major Al Williams; *Air Power;* Coward McCann, 1940

Articles

H. W. F. Bailey; *50 Years of Bristol Engines;* Rolls-Royce Engines plc, July 1970

Major G. P. Bulman; *The First Barnwell Memorial Lecture;* The Journal of the R.A.S. Volume 58, June 1954

A. Day; *Design Requirements of Military Aircraft;* R.Ae.Socy Journal, January 1966

F. Gerdessen; *Estonian Air Power 1918-1945; Air Enthusiast,* April/July 1982

Tony Harold; *Between the Wars Fighters; Flypast,* November 1981

H. B. Howard; *Aircraft Structures;* R.Ae.Socy Journal, January 1966

Alec Lumsden & Terry Heffernan; *Probe Probare No. 25; Aeroplane Monthly,* June 1986

Ron McAllister; *The White-winged Birds & the Intrepid Barnwells* Issue 3; *Stirlingshire Gazette,* July/August 1983

H. A. Mettam; *Fifty Years of Military Airworthiness;* R.Ae.Socy Journal, January 1966

Don Middleton; *Douglas Bader; Aeroplane Monthly,* November 1982

Don Middleton; *Test Pilot Profile No 12; Aeroplane Monthly,* May 1986

F. Owner; *Random reminiscences in Centenary Year;* R.Ae.Socy Journal, 1966

Alister Raby; *Duxford Review 1935; Flypast,* July 1985

RAAF News, March 1962; April 1963; September 1964

C. F. Shores; *Finland's Air War Pts 1 & 2;* 1968

C. F. Shores; *Air Pictorial Vol. 30 No 6 & 7;* 1968

Richard Ward; *Bristol Bulldog; Aircraft Modelworld,* December 1984/January 1985

John Weal; *The Bulldog Breed; Air Enthusiast,* January & February 1973

Documents

Air Publications AP1393, 1st edition — Air Ministry 1930

Air Publications AP1393/A Vol 1, 2nd edition — Air Ministry 1932

Operations Record Books (RAF Form 540) Air 27-32/-233/-252/-287/-341/-360/-424/-511/-527/-865

Key to endpaper illustrations

FRONT:

1. Mark II, No 3 Squadron, Upavon, June 1929-December 1932. No 3 Squadron also flew the Mark IIa from February 1931-July 1937 based at Upavon and Kenley.
2. Mark II, No 17 Squadron, Upavon, October 1929.
3. Mark IIa, No 19 Squadron, Squadron Commander's aircraft. Duxford, September 1931-January 1935.
4. No 19 Squadron.
5. Squadron Leader's pennant.
6. Mark IIa, No 23 Squadron, Kenley and Biggin Hill, July 1931-April 1933.
6. No 23 Squadron.
8. RAF.
9. RAAF.
10. Mark IIa, No 32 Squadron, Kenley and Biggin Hill, January 1931-July 1936.
11. Bulldog TM two-seater trainer, RAF College, Cranwell, 1933.
12. Mark IIa, No 29 Squadron, North Weald, June 1932-April 1935.
13. Mark IIa, No 41 Squadron, Northolt, October 1931-August 1934.
14. Mark IIa, No 56 Squadron, North Weald, October 1932-May 1938.
15. Mark II, Royal Australian Air Force, Point Cook, 1930.

BACK:

1. J7 Bulldog IIa, Swedish Air Force. The code indicates the 17th aircraft of the 2nd Squadron of the 1st Wing during the period 1931-1935.
2. J7 Bulldog II, Squadron Commander's aircraft, 2nd Squadron, 1st Wing, 1931. Swedish Air Force.
3. Latvia plan views.
4. Latvia alternative on silver dope, four positions.
5. Bulldog II, Latvian Air Force, first batch, September 1929.
6. Bulldog II, Estonian Air Force.
7. Latvia.
8. Bulldog Type 105D, Danish Royal Army Air Corps as delivered in March 1931. J-151 to J-154.
9. Bulldog Type 105D, No 1 Squadron, Danish Royal Army Air Corps, Kastrup in markings from 1933 until scrapped in 1942. J-1 to J-4.
10. Bulldog IV on skis, Continuation War, Finnish Air Force. *BU-63* pale blue undersurfaces.
11. Bulldog IV, Finnish Air Force used as a fighter trainer during the Continuation War. *BU-68* silver undersurfaces.
12. Finland undersurfaces pale blue or silver.
13. Bulldog JSSF built by Nakajima, Tokyo, in 1930, first of two built.
14. Bulldog JSSF the second aircraft built by Nakajima.
15. Japan.
16. US Navy.
17. Siam six positions.
18. Siam rudder.
19. Denmark.
20. Sweden 1931-.
21. Finland.
22. Latvia.

Index

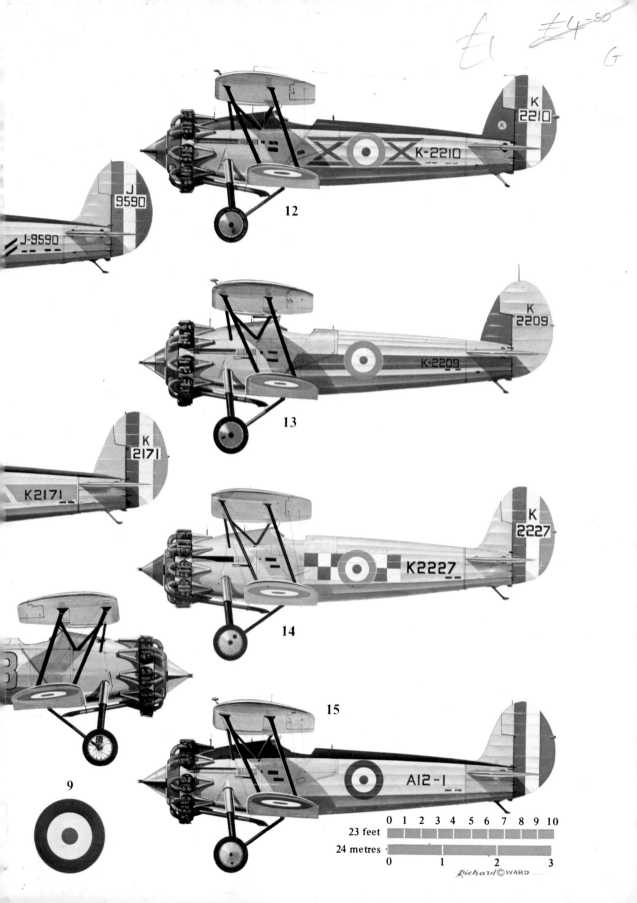

El £4-50
G

J 9590
J-9590

K 2210
K-2210
12

K 2209
K-2209
13

K 2171
K2171

K 2227
K2227
14

15

9

A12-1

0 1 2 3 4 5 6 7 8 9 10
23 feet
24 metres
0 1 2 3

Richard©WARD